Break Every Yoke

Break Every Yoke

Religion, Justice, and the Abolition of Prisons

JOSHUA DUBLER AND VINCENT W. LLOYD

OXFORD

UNIVERSITY PRESS

OXFORD
UNIVERSITY PRESS

Oxford University Press is a department of the University of Oxford. It furthers
the University's objective of excellence in research, scholarship, and education
by publishing worldwide. Oxford is a registered trade mark of Oxford University
Press in the UK and certain other countries.

Published in the United States of America by Oxford University Press
198 Madison Avenue, New York, NY 10016, United States of America.

Library of Congress Cataloging-in-Publication Data
Names: Dubler, Joshua, author.
Title: Break every yoke : religion, justice, and the abolition of prisons /
Joshua Dubler and Vincent W. Lloyd.
Description: New York : Oxford University Press, 2019.
Identifiers: LCCN 2019019521 | ISBN 9780190949150 (hardback) |
ISBN 9780190949167 (updf) | ISBN 9780190949174 (epub) | ISBN 9780190949181 (online)
Subjects: LCSH: Prisons—Moral and ethical aspects—United States. |
Criminology—Moral and ethical aspects—United States. |
Social justice—United States.
Classification: LCC HV9466 .D73 2019 | DDC 261.8/3360973—dc23
LC record available at https://lccn.loc.gov/2019019521

1 3 5 7 9 8 6 4 2

Printed by Integrated Books International, United States of America

For Jeffrey Stout

Contents

Introduction

The United States is not just a nation with an enormous number of prisons. In body and soul, it is—for the moment, anyhow—a prison nation. Millions face each day from the inside of a cage, millions more live under explicit state surveillance and control, and whole communities live in terror.[1] America's fever for punishment does not begin or end with the bodies of those who are, have been, and will be incarcerated. Rather, a network of ideas, feelings, and practices around the institution of the prison pervades American culture. As careful observers can diagnose, the knot of pathologies nestled in America's prisons are also endemic to the world outside the walls. Not all are equally impacted, but not one of us goes untouched. We have become a nation of jailers, of cops, of criminals and victims, of cheerleaders for vengeance, and of well-meaning but ineffectual standers-by. As a polity and as a culture, we embrace the necessity of social exclusion, and when we pursue justice, we almost invariably do so via violent means. The institutional configurations known to the general public as "mass incarceration"—and what, casting a wider net, prison abolitionists call the "prison industrial complex"—locks this culture down and, in turn, locks it in.[2]

The social consequences are devastating. By means of our systems of incarceration, policing, parole, and probation—and the carceral logics these institutions normalize—we punish our poor, prey upon the most vulnerable among us, perpetuate racial inequalities, enforce rigid gender norms, and contribute to the destruction of the earth—among a host of other effects, both direct and diffuse. Once, if asked to pinpoint the quintessentially American cultural entity, one might have reasonably pointed to the farm, the town, the church, or the marketplace. Asked nowadays to encapsulate what America is about, one could do far worse than hold up the prison as exemplum.

The prison is a particularly American problem, and America is particularly—peculiarly—religious. Coastal elites and the media these elites own and administer generally portray a country governed by fundamentally secular ideals, but many people are rightly skeptical of this conceit. In a variety of ways, Americans are a religious people. We say this not to speak for (and certainly not to valorize) those whom Fox News has been known to call the "real Americans." We are instead making an anthropological claim about the world—or indeed, the many worlds—that Americans imagine and actualize. By means of stories, ideas, and images (and via the institutions, media, and practices through which these stories, ideas, and images are transmitted) we come not only to *imagine* the world, but to actively *occupy* the world. In ways both obvious and less obvious, for the majority of Americans, religion is central to this process.

Even in ostensibly secular spaces, secularization in the United States is, at best, wildly incomplete. American culture is steeped in religious languages, practices, and themes: redemption, hope, self-transformation, love of your neighbor, hate of your other neighbor, beloved community, holy crusade. These and other religious tropes are woven into the national cultural fabric, and they furnish the tools by which we cobble together selves and collectivities. Like America's culture of punishment, which seeps out of prisons and courthouses into the culture at large, American religion cannot be contained merely by bolting the cathedral doors. Even those of us who would never be caught dead in church are not immune to American religion's languages and moods, dreams and dispositions. To be a subject of this great and grotesque nation is to be filled, to some degree, by the spirit of religion.

We say this not to debunk but to exhort. The spirit of religion infuses the ruling American order, but it also infuses—*especially* infuses—the collective projects of those who struggle to dismantle this order. In public and private, and in mass-mediated spaces, ruling elites carefully manage and repress religion—just as they manage and repress race, gender, sexuality, disability, immigration, and labor. Diked and rerouted, these sites of potential mass disruption are smoothly integrated into the reproduction of power structures and the flows of capital. But management is a tricky business, and the long arc of the universe bends in the direction of messier outcomes. We understand that religion has often been used to mollify, but religion may also ignite. We write with the hope of coaxing elements of the religious repressed back to the surface. We want to call forth and explicitly ponder the religious stories, symbols, feelings, and practices that have shaped—and pushed back against—the present civic order, a civic order in which carcerality is a predominant feature. In so doing, we hope to lend support for smashing those elements that engender mass harm and to open up space for alternatives that foster mass healing.

To understand the United States as a prison nation—and to cure the maladies that afflict us—it is imperative that we understand it as a *religious* prison nation, and more specifically, as a *Christian* prison nation. To designate the United States as such is not to endorse Christian triumphalism, nor is it to absolve non-Christians of responsibility. Rather, it is only to name properly the tradition that most informs Americans' interlocking senses of order, justice, virtue, and redemption. According to the ruling logics that inform American common sense, the state is authorized to inflict violence for the sake of the public good; violations of the law enact wounds to the collective that can only be healed through the deliberate infliction of suffering; and for those who violate the law, this suffering is potentially redemptive. In the American context, these ideas have particular Christian histories, and the practices that attend them are secularized Christian practices. Put somewhat crudely: the systematic criminalization of certain American lives is a product of racial capitalism, settler colonialism, and patriarchy, but it also takes place in the long shadow cast by Christ on the cross.[3]

What role did religion play in underwriting the explosive growth of prisons over the last five decades? What role does religion play in sustaining mass incarceration today? And most crucially, what potential role might religious ideas, practices, and communities play in destroying the mammoth carceral state and its attendant carceral culture, and in helping to foster in its place a culture of mutual care? These are the questions that animate the inquiry to follow.[4]

A Religious Prison Nation

The graph is familiar and baffling: a more or less flat line representing the US prison population into the early 1970s, followed by an almost vertical leap afterward.[5] The contrast borders on the cartoonish. Something happened, but what?

Among scholars, activists, and the general public, three stories currently circulate for what happened. Let us call these stories the "race account," the "politics account," and the "economics account." According to the first, the United States has always found ways to ensure a racial caste system in which Black people are disenfranchised and impoverished, their labor brutally extracted. When slavery ended, white terror installed a regime of segregation.[6] When the Jim Crow order was destroyed, a new way of controlling, marginalizing, and exploiting Black Americans came into being. As a one-two punch, the War on Drugs and consequent mass incarceration have supplied the necessary means. Unlike its predecessors, mass incarceration is nominally colorblind, but due to the racist ways that the drug war has been policed and prosecuted, it has served to perpetuate, and even intensify, America's racialized caste system. The expressly racist justifications are gone, but under what legal scholar Michelle Alexander has dubbed the "New Jim Crow," the net result of controlling Black bodies and subjugating Black communities remains more or less the same.[7]

According to the second story, mass incarceration has been a bipartisan political project. In this account, the forces of white supremacy team up with midcentury liberalism's bullishness about the power of state institutions to engineer equality of outcome. Under the Great Society, punishment outcomes were rationalized and standardized, and when the optimism curdled, prisons became an expedient solution to an ever wider set of social and political problems. Discipline and demonize, stoke up moral panics about crime, broaden the set of behaviors that are criminalized, toughen penalties, and limit people's power to contest their sentences: Richard Nixon developed this game, Ronald Reagan refined it, and after Michael Dukakis's shellacking in the 1988 presidential election, Bill Clinton went all in. The ratchet only turned one way.[8] What resulted was a political landscape in which no politician on the national stage was willing to waste an ounce of symbolic capital on the rights of incarcerated people or criminal defendants. Practice this brand of politics for a generation or two, and mass incarceration is what you get. Once locked in place, moreover, the narrow range of political remedies for dismantling mass incarceration lack the sweep and the teeth to do anything more than chip away at the edges of the problem.[9]

The third explanation for the rise of mass incarceration is economic. Before the prison explosion, the United States was experiencing the most robust economic growth in the country's history. Manufacturing, which had ramped up for the Second World War, continued to offer secure jobs. Income inequality was relatively low. For a variety of social sectors, prosperity reigned. But it did not last. The weakening of organized labor, the globalization of industrial manufacturing, and military downsizing in the waning days of the Cold War pushed up the unemployment rate and engendered warranted feelings of insecurity. A growing underclass, disproportionately living in urban centers and disproportionately Black and brown, found itself cut out of the labor market. Income and wealth inequality began to climb. Frustrated by their precariousness and demonstrably prone to uprising, this surplus population posed a problem for the smooth functioning of

American business. If class consciousness developed fully, the urban underclass might try to seize the means of production. The solution to this threat—
and the solution to surpluses of state capacity, land, and population—was to
build a mass public infrastructure for containing this underclass. This was
the prison building boom of the 1980s. By this read, mass incarceration is a
cunning adaptation to postindustrialization, a machine for containing the
urban underclass for whom viable work is no longer available, while simultaneously fostering economic opportunities for others, and for rural white
men in particular, many of whom were able to secure good union jobs in
the adjacent sectors of prison building and prisoner management. In time,
that which was emergent became entrenched. This system exploits incarcerated workers, and it rewards correctional officers' unions, prison contractors,
and private-prison shareholders. And these are merely the surface players.
In enumerable ways, the private and public sectors have come to depend on
incarcerated bodies. Though they destroy more communities than they sustain, mass criminalization and mass incarceration are thoroughly embedded
in the American political economy.[10]

In no respect does this book represent a repudiation of these accounts.
We are indebted to these frameworks, and in the pages to follow we make
ample use of them. But we worry about the ceiling that these three narratives
can place over possible political change. For good reason, the race account
and the politics account can lend themselves to cynicism, and all three accounts have a way of engendering a sense of powerlessness. In the event that
those who think with these frameworks evade defeatism and pursue political
mobilization, the carceral state has shown itself to be excruciatingly adept at
incorporating critique and converting vulnerabilities into new justifications
for growth. Focusing on racial disparities has been used to toughen penalties across the board, calls for improved prison conditions have led to new
prison building, and criticisms about the police invariably lead to more resources for law enforcement. Standard-issue politics has repeatedly failed,
and incarceration is one arena in which loosening the faucets of state
spending will only exacerbate the problem.[11] A turn to religion offers unique
potential. It is our hope that by weaving religion into the racial, economic,
and political accounts of mass incarceration, we will lend support to those
advocating for more fundamental institutional and cultural transformations.
In foregrounding religion we are not offering a diagnosis of what American
hyper-incarceration is *really* about, with the hope that demystification will
lead to redemption. More modestly, rather, we propose to actively and openly

engage with that which—for worse and for better—is inextricable from American life: religious traditions, practices, affects, and communities. We do not fetishize religion as in any way uniquely good or uniquely powerful. However, because of who we are as a country, religious stories, practices, and sentiments have the capacity to help us imagine and enact the sort of radical social transformation the situation demands.

But to move forward we must first look backward. What might a religious explanation for mass incarceration look like? Here's a preliminary gloss: Mass incarceration was born in the same historical moment as the megachurch and the big box store. Pathbreaking scholarship connects the rise of evangelical piety to the rise of Walmart and all it symbolizes, but the links between these developments and the rise of mass incarceration have yet to be fully explored.[12] In these newly supersized institutions of commerce, worship, and punishment, visions for the public good were shrunken down and distorted. Meanwhile, the role of the state was reconceptualized. During the New Deal and the period that followed, the state built social institutions intended to promote collective flourishing, but in the present era the state has been demoted to an auxiliary role.[13] With John Maynard Keynes shunted to the side and Milton Friedman afforded center stage, the state's job became to ensure a narrower set of freedoms for a narrower set of people. Tasked with fostering and protecting "free markets," the state buttressed the narrowing of economic opportunity with a heightened commitment to "security." The welfare state retracted, and the carceral state expanded. In the Reaganite taboo against "big government," the prison was granted a curious exception. The resulting world is the world in which we live: individualist, consumerist, identitarian, responsibilized, vigilantly concerned about "freedom" and "the economy" in the abstract, but all too agnostic about how social and material goods are distributed; where the wealthy live in securitized zones and act with relative impunity, while the poor are preyed upon by the police and confined to prisons in grotesque numbers and for obscene periods of time.[14]

At the first stirrings of mass incarceration a half century ago, American religious culture was also undergoing a dramatic transformation. Membership in liberal Protestant denominations began to nosedive, while evangelical and agnostic affiliations shot up. Along with this reconfiguration came a shift in public discourse. Henceforth, liberal Protestantism no longer formed the assumed backbone of American political culture. Prior to this point, a certain kind of religiosity pervaded American civic culture. God was thought to work through American history, and to participate in the collective work of

God—to pursue divine justice—meant laboring concertedly to make worldly law and society more just. It wasn't simply Martin Luther King Jr. who famously expounded this political theology. For the first half of the twentieth century, this political theology was expressed by mainstream politicians of all stripes. Beginning in the 1960s, American religion changed. With the waning of liberal Protestantism and the waxing of evangelicalism and secularism, religion ceased to a substantial degree to be public, collective, and socially minded. At both the individual and the communal level, American religion turned inward. Increasingly, religion was something private, personal, and spiritual—a matter principally between oneself and one's maker, or, in the case of secular spirituality, between oneself and oneself. As imagined and as practiced, religion came to designate an individual's belief—in a personal God with a plan for *your* life, or in a self bound primarily by the duties of experience and self-actualization. Not all succumbed to pietism or solipsism, but fewer and fewer felt compelled by a robust kind of collectivism.[15]

With personal conviction brought to the fore, divine justice was cut off from American politics. Religion's primary place (and many on the left would come to question whether religion has a place at all) was in the individual's heart. If, on the evangelical right, neoliberal economics and neoconservative foreign policy became constitutive of an alleged divine plan (with pastors rallying the laity to vote accordingly), for those on the secular left, God absconded and community power withered. The evacuation of religion from the left did not "cause" mass incarceration, but it substantially weakened the capacities of the left to push back against its emergence and eventual predominance. In stark contrast to the civil rights era, during the era of mass incarceration, progressive politics came to be pursued on a purely secularist plane. Rather than pursuing ideals, liberals chose to tackle problems. In a political milieu which demands that social programs intended to assist poor and working people be means tested, and their costs offset with comparable cuts to government spending, the unapologetic declaration of universal ideas about justice was put aside like a childish thing.

What religious ideals have remained have been hollowed out into thin branding slogans like Bill Clinton's "New Covenant" and Obama's "Hope." On the left, policy reigns. Moralists have been banished from the table, and wonks and administrators are the only ones left. To focus on ideals and stress moral principles was made into the purview of cranks and fools. In such an impoverished landscape of ideas, the ideal of "justice" was ceded almost in full to the "criminal justice *system*." This system is now everything. Justice has come to mean little more than the proper functioning of the law. Albeit neutral in theory, in practice this law shields those with property and gashes those without. The possibility for sweeping critique has been surrendered. With prophets relegated to silence, officers and administrators of legal state violence come to resemble gods on earth. For some, these gods are thought to be benevolent; for others, they are plainly demonic. Collectively deprived of the concepts necessary for imagining otherwise, however, few would question their sovereignty.

As a handmaiden to neoliberal economics and apologist for state violence, American religious culture has been partially responsible for sustaining the carceral state, but attending to religion may help us summon the power necessary for toppling this order. By foregrounding religion in the analysis of (and mobilization against) America's prison culture, we might tap new resources and, in the process, make new alliances. As we hope to show, religion has been intimately involved in enabling and sustaining the American carceral state, but religious languages, practices, and communities have also challenged the carceral state. Going forward, these forces can be harnessed to end mass incarceration or even abolish the prison in its entirety. On the one hand, this is simply a matter of getting bodies into the streets, but it is also more substantive than that. For our proposed intervention to work, it is not enough to relegate religious communities to one coalition partner in a pragmatic, secular movement for prison reform. Rather, we believe it is incumbent for the movement against prisons itself to "get religion." The movement against prisons needs to understand religion and it needs to harness religion's spirit. For the monumental challenge we face, a secular, pragmatic frame isn't enough. To win, we must go deeper than surface symptoms, and we must go larger than policy. To win, we must wage a war that roots itself in and pushes for a fully transformative vision of what justice is and must become. Religious traditions enjoy no monopoly in this regard, but they have troves to offer the struggle. Religious dissent animates some of our most powerful national myths and provides a potent toolkit for reimagining justice. Only by *getting religion* can the movement against prisons sufficiently empower itself to break the prison's stranglehold on "justice" in America, making it possible for us to imagine and build an alternative justice—a *real* justice—worthy of that name. Religiously fueled abolitionists transformed the national conversation about slavery in the nineteenth century and ignited the civil rights movement in the twentieth. So, too, today, an abolitionism doused in religion may be uniquely able to revolutionize the public conversation about prisons, and energize the mass movement necessary for eviscerating the prison industrial complex and the broader punitive culture that sustains it.

Abolition, Not Reform

For some reading these words, connecting religion to the ascendency and maintenance of mass incarceration will be the easy sell. But this is only half of our agenda. The other half entails thinking religion into the political project of abolishing prisons. Abolition, not reform.

The prison, and the society that depends on the prison, is violent and cruel. Prisons break people. They ravage communities. They are brutal and unjust, and they should be abolished. For reasons we will lay out in chapter 1, both on its merits and as a matter of strategy, prison abolition is the solution that mass incarceration rightfully demands. Our prison system is a moral abomination and it should be erased from the face of the earth. This is the negative case. Meanwhile, as an affirmative political project, abolition (as opposed to reform) is far-sighted and potentially transformative. Though necessarily fuzzy on the details, abolition provides a horizon for struggle without which transformative change is impossible.[16] As an idea, abolition is individually and collectively activating, a principle around which a winning movement can organize. As a set of practices, abolitionism has the power to remake the world. As we see it, the principal problem with prison abolition rests on one thing and one thing only: its manifest impossibility. But impossibility is only a starting point, and here the abolitionists of old have everything to teach us. Two hundred years ago, it was merely a fact of life that some people were owned by other people. On the strength of the greatest mass movement in US history, a radical principle was inscribed by men and women into the nature of things: *slavery is a moral abomination*. Not merely chattel slavery as it then existed in the United States, but slavery as such. This simple and uncontestable moral fact is a monumental historical achievement, and absent the courage and genius of generations of clear-seeing and brave people pulling together in the same direction, nature would to this day remain mute on the subject.

Is locking a human being in a cage a moral abomination on a par with a human being owning another human being?[17] We believe that it is, and we also believe that the world of our children's children that doesn't embrace this fact as natural and obvious is odds on a dystopia. The moral reasoning that condemns the unfreedom of enslavement but condones the unfreedom of human caging is plainly perverse. If justice demands that all slaves need be free, then justice also demands that all prisoners be free. We recognize that this is a radical position, but it is also, we believe, the just position. That people are caged by the state rather than by individuals, and that they are caged—nominally—for things they have done, should not distract from the basic proposition that placing a human being in a cage is wrong. If at this point you disagree, that is okay; but please don't discard us yet. Even if all you wish to do is "end mass incarceration," prison abolition is still a necessity. As we explain in chapter 1, only by calling for truly transformative change can the narrower goal of ending mass incarceration be won.

Making the impossible possible calls for an exercise in radical imagination, and it is precisely in this regard that religious faith, or something closely related to religious faith, becomes essential. To remain trapped in secularist conversations about policy is to doom ourselves to defeat. We must argue at the level of unyielding moral principle. Without religious dreams, we will not even be able to envision what a truer, more just justice will look like. As Angela Davis has persuasively argued, abolition is much more than the singular act of eliminating prisons.[18] Simply opening up the gates and setting everyone free is not nearly enough. We must also reconfigure our political system, economy, society, and culture to ensure safety, health, and well-being for all of our communities. A reform agenda may well improve individual lives, but social change this transformative requires abolitionist dreaming and abolitionist organizing. It requires that we decry abominations and declare the sacred values upon which true justice may be instantiated.

In so doing we play to one of our country's great strengths. Just as America has a prison culture—which in recent decades has grown ever more powerful—America also has an abolition culture. Just as American prison culture is imbued with religion, American abolition culture is also imbued with religion. Abolitionism's revivalist spirit catalyzes social movements. It speaks the languages of divine coercion and absolute principle, and by doing so it challenges and reshapes the taken-for-granted ways of the world. It addresses concrete injustices, but its vision exceeds (and, when called for, even scorns) the pragmatic. In the end, this revivalist spirit has the capacity to drive institutions for social democracy into existence. Abolitionism is the fiery spirit of John Brown and Nat Turner, of Harriet Tubman and Frederick Douglass, of shirtwaist strikers and Stonewall rioters, of Occupy Wall Street and Black Lives Matter. To win, it must also become the prevailing spirit of the movement against prisons. Today's prison abolitionists are already moved by this spirit, but without getting religion—and igniting whole religious communities with abolitionist fire—prison abolitionism will never acquire its necessary force. Only a mass abolition-steeped fury will be able to tumble the walls down.

American history is rich with resources for thinking about divine justice and for interrogating worldly practices that run afoul of God's law. These religious resources have been essential to American democracy, and they remain salient today even as they are drowned out by loud professions of personal faith or personal disbelief. Even communities seemingly animated by evangelical or secularist commitments are formed by deep, old, rich currents of American religion with strong collectivist potential. It is these currents, these lower frequencies of American religious life to which we must attune ourselves today. The justice we want, the justice we need, is larger than ourselves. It is a justice that takes the state to task, asserts that every one of us is entitled to safety and sustenance, and insists without qualification that no human life is disposable. We must own this version of justice, testify to it, and enact it here on earth. These are the frequencies of abolitionism: as it fought slavery, as it fought segregation, as it fights patriarchy, homophobia, and transphobia, and today as it fights not only *mass* incarceration but incarceration as such.[19]

Complications, Openings, Itinerary

For some, we realize, our proposed turn to religion might prove a tough sell. Secularism is so entrenched in our discourse that it distorts our collective memory and makes many recoil at the prospect of religious ideas, practices, and actors actively shaping history. Religion, as many on the left see it, is a toxic entity, something to be combatted. For such progressive secularist readers, the notion that in order to effectively combat incarceration we might have to actively engage with religious ideas is perhaps off-putting. Interfaith activism is one thing—bringing progressive Christians, Jews, Muslims, and "others" to a table defined by shared secular values is not particularly threatening—but tapping into expressly religious histories and beliefs would seem to many a bridge too far. But one builds a mass movement with the culture one has. Without religious ideas, practices, and communities, neither nineteenth-century abolition nor twentieth-century civil rights could have gotten off the ground, and until it learns how to make the most of American religion, neither can prison abolition.

We hope this level of abstraction is not too alienating. Given the brutal materiality of the millions of Americans directly affected by the criminal justice system, clearer lines of causation would seem appropriate and necessary. Might a focus on America's religious culture distract from what many find to be the fundamental problem with prisons: that they violate human dignity? The pages to follow do not offer graphic descriptions of the size or smell of prison cells, of the humiliation of strip searches, of rape, of tortured children, or of women shackled during childbirth. Shining a light on these disgraceful particulars is vital work, and is an invaluable tool for movement building, but we leave this work for others to do.[20] Our contention is that a different kind of analysis might help foster the conditions for wholesale transformation. The myriad indignities associated with prisons are impossible to remedy if our very sense of justice has been corroded beyond recognition. By attending to religion, we hope to bring into relief just how desiccated American "justice" has become, and to point to religious resources as vital tools for imagining a version of justice worthy of its name.

Many stories may be told about religion's entanglement with mass incarceration, and in the chapters to follow we tell only a few. We hope that the conceptual and historical territory we chart will inspire others to dig deeper, to ask new questions and develop new frameworks that braid together the religious and the carceral, so as to further unleash the spirit of abolition. Among others, important stories must be told about religion, prisons, gender, and sexuality;[21] about American religion, nativism, and the demonization of immigrants;[22] and about the American prison state in the context of global Christianities and carceralities.[23]

Thinking religion into the history of mass incarceration and thinking religion in prison abolition has required us to chart two separate historical arcs. In the first and last chapters, our timeline is the entire sweep of incarceration in America: from the early republic, through the Progressive Era, to the present. Most crucial here is the antebellum period, a period of religious awakening and the ambivalent moment at which an old institution—slavery—was being rendered expendable, and a radically new institution—the prison—was being made essential.

Scholars of incarceration have long attended to the prison's religious origins, but the explosion of scholarly interest in the prison over the past two decades has rarely considered connections between religion and prisons. In part, this is because much recent historical scholarship has focused on the South, where the connections between prison growth, anti-Black racism, and slave labor rightly dominate the historical narrative.[24] It is our aspiration to bring this story together with the religious history of the prison told by those whose focus is the North. We do not approach this material as historians proper. We engage this material rather as scholars of culture, scholars of religion, and genealogists. As the term is employed by Nietzsche and Foucault, *genealogy* is the analytic procedure by which the taken-for-granted facets of one's culture can be shown for the contested, historically contingent stuff that they, in fact, are. As genealogists, we believe very much in history's incendiary value. Just as history is frequently used to justify existing institutional configurations, history can, in a critical mode, serve to call our existing institutions into question.[25] Neither mass incarceration nor incarceration as such, which is to say incarceration as the default response to certain sorts of deviance, was in any way foreordained. Neither condition will persevere forever. Embracing the perspective that, historically speaking, our present moment resides someplace in the middle of the story is an empowering orientation, and also an essential one if we are to successfully do what must be done.

The historical material of the book's middle chapters is presented in a finer-grained manner. The story here tracks the emergence, beginning in the 1960s and gathering speed thereafter, of a particular swirl of religious and secular speech, practices, and feelings. Chief among these are new ways of talking about and administering justice. Whereas in the era that preceded our own, justice was an expressly theological concept, in the present era, justice means the "criminal justice system." Similarly, law, which used to strain toward a higher justice, has come to narrowly mean "law and order." As an organizing framework, law and order acts to protect the property of the wealthy and powerful and to sanctify the state violence that is systematically deployed against certain vulnerable populations deemed as problems. Prior to the emergence of this framework, the prison population in the United States was more or less in line with its global economic peers. After it, the US prison population grew exponentially, and the country now has an incarceration rate more than four times as high as the next highest nation in its peer group.[26] Prior to this emergence, liberal religion dominated the American public square and mingled freely with the practices of politics; after it, evangelicalism and secularism dominated the public square. Our foundational hypothesis is that this shift in religious and political discourses about justice is not unrelated to the rise of mass incarceration.

Pursuant to this hypothesis, chapter 2 focuses on high-profile political rhetoric and tracks the ways that during the era of mass incarceration the notion of justice was subsumed under the notion of law. Absent the horizon of a divine law against which state law might be contrasted and critically assessed, the criminal justice system became the only available means for effecting justice. In search of a cultural diagnosis and resources for resistance, chapter 3 focuses on religious communities: how they participated in, pushed back against, and accommodated themselves to mass incarceration. Chapter 4 focuses on religious language and practices among the incarcerated and shows how, over the duration of mass incarceration, law was used as a tool to manage radical, abolition-minded prisoners' religion out of existence—and how, at present, this barrier is beginning to crack.

In sum, these chapters track the disappearance of one notion of justice and the emergence of another. Prior to the 1970s, Americans from top to bottom, from the White House to San Quentin Prison, employed the language of justice to mark higher—often divine—ideals. The shift to justice as law-following, a shift marked by Barry Goldwater in the political domain, Eldridge Cleaver's conversion behind bars, and the rise of Charles Colson's Prison Fellowship ministry, corresponded to economic, political, and racial shifts in the nation. During the era of mass incarceration's ascendency, combative conceptualizations of justice that pushed beyond mere law-following were repressed. In our prisons and out, the law was used to separate politics out from religion. By the end of the twentieth century and the start of the twenty-first, Presidents Clinton and Bush fully embraced a law-and-order political paradigm, and celebrity death-penalty victim Stanley Tookie Williams painted himself as a law enforcer.

The landscape, however, is not quite so uniform. During the period we investigate, the evangelical Jimmy Carter hinted at higher ideals of justice, religious advocates of restorative justice grasped at prison abolition, and incarcerated religious men and women creatively pursued the good and the just in spite of their conditions of captivity. More recently, a new generation of protesters and organizers has transgressed the sacred-secular divide. New practices generated by the incarcerated and the free gesture toward new configurations of justice-seeking religion that strive for a world in which everyone is free.

Using different sets of sources, the three historical chapters track the rise of a dominant carceral logic. Simultaneously, each chapter tries to identify anomalies and fragments that might help us shift to something new and better. These anomalies converge in our final chapter. For most Americans living today, it is impossible to envision higher justice as it was widely envisioned in the period prior to mass incarceration's emergence, just as, for the overwhelming majority of Americans, it is now impossible to envision a world without prisons. Putting the specific features of our current world into historical relief necessarily shows that what we take for granted today has not always been so. By drawing out the historical contingency of our common-sense assumptions about justice and religion we open ourselves to new possibilities.[27] We open ourselves to witnessing, and enacting, a new emergence, a transformation that may be impossible for us to fully see or comprehend, but which we may intuit in anomalies and eruptions here and there. These crazy ideas, these radical improvisations, these moments of possibility, which do not quite fit in the ordering of our contemporary world, are embers of unrealized futures past.[28] In this book we seek to gently rake these embers together and fan them gingerly to a flame, with the hope that, one day soon, they will catch fire and consume the world. One day, not too long from now, we will collectively think and do justice differently. One day, not too long from now, there will be no more prisons. We assert these things to be true with the knowledge that these emergent truths are by no means foreordained, and that, therefore, it is our sacred civic duty to help make them true.

We do not aim at exhaustiveness. Our project, rather, is to construct a framework, show how it is plausible, and show how it might open new possibilities for those grappling with the moral and social catastrophe that is American mass incarceration and the larger prison industrial complex. As we gesture toward new possibilities, we are acutely aware of the necessary limits on our vision and our imagination. The justice we are hoping to nurture is not yet a live option; it is impossible and, to a substantial degree, unthinkable. Though we look backward for inspiration, we write without nostalgia. By revisiting the ideas and practices of an earlier moment, we are not hoping to resurrect a lost world—most certainly not the liberal Protestantism or Eisenhower politics of the 1950s. Instead, we scour the past for usable pieces for a better justice and to understand the world that is ours, in which "criminal-justice reform" can receive bipartisan endorsement but utterly fail to address the fundamental injustices of imprisonment itself.

Like all writers, we hope that our words will travel far and wide, but we write for a few audiences in particular. We write first of all for scholars and students of justice and injustice in America. The second decade of the twenty-first century has seen a welcome surge of attention among humanists and social scientists to mass incarceration. In focus and in orientation, this scholarship has been decidedly secularist. We are not disciplinary imperialists, and we do not believe that every scholar must focus on religion, but we do think that all scholars of mass incarceration should be sensitive to its religious dimensions, just as they are already sensitive to its racial, political, economic, and gendered dimensions. Simultaneously, by foregrounding religion, we also hope to offer religious studies scholars a pathway into the vital conversations about America's broken justice system.[29]

In departments of religion and in divinity schools, theologians have been doing excellent work in marshaling the resources of the Christian tradition to reframe the gigantic US prison population as a moral and religious challenge.[30] We seek to advance this conversation by showing how mass incarceration is not just one among many social problems out there for religious communities to address. Instead, religious ideas and practices have played a particular role in the development of this problem, and they are particularly well positioned to help end it. Moreover, we invite those who think with religious ideas to reflect on the ways that religiously motivated reform projects, such as opposition to the death penalty or the promotion of restorative justice, at times turn away from riskier and more exacting, but also more comprehensive, movements toward justice. We invite thinkers from non-Christian faith traditions to investigate their own traditions' relationships to the swirl of ideas, feelings, and practices that accompany mass incarceration, and to investigate how what we argue about American Christianity might or might not apply to their traditions.

Last, but in no way least, we write for activists and organizers, those with explicit faith commitments and those without them.[31] In places of worship across the denominations and across the country, social-justice committees are reading books by Bryan Stevenson, Michelle Alexander, and others. How can they respond? They should, we argue, welcome the radicals in from the cold, and join the growing movement to abolish prisons. Meanwhile, many on the American left have been opposing incarceration for decades, and some of the most vibrant organizing efforts today draw explicitly on Marxist, feminist, and Black radical traditions. Largely, these are today's abolitionists. Because of the association of Christianity with homophobia, patriarchy, militarism, and conservative politics more broadly, much of the abolitionist left has little patience—and little aptitude—for religion. We try to show why this should change. As we see it, secular prison abolitionists need not compromise their values to work in coalition with religious communities. These coalitions have long been vital, and we have everything to gain from deepening and expanding them.

Looking Backward, Looking Forward

Eventually, if we push hard enough, mountains may be moved. For two centuries abolitionists represented a radical fringe of American discourse, but around 1830, their ideas began to gain traction and followers. Black and white, enslaved and free, these abolitionists used a blend of religious, social, and political institutions to shift public opinion. A generation's worth of organizing later, the end of slavery had moved from practical impossibility to pressing moral necessity. It is this unfinished project to abolish slavery that must be our model and guide. In this respect, the Jim Crow metaphor, which in recent years has gained a powerful foothold in the public conversation around prisons, represents but a partial awakening. Our firm belief is that today's reformers who speak of the New Jim Crow, or, more recently, of the Thirteenth Amendment as the loophole that preserved slavery under another name, are tomorrow's abolitionists.

The spirit of abolition is both a spirit of righteous protest and a concrete, grassroots organizing practice. As such, it stands astride the secular-sacred divide, pushing us to envision the impossible, and to have faith in our power to make the impossible a reality. A religious attitude is here an essential component of the abolitionist cause. For the abolitionist, justice cannot be reduced to worldly terms (not the terms of *this* world, anyway). The norms and laws of worldly justice are no match for the abolitionist's justice, and the abolitionist's faith marks a commitment to shatter these norms and laws. What precisely lies "beyond" need not as yet be fully filled in—indeed, so as to allow for the broadest possible coalition, justice is advanced most effectively when it is not—but the existence of something "beyond" must be affirmed. Abolitionism builds on the shared intuition that there is more to justice than even the best policy proposals can achieve. Abolitionist faith is experienced and developed, collectively, through struggle and organizing in the world, with friends and neighbors and coreligionists and strangers, to advance that vision of justice. This necessarily involves difficult decisions, experimental failures, uncomfortable coalitions, and sometimes pyrrhic victories. As a collective endeavor, it also involves participation in community that cultivates the virtues needed for struggle. These include, among others, the virtues of faith, hope, and love. The abolition spirit can be found in religious institutions and in secular political groups, but it invariably transgresses such institutional boundaries. It gathers those dissatisfied with the menu of options on offer, those who feel the violence of unjust systems and know that incremental amelioration—though also necessary—is not nearly enough. Properly honoring human sacredness obligates us to destroy the idols propped up by the wealthy and powerful and to assemble in their place a world where all people are safe and all people are free.

The abolition spirit haunts the American spirit, the former rejecting the latter's unearned confidence and toxic triumphalism while at the same time embracing its suspicion of authority, its orientation toward the future, and its resolve to reshape the world. Religious communities also have within them— within their histories and values, their sacred texts and worship practices, their messianic dreams—the abolition spirit, and it haunts them, too, challenging any easy alignment between the world as we find it and the world as it ought to be. We cannot predict what shape the abolition spirit will take next, but we know that this spirit is once again upon us, and that we have everything to gain by embracing it. In forms that refuse classification as either purely secular or as conventionally religious, we can see the abolition spirit in the mass protests that have risen up in our streets and in our prisons, in the widespread re-embrace of grassroots organizing as our last best democratic hope, and in the seeming re-emergence of sacred values as declared in the public square.[32] We write with the hope of shedding light on this resurgent spirit. We write with the hope of fanning its flames.[33]

Notes

1. For a breakdown of the 2.3 million people incarcerated in American jails and prisons, and of the almost seven million under the criminal justice system's control, see Peter Wagner and Wendy Sawyer, "Mass Incarceration: The Whole Pie 2019," press release, Prison Policy Initiative (March 14, 2018), https://www.prisonpolicy.org/reports/pie2019.html.

2. We largely concede Loïc Wacquant's argument that "hyperincarceration" might be a more accurate term than "mass incarceration," for how it properly indicates the ways that the American prison population is radically uneven in its distribution. We appreciate the argument made by abolitionist organizer Mariame Kaba and others that for the attention it pays to the millions on probation and parole, and who live under government surveillance and control in targeted neighborhoods, "mass criminalization" is the appropriate term. Nonetheless, in the present volume we have by and large stuck

with "mass incarceration." We have done so because the religious and secular facets of America's carceral culture that supply our subject matter *are* mass phenomena, and the attention we pay is largely to prisons and to the incarcerated. In addition, with an eye toward strategy, we deploy the language of "mass incarceration" because that is the organizing category around which the energies of the public discourse are currently focused. See Loïc Wacquant, "Class, Race & Hyperincarceration in Revanchist America," *Daedalus* 139, no. 3 (2010), 74–90.

3. For a Christian theological development of this point, see James Cone, *The Cross and the Lynching Tree* (Maryknoll, NY: Orbis, 2011).

4. In what follows, we deploy the category of "religion" elastically and pragmatically. In refusing to pin down religion, it is not our intention to be slippery. Consistent with the spirit of this enterprise, it is our intention rather to open up as much analytic space as possible with the hope that some of the resulting connections will prove useful to the struggle. In some places, "religion" will allude to doctrines, in some it will allude to practices, and in others it will allude to communities. By the same token, "religion" will sometimes index discrete "religious" traditions and will sometimes allude to the spirit or mood of practices more commonly thought of as secular.

5. See, for example, the first graph in this useful set of infographics: https://www.vox.com/2015/7/13/8913297/mass-incarceration-maps-charts.

6. See Douglas Blackmon, *Slavery by Another Name: The Re-enslavement of Black Americans from the Civil War to World War II* (New York: Doubleday, 2008). For the role prisons played in this process, see Mary Ellen Curtin, *Black Prisoners and Their World: Alabama, 1865–1900* (Charlottesville: University of Virginia Press, 2000); and Sarah Haley, *No Mercy Here: Gender, Punishment, and the Making of Jim Crow Modernity* (Chapel Hill: University of North Carolina Press, 2016).

7. See Michelle Alexander, *The New Jim Crow: Mass Incarceration in the Age of Colorblindness* (New York: New Press, 2010). Troubled by the ways that this movement narrative erases Black agency, recent scholars have made important interventions and offered new nuances and wrinkles to this story. See Michael Javen Fortner, *Black Silent Majority: The Rockefeller Drug Laws and the Politics of Punishment* (Cambridge, MA: Harvard University Press, 2015); James Forman Jr., *Locking Up Our Own: Crime and Punishment in Black America* (New York: Farrar, Straus and Giroux, 2017); and Vesla Weaver, "Frontlash: Race and the Development of Punitive Crime Policy," *Studies in American Political Development* 21, no. 2 (2007), 230–265.

8. On the "ratchet effect," see Robert A. Ferguson, *Inferno: An Anatomy of American Punishment* (Cambridge, MA: Harvard University Press, 2014), 32–64.

9. See Marie Gottschalk, *Caught: The Prison State and the Lockdown of American Politics* (Princeton, NJ: Princeton University Press, 2015); Elizabeth Hinton, *From the War on Poverty to the War on Crime: The Making of Mass Incarceration in America* (Cambridge, MA: Harvard University Press, 2016); and Naomi Murakawa, *The First Civil Right: How Liberals Built Prison America* (New York: Oxford University Press, 2014).

10. See Ruth Wilson Gilmore, *Golden Gulag: Prisons, Surplus, Crisis, and Opposition in Globalizing California* (Berkeley: University of California Press, 2007);

Brett Story, *Prison Land: Mapping Carceral Power across Neoliberal America* (Minneapolis: University of Minnesota Press, 2019); Loïc Wacquant, *Punishing the Poor: The Neoliberal Government of Social Security* (Durham, NC: Duke University Press, 2009); and Jackie Wang, *Carceral Capitalism* (Cambridge, MA: Semiotext(e), 2018). See as well Brett Story, dir., *The Prison in Twelve Landscapes* (2016). For teaching purposes, Jackie Wang's consideration of the criminalization of the poor through fines and fees alongside the student-debt regime and the financialization of municipal debt is especially productive.

11. Striking a cautionary note to would-be reformers, abolitionist luminaries Ruth Wilson Gilmore and Angela Davis each routinely note how the carceral state has long been adept at converting critique into grounds for further expansion. In particularizing this critique, Marie Gottschalk notes how preoccupation with "the three Rs—reentry, justice reinvestment, and recidivism," does little to shrink the ranks of the incarcerated. See Gottschalk, *Caught*, 3.

12. Bethany Moreton, *To Serve God and Wal-Mart: The Making of Christian Free Enterprise* (Cambridge, MA: Harvard University Press, 2010).

13. We readily concede the limitations of the New Deal, paradigmatically with its exclusion of domestic and agricultural workers from the Social Security Act, but we refuse to define the New Deal only by its shortcomings. For a defense along the same lines see Cedric Johnson, "What Black Life Actually Looks Like," *Jacobin* (April 29, 2019), https://www.jacobinmag.com/2019/04/racism-black-lives-matter-inequality.

14. For accessible conceptualizations and histories of neoliberalism, see William Davies, "The New Neoliberalism," *New Left Review* 101 (2016), 121–134; Bernard Harcourt, *The Illuison of Free Markets* (Cambridge, MA: Harvard University Press, 2012); David Harvey, *A Brief History of Neoliberalism* (New York: Oxford University Press, 2007); and Naomi Klein, *The Shock Doctrine: The Rise of Disaster Capitalism* (New York: Picador, 2008). On "responsibilization" as a mode of neoliberal domination, see Jennifer Carlson, "States, Subjects and Sovereign Power: Lessons from Global Gun Cultures," *Theoretical Criminology* 18, no. 3 (2014), 335–353.

15. On the waning of liberal Protestantism and the ascendancy of conservative Protestantism in the public square, see Darren Dochuk, *From Bible Belt to Sunbelt: Plain-Folk Religion, Grassroots Politics, and the Rise of Evangelical Conservatism* (New York: W. W. Norton & Company, 2012); David A. Hollinger, *After Cloven Tongues of Fire: Protestant Liberalism in Modern American History* (Princeton, NJ: Princeton University Press, 2015); and Molly Worthen, *Apostles of Reason: The Crisis of Authority in American Evangelicalism* (New York: Oxford University Press, 2016).

16. Jodi Dean develops this concept of "horizon" in *The Communist Horizon* (New York: Verso, 2012), 1–22. For its application to abolitionist organizing, see "Towards the Horizon of Abolition: A Conversation with Mariame Kaba," The Next System Project (November 9, 2017), https://thenextsystem.org/learn/stories/towards-horizon-abolition-conversation-mariame-kaba.

17. On "human caging," particularly as a settler-colonialist technology, see Kelly Lytle Hernández, *City of Inmates: Conquest, Rebellion, and the Rise of Human Caging in Los Angeles, 1771–1965* (Chapel Hill: University of North Carolina Press, 2017).

18. Angela Y. Davis, *Are Prisons Obsolete?* (New York: Seven Stories Press, 2003); Davis, *Abolition Democracy: Beyond Empire, Prisons, and Torture* (New York: Seven Stories Press, 2005). It might be asked why we embrace abolition but not reconstruction, particularly given the embrace of the latter by the powerful organizing in North Carolina around Moral Mondays—see, for example, William J. Barber II, *The Third Reconstruction: Moral Mondays, Fusion Politics, and the Rise of a New Justice Movement* (Boston: Beacon Press, 2016). We certainly agree that the deep social transformation and institution-building connoted by reconstruction is essential, and we commend those engaged in such work. Our argument is that abolition, as a rhetoric and a strategy, is also necessary, and that especially with the help of religious resources, there is a good chance for abolition to move even further into the mainstream.

19. Similar to our reasoning vis-a-vis our use of the category of religion, the notion of prison abolition we are working with here is also intended to be elastic and pragmatic. As will be addressed in chapters 1 and 5, while the difference between prison reform and prison abolition is substantive and meaningful, the two organizing orientations share much common ground. We hope that prison reformists reading these words feel welcomed rather than chastened by the abolitionist call. Simultaneously, with our abolitionist fellow travelers, we don't want abolitionism to be made so accommodating as to be evacuated of its substance and power. In what follows we have tried to honor these two competing imperatives.

20. See, for example, Mohammadou Slahi, *Guantanamo Diary* (Boston: Back Bay Books, 2015); Jill McCorkel, *Breaking Women: Gender, Race, and the New Politics of Imprisonment* (New York: New York University Press, 2013); and Keramet Reiter, *23/7: Pelican Bay Prison and the Rise of Long-Term Solitary Confinement* (New Haven, CT: Yale University Press, 2016).

21. See Regina Kunzel, *Criminal Intimacy: Prison and the Uneven History of Modern American Sexuality* (Chicago: University of Chicago Press, 2008); Joey L. Mogul, Andrea J. Ritchie, and Kay Whitock, *Queer (In)Justice: The Criminalization of LGBT People in the United States* (Boston: Beacon Press, 2011); Eric A. Stanley and Nat Smith, eds., *Captive Genders: Trans Embodiment and the Prison Industrial Complex* (Oakland, CA: AK Press, 2015).

22. Overlapping with the issue of immigrant detention is the issue of private prisons. Ending private prisons is a potent rallying cry—and one that we endorse—but private prisons play a relatively small role in the larger American prison ecology. As others have argued, the narrow demand to end private prisons should not obscure the much larger moral challenge presented by the prison industrial complex in its totality. See Ruth Wilson Gilmore, "The Worrying State of the Anti-Prison Movement," *Social Justice: A Journal of Crime, Conflict, and World Order* (February 23, 2015), http://www.socialjusticejournal.org/the-worrying-state-of-the-anti-prison-movement/.

23. The international component of American religion's encounter with incarceration is another topic we do not adequately address here. American capital and culture flow easily across borders, and the American prison is no different. Troubling echoes of the American prison boom are being heard the world over, especially in

the most vulnerable corners of the world. Important stories may be told about the way American economic policies and American security policies are exported in tandem, not infrequently along with American modes of piety. See, for example, Kevin Lewis O'Neill, *Secure the Soul: Christian Piety and Gang Prevention in Guatemala* (Berkeley: University of California Press, 2015); Chris Garces, "The Cross Politics of Ecuador's Penal State," *Cultural Anthropology* 25, no. 3 (August 2010), 459–496; and Andrew Johnson, *If I Give My Soul: Faith behind Bars in Rio de Janeiro* (New York: Oxford University Press, 2017).

24. See note 6.

25. On genealogy, see Friedrich Nietzsche, *On the Genealogy of Morals and Ecce Homo* (New York: Vintage, 1989), 15–166; Nietzsche, *On the Advantages and Disadvantages of History for Life* (Indianapolis, IN: Hackett Publishing, 1980); and Michel Foucault, "Nietzsche, Genealogy, History," in *Language, Counter-Memory, Practice: Selected Essays and Interviews*, ed. Donald F. Bouchard (Ithaca, NY: Cornell University Press, 1977). See also Wendy Brown, *Politics Out of History* (Princeton, NJ: Princeton University Press, 2001).

26. For resources on international incarceration rates, see Marc Mauer, "Incarceration Rates in International Perspective," The Sentencing Project (June 28, 2017), https://www.sentencingproject.org/publications/incarceration-rates-international-perspective/.

27. We follow Michel Foucault in a commitment to historical inquiry that seeks to identify patterns in the ideas circulating at a given historical moment: circulating through institutions, social practices, media, speeches of the elite, ordinary individuals' common sense, and everything else that makes up the substance of culture in a particular place, at a particular time. These patterns form the *conditions of possibility*: they determine how one accesses the world, what can (and, at the same time, what *cannot*) be imagined, be seen, be said, and be felt. These conditions vary dramatically from time to time and from place to place, and reflection on them serves as a reminder that our own world could, and will, be radically different. See Michel Foucault, *The Order of Things: An Archaeology of the Human Sciences* (New York: Pantheon Books, 1970).

28. Walter Benjamin writes, "Articulating the past historically does not mean recognizing it 'the way it really was.' It means appropriating a memory as it flashes up in a moment of danger. . . . The danger threatens both the content of the tradition and those who inherit it. For both, it is one and the same thing: the danger of becoming a tool of the ruling class. . . . The only historian capable of fanning the spark of hope in the past is the one who is firmly convinced that *even the dead* will not be safe from the enemy if he is victorious." Walter Benjamin, "On the Concept of History," in *Selected Writings*, vol. 4, *1938–1940* (Cambridge, MA: Belknap Press of Harvard University Press), 391.

29. In so doing, we draw inspiration from our friends and colleagues who have broken parallel ground with respect to the creative and pathbreaking (but also at times regressive and heartbreaking) ways that Christian communities responded to the AIDS crisis and participated in the movement for gay rights. See Anthony Petro, *After the Wrath of God: AIDS, Sexuality, and American Religion* (New York: Oxford University Press, 2015); and Heather White, *Reforming Sodom: Protestants and the Rise of Gay Rights* (Chapel Hill: University of North Carolina Press, 2015).

30. See Amy Levad, *Redeeming a Prison Society: A Liturgical and Sacramental Response to Mass Incarceration* (Minneapolis, MN: Fortress Press, 2014); James Samuel Logan, *Good Punishment? Christian Moral Practice and U.S. Imprisonment* (Grand Rapids, MI: William B. Eerdmans, 2008); Mark Lewis Taylor, *The Executed God: The Way of the Cross in Lockdown America* (Minneapolis, MN: Augsburg Fortress, 2001); Kathryn Getek Soltis, "The Christian Virtue of Justice and the U.S. Prison," *Journal of Catholic Social Thought* 8, no. 1 (Winter 2011), 37–56; Lee Griffith, *The Fall of the Prison: Biblical Perspectives on Prison Abolition* (Grand Rapids, MI: William B. Eerdmans, 1999).

31. For a defense of the term "organizers" instead of "activists," see Astra Taylor, "Against Activism," *The Baffler* 30 (2016), http://thebaffler.com/salvos/against-activism. See also Andrew Sable, *Ruling Passions: Political Offices and Democratic Ethics* (Princeton, NJ: Princeton University Press, 2002).

32. On democratic hope and grassroots organizing, see Jeffrey Stout, *Democracy and Tradition* (Princeton, NJ: Princeton University Press, 2004); and Jeffrey Stout, *Blessed Are the Organized: Grassroots Democracy in America* (Princeton, NJ: Princeton University Press, 2010).

33. For the category of "abolition spirit," we are very much indebted to Mark L. Taylor, who suggested the category at our 2016 manuscript workshop.

1

Why Not Prison Abolition?

Juan G. Morales belonged to the 1970s crush of incarcerated men and women who turned to the courts for the protection of their rights and to ease the harshness of prison life. Morales was incarcerated in the state of Wisconsin, and his jailers were not allowing him to exchange letters with his lover. In 1972 he sued in federal court to restore his right to correspondence. His case came before Judge James E. Doyle, the father of a future governor. Doyle sided with Morales, and the language he employed says much about how the prison system was viewed at that time: "I am persuaded that the institution of prison probably must end. In many respects it is as intolerable within the United States as was the institution of slavery, equally brutalizing to all involved, equally toxic to the social system, equally subversive of the brotherhood of man, even more costly by some standards, and probably less rational."[1] The question Doyle believed he needed to address was how, given the imminent demise of the prison as a mode of punishment, judges were to treat this moribund institution. By today's standards, for a jurist to speak so bluntly of the prison's intolerability and brutality is as surprising as Doyle's sense of the prison's imminent disappearance is, in light of what was coming, ironic. Yet Doyle's sentiments reflect a relatively widespread belief in the early 1970s among policymakers and academics: the end of the prison could be close at hand.

In the years following the 1967 Kerner Report on the causes of urban uprisings, a raft of popular and scholarly literature challenged the very existence of prisons.[2] As is true of today, from the late 1960s to the early 1970s, there were many prison-related publication events. Unlike today, when critical attention is generally directed against the problem of *mass incarceration*—how and why it happened and how we might begin to end it—the critical attention of the previous era was trained on the scourge of imprisonment *as such*. Karl Menninger's *The Crime of Punishment* (1968), Nigel Walker's *Sentencing in Rational Society* (1969), Richard Harris's *The Fear of Crime* (1969), former US attorney general Ramsey Clark's *Crime in America* (1970), and Jessica Mitford's *Kind and Usual Punishment* (1973) are but a few of the works on this subject.[3] To a wide and receptive public, these opponents of incarceration argued that prisons simply do not work. Prisons attempted to rehabilitate, but high recidivism rates proved they were failing. Prisons were also cruel and unjust, according to these opponents—not merely as they were currently administered, but essentially and unalterably. Prisons were presented not only as fundamentally harmful to the captives, but as demonstrated by the infamous Stanford Prison Experiment, as machines that manufactured evil in the captors.[4] Jessica Mitford, an English aristocrat and journalist, went further, and offered a more structural critique: prisons are "essentially a reflection of the values, and a codification for the self-interest, and a method of control, of the dominant class in any given society."[5] Public attention was focused on the prison system, stoked by highly visible prison rebellions in New York City in 1970 and in Attica in 1971, and there was a sense among many that transformational change was inevitable. The system was an abject failure. It was now just a question of sorting out the practicalities.[6]

Forecasting the coming decarceration, in 1971 historian David Rothman optimistically asserted, "We have been gradually escaping from institutional responses and one can foresee the period when incarceration will be used still more rarely than it is today."[7] Two years later, in his widely circulated exposé *The New Red Barn: A Critical Look at the Modern American Prison*, reformer William G. Nagel prescribed as the only appropriate policy response a moratorium on all prison construction.[8] This proposal was broadly considered plausible and seemed to reflect an emergent common sense. In April 1972 a moratorium was endorsed by the board of the National Council on Crime and Delinquency, a centrist criminal justice think tank, as well as by the National Advisory Commission on Criminal Justice Standards and Goals a year later. Operating under the Department of Justice, this commission added a call for the closure of all juvenile prisons. Explicating the emerging consensus about American prisons, the commission wrote, "There is overwhelming evidence that these institutions create crime rather than prevent it."[9]

With such broad public concern, elites wanted to gain firsthand knowledge of the experience of incarceration. To get an impression of the conditions, lawyers, judges, and politicians would spent a day or two in prison. Emanuel Margolis, a prominent Connecticut civil rights lawyer, emerged from his own experience of being encaged fully shaken. The son of a rabbi, Margolis concluded from his brief prison experience that in incarceration "the total being is involved and affected—his dignity, even his soul."[10] Though acknowledging that his prison stay was short and relatively benign, Margolis nonetheless reported having gotten a taste of the indelible damage prisons inflict: "I began to feel, simply, like an un-person. . . . Having been assigned a number, I felt like one."[11] Prison reform, Margolis therefore concluded, was insufficient; the goal must instead be to eliminate prisons altogether. To understand what everyone was talking about, Congressman Stewart McKinney, a Republican from Connecticut, decided to spend thirty-six hours in a prison. The congressman "emerged from prison an emotionally strained man," the Associated Press reported. McKinney concluded that the current prison system is "a big waste of money and human life." Upon his "release," he told reporters, "I can't see consigning any human being to this kind of existence."[12]

Prison abolition was also on the feminist agenda. "How Many Lives?" asked an essay in a 1971 issue of the feminist newsletter *off our backs*, referring to lives snatched by the prison system. Written in the immediate wake of the massacre at Attica, the essay offers a list of possible reforms, including ending pretrial detention and the promotion of viable alternatives to incarceration. Carceral policies, the authors diagnose, are a product of the fears conditioned by patriarchy, capitalism, and racism. "The ethics of this society have been distorted by this fear, and are then imposed on nonwhite people, poor people, young people and women to make survival and experimentation crimes."[13] In concluding, the authors of "How Many Lives?" underscored on intersectional grounds the need for prison reforms to be pursued in haste and with an eye toward an abolitionist horizon: "Whatever approaches are used, the goal should be prison abolition. To have no alternative at all would be better than to continue the present reality. And we can't wait for the ending of racism and sexism and poverty in this country before we begin tearing down the walls."[14]

If those more accustomed to being on the receiving end of state violence didn't necessarily share the elites' blithe optimism, self-described revolutionaries were all the more determined to bring the prison to its necessary end. On June 9, 1972, five days after she was acquitted of all the charges for which she had languished for sixteen months in jail prior to trial, Angela Davis exhorted some 1,500 supporters in Los Angeles' Embassy Auditorium:

> A very long struggle awaits us. And we know that it would be very romantic and idealistic to entertain immediate goals of tearing down all the walls of

all the jails and prisons throughout this country. We should take on the task of freeing as many of our sisters and brothers as possible. And at the same time we must demand the ultimate abolition of the prison system along with the revolutionary transformation of this society.[15]

With voices from below and above declaring the prison to be a failure and a disgrace, concrete steps were taken to put it out of existence. In 1974 the Juvenile Justice and Delinquency Prevention Act was signed into law, creating an office within the Department of Justice charged with minimizing the juvenile prison population.[16] That same year, radical Norwegian criminologist Thomas Mathiesen's *The Politics of Abolition* was translated into English. The book recorded the struggles and triumphs of the Norwegian prison abolition movement, and it showcased the organizers' success in eliminating both youth incarceration and forced prison labor.[17] Following these leads, state legislatures took up the project of ending imprisonment for juveniles. Under the leadership of Jerome Miller—a reformer who left his training for the priesthood to become a social worker and administrator—the state of Massachusetts led the way with its closure of all youth-incarceration facilities.[18] Juvenile facilities weren't the only prisons placed on the chopping block. The vice-chairman of Pennsylvania's state-sponsored Justice Commission surveyed 103 "of the newest correctional institutions in America" and discovered that "the institutions were new and shiny, but for all their finery they still seemed to harden everyone in them."[19] He endorsed a moratorium on prison construction.

We begin this chapter with the abolitionist moment of the early 1970s to make a simple point. Not too long ago, prior to the madness that we have come to call "mass incarceration," a wide array of Americans looked upon the institution of the prison as a grave mistake, a barbarous relic that had outlasted its time. That sooner or later we would cease entirely to put human beings in cages was anything but a radical proposition. Fifty years on, for most of us, conjuring such a clear and simple moral vision requires a great deal more effort.

The Folly of Prison Reform in the Era of Mass Incarceration

Fifty years before Angela Davis's call for abolition in Los Angeles, Orlando Lewis, then general secretary of the pioneering Prison Association of

New York, reflected on the estranging awe he felt upon glimpsing Sing Sing prison by train:

> [T]he gray, bastille-like prison . . . loom[s] like a monolith beside the rail-road track. Its many small windows, that look like loop-holes; its cheerless granite walls, worn by the elements during an entire century; its extraordinary architectural construction, and its notorious history as a place of punishment, all lead the mind of the traveler to ponder upon the prison as a necessary institution in our American life.[20]

How and when did the prison become a necessary institution in—and arguably the defining institution of—American public life?

Still comparatively close to the prison's beginnings, Lewis was able to observe that the prison's necessity had been hard won. As a Progressive reformer—after his stint at the New York Prison Association, Lewis went on to become general secretary of the American Prison Association—his preoccupation was with finishing the job right.[21] "Sing Sing is passing," he wrote. "Built in 1825, by 1925 it will undoubtedly have been superseded by the most modern, most humane and most scientific institutions for the treatment of delinquents yet projected upon the North American continent."[22] Lewis was at best half right. The twentieth century would bring a raft of new prisons, but these facilities would supplement and not replace those that that already existed, and though decidedly modern, they would be designed less to treat than to control.

Nearly a hundred years after Lewis's reflections, New Yorkers still train past Sing Sing, but few would entertain the possibility of its passing. Prisons have become necessary to a degree that Lewis couldn't possibly have foreseen. The numbers speak clearly. By the 1923 census, the United States had 109,619 people in prison and jail, a figure that represented less than a tenth of 1% of the population. Today, we have 2.3 million, with a rate more than seven times that of Lewis's day. Thus, a nation with just 5% of the world's population incarcerates nearly a quarter of the world's prisoners.[23]

There is little historical precedent for what we are collectively up to. Devastating in absolute terms, the crosstabs are yet more discouraging. Because our laws and carceral procedures are enforced with gross unevenness, mass incarceration punishes poor people, and Black and brown people, the hardest. And while we know incarcerated and formerly incarcerated people who emphatically maintain that if not for prison they would surely be dead, few would claim beneficence as being what prisons are primarily for. As the number of prisons boomed, the administrative ambitions of these institutions grew ever more modest. Whereas in the era that preceded our own, prisons were said to be places for rehabilitation, few on either side of the bars would make that claim today. At its most philosophically ambitious these days, human caging is said to deter future crime, but this too is a waning doctrine. To inflict retributive suffering and to warehouse the variously "dangerous" and unwanted—in the era of mass incarceration, this is what prisons are said to be for. For those willing to think remotely critically about these claims, the composite picture is unambiguous: prisons are where people who have already been neglected and brutalized are placed for further neglect and brutalization. This, it seems, is merely how things must be.

The good news is that the moral and social catastrophe called "mass incarceration" is now an open secret. Beginning around 2015, politicians from across the spectrum—from Bernie Sanders on the left, to Hillary Clinton, Barack Obama, and Eric Holder in the center, to Chuck Grassley and Mike Lee on the right—declared their intention to do something about it. Even the Koch brothers were in.[24] With such a broad coalition in place, if we can just muddle through the Trump era (a sizable "if"), then mass incarceration's days are surely numbered, right? Not remotely. And this is the bad news: from the sort of proposals on offer, prison reform proponents seem to have absolutely no appreciation of just how massive the problem is.

What would it take to truly "end mass incarceration"? As a thought experiment, let us consider three radical policy proposals—proposals specifically tailored to mass incarceration's political, racial, and economic dimensions. First, to scale down the War on Drugs, we might release every person in state and federal custody who is incarcerated solely on the basis of a nonviolent drug offense. Second, to stop incarcerating people simply because they're poor, we might release every pretrial defendant who is sitting in jail solely because he or she has been unable to make bail. Third, to end the New Jim Crow, we might release the 36.2% of state and federal prisoners who are Black.[25] Between state and federal prisons and county jails, this means releasing 367,000 nonviolent drug offenders, half a million pretrial defendants, and the remaining 75% of the 549,100 Black men and women in state and federal prison that we haven't already accounted for under provisions one and two.

By committing to these three measures, the United States could reduce its prison population by over 50%, to a tick over one million people. Were it legislatively feasible, and were it enacted in every state and at the federal level, an outcome of this scale would be an outsize achievement politically, and a monumental good. What it would *not* do, however, is end mass incarceration. Even at half its current size, the US incarceration rate would remain three times that of France, four times that of Germany, and similar degrees in excess of where it was for the first three-quarters of the twentieth century.[26]

Here is what an actual piece of state or federal legislation touted as "ending mass incarceration" would be likely to do: reduce mandatory minimums for nonviolent drug offenses; decriminalize marijuana; limit cash bail; provide block grants for local law enforcement for trainings and tech; and otherwise offer a slew of other modest provisions to reshape (rather than shrink) the carceral state.[27] Some systemic injustices would be rectified, others may well be exacerbated.[28] Tens of thousands of people would be helped, and victory would be declared. What will not take place in any real sense is the end of mass incarceration. Given how far down this insane path we have ventured, no reform agenda is capable of that.[29]

Why Not Prison Abolition?

Why not prison abolition? What would seem to be a policy question is in actuality a historical question: When, by what means, and to whose ends did the prison become socially indispensable, and, consequently, its abolition supposedly impossible? How does an oddball idea—locking human beings in cages for inordinate periods of time to "reform" them—come to take on the sheen of immutability? These are questions of genealogy. What, Nietzsche asked, makes self-sacrifice "good?" How is it, asked Foucault, that we all come to see ourselves as having an innate "sexuality?"[30] By untangling these knots, genealogy allows us to think not only about what people do, and to think about why people do the things that they do, but also, and most consequentially, to think about what in sum all this doing collectively *does*.[31] In the pages that follow, we return to the religious beginnings of modern incarceration and attend to the Quakers and Calvinists that made punishment edifying, but genealogy's primary object is less *them* than it is *us*. In this spirit, the question we wish to pose is as follows: What, according to your friends and neighbors, makes prison abolition not merely impossible, but, for many, unthinkable?

As we see it, the impossibility of prison abolition is secured via two primary means: It is secured via the coupling of crime to incarceration procedurally, and via the coupling of incarceration to justice conceptually. In the first, incarceration is presupposed as the primary strategy for securing public safety. The linchpin for this is incarceration's purported target: the "bad man." It is simply a matter of fact, most of us believe, that as a society we require protection from bad men (and increasingly, it would appear, bad women).[32] A more holistic and humanistic conceptualization of crime and delinquency as a function of broken environments, and therefore a matter of collective rather than individual responsibility, returns now and again as a leitmotif, but it hasn't had, for the duration of mass incarceration anyway, any measurable presence in policy conversations. In the public square and in court proceedings, lip service is paid to the role of adverse circumstances as an incubator to criminal conduct, but we fight crime at home like we fight terrorism abroad: peaceful ends are pursued with violent means. Achieving public safety first and foremost requires the incapacitation or outright elimination of bad men.

This approach is wrongheaded, we believe, even in the best of times. When the welfare state retracts and the carceral state emerges, making prisons the primary tool for battling a wide range of social ills, such conventional wisdom is catastrophic. We think of the prison as a place for "murderers" and "rapists"—which is to say, people that we brutally essentialize as being nothing more than the personifications of these crimes—but the number of incorrigibly demonic people in our prisons surely is vanishingly small. Prisons aren't primarily about managing incorrigibly bad men. They are about managing the poor and the sick, the neglected and the unruly. Prisons are said to protect us from evil people, but whom they truly "protect us" from are poor people, people addicted to drugs, homeless people, shell-shocked war veterans, and, when they get a little bit older, the poisoned children of Flint, Michigan.

Thornier still than disentangling prisons from "security" is challenging retributivism's near monopoly on how we've come to think, talk about, and *feel* justice and injustice. As a privileged case in point, consider Ta-Nehisi Coates's *Between the World and Me*. It is not by accident that the soul-wrenching instance of injustice at the heart of Coates's essay is the nonindictment of police officer Darren Wilson for the 2014 killing of Michael Brown. Coates intones, "The men who had left his body in the street like some awesome declaration of their inviolable power would never be punished. It was not my expectation that anyone would ever be punished. But you were young and still believed." "You" here is Coates's fifteen-year old son who, newer to being Black in America, announces his departure and retreats to his room to cry. "I came in five minutes after," Coates writes. "I didn't hug you, and I didn't comfort you, because I thought it would be wrong to comfort you. I did not tell you that it would be okay, because I have never believed it would be okay."[33]

Coates isn't wrong to see in the killing of Michael Brown and the non-punishment of his killer the unbroken legacy of white supremacy, but in his disappointment we read something else as well, something indicative of an age in which prison abolition is a manifest impossibility. Not all too long ago, Martin Luther King Jr. and those who stood alongside him appealed to an as yet unrealized higher law, and they strove to realize this divine justice here on earth. Two generations into mass incarceration, the greatest justice that most of us can imagine is a justice where avaricious bankers and virulent racists are treated with the merciless severity generally reserved for Black and brown youth. To honor justice and discourage such horrors from happening in the future, there certainly may be value in sending cops who murder to prison. But as an icon for injustice, the despair-inducing non-incarceration of Darren Wilson testifies not only to our country's unpassed history of systematic racialized terror, but also to what it is to live in a culture where the notion of justice has been shrunken down to the size of a jail cell.

The 2016 brouhaha over the inadequate sentencing of Stanford freshman Brock Turner evinces the same logic. Because he was deemed by the court to be guilty of rape, and because the victim's powerful impact statement went viral, Turner's six-month sentence was widely treated by progressives as a grave injustice. Testimonies of righteous outrage flared across social media, engendering more outrage. Progressive feminists demonized Turner and clamored for the judge's removal. Spurred by the public outrage, California's state assembly unanimously passed a bill raising mandatory minimum sentences for people convicted of rape where the victim is unconscious or too drunk to grant consent.[34]

The campaign against Brock Turner and the broader legislative fallout is what abolitionist feminists call "carceral feminism."[35] Whether or not the state's repressive wings have an affirmative role to play in promoting women's safety is a complicated question, and not one we have the capacity to adjudicate here. We reference the outcry against Brock Turner's short jail sentence to draw into relief a set of carceral assumptions that are now second nature, even on the left. Among these we would include the assumptions that crime is to be conceptualized as a product of individual moral failing (rather than as a matter of public health), that the only just response to crime is a lengthy prison sentence, that such sentences necessarily have a deterrent effect, and that such sentences are vital for victims' healing.

Why must the healing of victims be tethered to the punishment of perpetrators? Because the necessity of incarceration for justice has been so deeply ingrained, this question has been rendered more or less unaskable (and those that *do* ask are generally legible only as reactionaries). Almost entirely absent from the discourse, too, is the acknowledgment of the relative newness of the civic procedures upon which these assumptions depend. To take but one example, the first "victim impact statement" was presented in 1976, in California, and only in 1991, in a gathering swirl of laws and procedures that punished those charged and convicted of crimes, did the Supreme Court determine such statements to be admissible in court.[36] As moving as the viral statement of Brock Turner's victim might have been, in fact and in spirit, as a legal genre that mobilizes the spectacle of suffering for the purpose of harsher punishment, the victim's impact statement is a quintessential exemplum of the policies and culture of American mass incarceration.

In these ways, the impossibility of prison abolition pays profound tribute to mass incarceration, which even in its manifest failure has been utterly triumphant. Progressives rail against disparities of treatment, and they demand—for justice's sake—that rapists and racists be subjected to the sorts of brutality that the state levies on people of color, as though the principal problem with prisons is that their wantonness for human life isn't evenly enough distributed. Something bad happens? Someone must pay. Meanwhile, at the policy level, tepid reformism is the standing rubric for "ending mass incarceration" because, having been collectively acculturated over forty years, nips and tucks are generally all that most can imagine. This failure of imagination is to our collective discredit, but also at our direct expense. To languish in this failure of imagination is to sustain an America in which the mass caging of humans is a predominant feature.

How can we whittle away at abolition's impossibility? As an exercise, we would ask you to consider prison abolition alongside two other positions: death penalty abolition and an anti-militarism that stands ready to say "no" to whatever the next imperialist venture might be. Just as you might imagine a crime so heinous as to warrant death but balk at giving your governor the right to make that determination, or just as you might imagine the possibility of a truly necessary war but mistrust (in light of the track record) our commander-in-chief to make that call justly, so too might you regard imprisonment *as such*. Tools for domination are used to dominate. Opposing domination demands that we reject these tools.

Does the public good require some small number of people to have their movements restricted for reasons of public safety? For argument's sake, let us concede that perhaps it does. But is our prison system to be trusted as a proper means to go about doing that? As with the death penalty and whatever the next war on offer happens to be, as an ordinary American citizen in the age of mass incarceration, the best move available politically is to stand up—together—and to categorically declare "No."

Whether, like us, you regard locking a person in a cage as a moral abomination categorically, or whether you regard imprisonment as perhaps socially necessary but recognize the racism and classism that haunt our systems of imprisonment from top to bottom, by collectively assuming an abolitionist stance against human caging we open up space for moral imagination and practical experimentation, *and* we gain leverage for securing marginal political victories. Consider the three policy proposals we offered earlier—releasing all nonviolent drug offenders, ending cash bail, and the mass release of incarcerated Black people—and the degree to which such proposals seem to you impossible. Now consider the emergence of a robust movement that demands abolishing prisons outright. How impossible might those measures seem were prison abolition a recognizable position in the public conversation? Framed in this manner, prison abolition is anything but a pie-in-the-sky proposition. It is the leveraging of principle and moral clarity in service of practical politics. As the pragmatic rejection of pragmatism, abolitionism is the orientation we require if we are to actually win the struggle at hand.

However, prison abolition is no mere strategic posture. It means what it says: every jail and prison in your town and state will eventually be closed. We are not necessarily committed to doing this tomorrow. As the afterlives of American slavery perhaps suggest, there may well be credible reasons to take a gradualist approach to ending mass incarceration. However, we are unwilling to concede them out of hand. Would throwing open the gates and setting two million plus people free immediately be a manifestly insane course of action? Undoubtedly it would be. Still, we ask, would such a mad prescription be measurably *more* mad than simply pushing the brutal and wasteful *status quo* along for another day? We pose this question non-rhetorically. But

what a salutary development it would be if a question of this magnitude—
the question of *immediate* radical decarceration versus *gradual* radical
decarceration—were the one that those pushing to "end mass incarceration"
forced our elected representatives to answer.

A Peculiar Secularity

The history of human caging in the United States is saturated with the spirit
of white supremacy, capitalism, and settler colonialism, but it is also infused
with the spirit of American religion.

As we know from his prison records, Austin Reed was born in Rochester,
New York, in 1823. By age ten, this "bright looking little negro" was already in
jail, convicted of arson and housed in New York City's House of Refuge, the
nation's first youth detention center.[37] Freed at sixteen, Reed was convicted
again a year later, this time for larceny, and returned to state custody, upstate
this time, in Auburn Prison.

Some months into his imprisonment, Reed is caught talking to another
incarcerated man. As punishment, he is subjected to forty lashes with a cat-
o-nine-tails, then squeezed into a small box barely big enough to fit his body.
There he is left for the rest of the day. After dark, half-naked and covered with
cold clods of blood, Reed is returned to his cell. Huddling in the corner of
his cell, weeping, his face in his hands, he is interrupted "by a kind and sweet
voice that struck upon my ears like a band of music proceeding from the
white milk throne of heaven."[38] It is the venerable chaplain.

The chaplain extends his arm through the iron grate and takes Reed's
"black paw into his milk white hand." The old man exchanges greetings with
the young prisoner, barely a man but long since, if ever, a child. "You look
very pensive and sad this evening," the chaplain observes. "Yes sir," Reed
replies. "I've been drinking from the cup of sorrow, and now tonight I'll have
to taste the bitter bread of pain." The two men talk religion, and then the
chaplain asks after Reed's parents. Calling to mind his father, now passed,
and his mother, only a handful of towns down the Erie Canal but years away,
Reed is again undone by tears. The chaplain's presence brings solace and
bestows a grace—and indeed, a freedom—that Reed charitably reflects back
upon its source. "As the chaplain stood in front of my iron grated door," Reed
writes, "he seemed to me like a new born angel, sent from the portals of the
sky to come and unlock the prisoner's door, unbind his chains and let the

prisoner free."[39] Evoking the language of the Prophet Isaiah, Reed declares, "How beautiful are the feet of those that bring glad tidings."

For those caged in their gloomy cells, the chaplain's arrival indeed brings glad tidings. Even absent the brutalities of the cat, to lock a person in a cage is a form of torture. In forced solitude with one's thoughts, denied the stimulation of movement, all but the most disciplined mind will turn viciously inward.[40] Traumata return, shame and regret rattle, and despair rolls in. Against such crippling solitude, the chaplain's ministry is a ministry of presence, a presence that consoles and uplifts. For Reed, the chaplain's arrival delivers nothing less than freedom—freedom of seemingly two different varieties, one religious and one secular. In the first, the chaplain offers the radical freedom endowed through Christ's blood on the cross. But just as important, if not more so, the chaplain extends to men otherwise denied it the quotidian freedom of human touch and human recognition. To feel oneself seen, for once and correctly, as a child of God and as a man among men: these are the glad tidings delivered by the gentle pad of the chaplain's feet.

Reed's testimonial would seem to be a strong brief in defense of religion as a place of opposition within the carceral state. Amid the darkness, the chaplain is a light; amid the suffering, the chaplain is a lifeline. Though of the system in body, the chaplain is decidedly not of the system in spirit. Or so it would appear on the face of it. In Reed's account, the chaplain is a healer, but he is also an agent of torment. This is so not merely because he hangs his hat beside that of Reed's torturer, but also, quite simply, because as often as he arrives, he departs, and once he has left, the prison is no better than it was prior to his arrival. Even as he experiences his relief, Reed understands its fleeting character: "How lonesome, sad, and pensive I'd feel again when he was gone."[41]

It is tempting to see religious healing as the antidote to prison suffering, and, at times to a life-saving degree, for those in captivity, it is.[42] Assessed systemically, however, the temptation doesn't withstand scrutiny. In theory and in practice, the religious healing the chaplain provides belongs squarely to the prison system that is the cause of Reed's suffering. Whether in making this claim we are reading with the grain of Reed's testimony or against it, we are uncertain. But the judgment stands in either case. In effect, the torturer and the chaplain administer their services in complement.

Is there a more secular institution than the modern prison? Even though today they have swelled into corporatized behemoths, the marketplace, the stadium, and the state capitol all gesture back to their own antiquity. In its brutal efficiency, by contrast, the prison would seem uniquely and paradigmatically modern. Or this, in any event, is one of the principal stories that we tell about the prison. In Michel Foucault's touchstone formulation, as an institution the prison is the very archetype of secular modernity. It is a machine engineered to produce disciplined bodies and the modern souls that animate them from the inside out. As functional progenitor of the hospital, the school, and the military barracks, the prison is the institution after which all other modern institutions are crafted.[43]

But if the prison is emblematic of secular modernity, it is also emblematic of the ways that immanent to secular modernity we find preserved religious themes, tropes, and values. While Foucault might urge us to imagine modernity as a break with what preceded it, other theorists help us to muddy these waters. On their account, secularity in the sense we mean it is essentially a development within the history of Christianity.[44] As was claimed by German jurist Carl Schmitt, the ostensibly secular political concepts of modernity—individuality, justice, sovereignty—are deeply connected with our ideas about God.[45] Where once God was sovereign from on high, and the king ruled from above the people, now God dwells among us and sovereignty resides in the will of the people. This way of figuring the relationship between secularity and religiosity would seem to fit the prison to a T, in theory and in practice. As an earlier generation of scholars was keen to remind us, the Philadelphia reformers who in the early republic spearheaded a new form of punishment imagined the prison to be a disciplinary place of silent reflection and reform—a *penitentiary*.[46] In its inception, the modern prison was intended as an explicitly religious enterprise, and long after this generative rationale receded, the spirit of religion continues to haunt it.

To see the modern prison as at once profoundly secular and profoundly religious is no contradiction. Rather, this Möbius configuration is characteristic of the peculiar shape religion tends to take in American public life. For students of American culture, the snug interdependence of the religious and the secular has long been a dominant trope. As Alexis de Tocqueville observed: take the voluntarist spirit that allows the American republic to run, turn it around, and what you find is a version of American Protestantism, disestablished perhaps, but thoroughly pervasive.[47] In the spirit of Karl Marx's Martin Luther, who freed the Christian's body only by enchaining the Christian's heart, for free Americans in the antebellum period, newly unshackled from the coercions of crown and cross, it fell to Protestant faith to ensure that what these Americans wished for did not veer too far from the law. Meanwhile, those who proved themselves unable to self-govern would, by implication, find themselves subject to Protestantism's more brutal proclivities.[48]

In its formative years, the modern prison was inspired precisely by this sort of religious secularity. As historian Jennifer Graber notes of the religious men and women who brought Auburn Prison online, "The experience of Protestant prison reformers reveals the early national period's great paradox. It was a society marked both by the disestablishment of religion and the citizenry's commitment to the nation's Christian character."[49] For a secular nation to survive, it was imperative that this Christian character be instilled, and nowhere more acutely than in the bodies and minds of those who transgressed. If, for Philadelphia's optimists, individual reform necessitated isolation and the restorations of penitence, for the progenitors of the competing Auburn model, the recipe for individual reform was bodily suffering.[50] In language they drew from Isaiah 48:10, Calvinists spoke of the prison as "a furnace of affliction," one "in which God-ordained sufferings paved the way for receiving grace and reforming behavior."[51] Suffering was not incidental to the state project of reforming deviants. It was essential and, by its own light, benevolent. As Graber puts it, the "theology of redemptive suffering" did not merely allow for degradation and abuse; it "demanded these degrading practices."[52] And this perspective was that of the *reformers*! Even among the ranks of the afflicted, there were men who saw the whippings they endured as being "inflicted in mercy, designed for my good" (or so, when prompted to speak, these men proclaimed).[53]

As Graber convincingly tells it, over the course of the antebellum period, Protestant prison reformers found themselves increasingly sidelined from policy discussions. As time went by, suffering ceased to be a means to a theological end and became instead an end unto itself. Inevitably, new religious forms sprouted. For the Puritans, punishment was public but the transgressors on the receiving end were seen as belonging to the broader collective. With the birth of the prison, however, punishment was removed from the scope of public scrutiny, and the punished were separated out from the community at large. Meanwhile, ideas about God, the self, and the body politic were also in motion. Whereas during the colonial period, sin and redemption were, to a substantial degree, collective endeavors, in the ambient Protestantism of the early republic, salvation was made into a matter of individual responsibility. In the Second Great Awakening, religious conversion became a personal mandate. For members of the emerging class of free workers, a newly "democratized" notion of salvation was placed within reach. With a sufficiently temperate lifestyle and a spirit susceptible to religious enthusiasm, any man was redeemable.[54] Marked with the stain of their criminal convictions, prisoners came to be regarded as especially in need of ministry, and hidden carceral spaces became alluring grounds for evangelism. But as the emergent cultural logic would have it, such efforts were increasingly doomed to failure. Once they had been separated out in body, the people who were incarcerated came to be seen as fundamentally distinct from the rest of us.[55] Good religious folk became avid about redeeming prisoners' souls, but this religious zeal was itself a reflection of just how damned they took these incarcerated men and women to be.

Then and now, Americans' civic faith in the power of brutal state violence to effect positive social outcomes is also a religious faith.

Before Prisons Were Necessary

Perhaps nowhere is the braided character of the *is* and the *ought* more transparent than in the stories we tell about how "necessary" things came to be what they are.

In accounting for the prison's rise to necessity, Progressive Era prison reformer Orlando Lewis looked to the heady days of the early republic. Setting the scene at the precise hour of the Constitutional Convention, Lewis's posthumously published 1922 book *The Development of American Prisons and Prison Customs* zeroes in on a group of Philadelphians, Quakers mostly, who, under the banner of the Philadelphia Society for Alleviating the Miseries of Public Prisons, directed their revolutionary zeal onto the problem of punishment. Penalties for breaking the law were still meted out in pain back then, and crimes as meager as burglary and sodomy warranted death. Laden in iron collars and chains, prisoners were public spectacles, and the jails where they were housed were chaotic "centers of promiscuous herding."[56]

The Philadelphia idealists saw in the prison not only the occasion for inflicting punishment, but also the chance to enable improvement. This humanism wasn't motivated solely by an impulse toward mercy. It was informed as well by an environmental theory of social good that regarded public depravity as a collective product and saw the penchant for criminality as a function of a corrosive social environment. If instead of further afflicting criminal offenders, a society might repair them, the problem of crime could be ameliorated if not solved. In the simple but radical words of Constitution signatory and Society founder Benjamin Rush, the prison was to be, in short, "a reformative institution."[57] The raw materials for such reformation lay within the incarcerated man himself. Taken out of his environment and placed in solitary confinement with only his maker as a companion, a prisoner's inner goodness, repressed by the adverse social conditions that precipitated his crime, would be restored to sovereignty.

Public tortures and hangings were judged the stuff of kings and tyrants. As democrats and republicans, the Philadelphia reformers vowed to do punishment better. "Effective custody and punishment of criminals with humane treatment"—this was the administrative ambition of Philadelphia's Walnut Street Jail, which under its new reformist mandate commenced operations in 1790.[58] Solitary reflection and solitary labor were the tools by which reform was to be effected. The prison population was classified and stratified, with major offenders placed in isolation and lesser offenders housed in dormitories. During the day, residents labored in carpentry, joinery, weaving, shoemaking, tailoring, and making nails. Corporal punishment was unknown, and in the streets of Philadelphia, crime was down.

Success, however, proved short-lived. As admissions spiked, overcrowding followed. Discipline fell away and cruelties became commonplace. The prisoners responded with recalcitrance and riots.[59] Public opinion quickly shifted: for the "desperately wicked" at Walnut Street, one local expert was quoted as saying that "reformation is out of the question."[60] No longer a tactic for improvement, solitary confinement became an end unto itself.

Antithesis, that is to say, followed upon thesis. The synthesis was reconciled to the north in New York's Auburn system, or as it was also known, "the silent system." Auburn Prison was sanitary, and the discipline strict. "Day-association" consisted of silent group labor, and "night-separation" meant solitary confinement.[61] In 1821, with what Lewis characterizes as "penological faith" rooted in and conducive to "the deliberate elimination of hope," Auburn's board of inspectors glossed their administrative logic as follows:

The end and design . . . is the prevention of crimes, through fear of punishment, the reformation of offenders being a minor consideration. . . . Let the most obdurate and guilty felons be immured in solitary cells and dungeons; let them have pure air, wholesome food, comfortable clothing, and medical aid when necessary; cut them off from all intercourse with men; let not the voice or face of a friend ever cheer them; let them walk their gloomy abodes, and commune with their corrupt hearts and guilty consciences in silence, and brood over the horrors of their solitude, and the enormity of their crimes, without the hope of executive pardon.[62]

Lewis grudgingly concedes to the Auburn system its grim brand of genius. The great success of the Auburn system lay in the fact that it *worked*—but how? The Auburn system "had the beauty of a finely-functioning machine. It had reduced the human beings within the prison to automata."[63] In contrast to the "foul-mouthed recidivists" fashioned by Walnut Street and New York City's similarly styled Newgate Prison, Auburn's unrelenting discipline made prisoners manageable.[64]

By 1840, the year that Austin Reed arrived, the Auburn system had become simply how things were done. As Lewis put it, this "insurgent and reactionary movement against the failure of the first prison system" achieved "sudden and almost complete dominion."[65] For the century that followed its christening, Auburn Prison furnished the prototype for prison architects and administrators in the United States and beyond, and when Lewis himself visited Auburn nearly a hundred years later, he found the 1821 disciplines still very much in effect.

Reading Lewis's history over his shoulder almost a century later, a cluster of themes pop into relief. For one, the fate of the American republic has been awkwardly tethered to its prisons from the start. This is true as per the old saw (often attributed to Dostoyevsky) that the measure of a civilization may be found in how it treats its prisoners, it is true given America's self-regard as being "the land of the free," and it is true as a simple historical matter. As Lewis characterized it, the two births "occurred practically simultaneously."[66]

What makes Lewis's yellowed history eminently usable still is its capacity for demonstrating just how contingent "necessity" really is. Before prisons were rendered necessary, committed cliques had to struggle to make it so. In their crusade against public misery, the Philadelphia reformers dreamed big and overshot. But in the process incarceration was normalized as the primary tactic by which offenders were to be punished and public safety was to be secured. When Revolutionary-era perfectionism curdled into Jacksonian vindictiveness, the Auburn successors sought only to clean up the mess left behind. Which they did. Supplemented by liberal doses of torture both by the book and ad hoc, the Auburn system triumphed, but its achievement entailed neither healing its charges nor effecting public safety. On these social imperatives the Auburn administrators merely punted. Broken wills and docile bodies were what they wrought, and manageable prisons were their yield. By doing this reliably and by offering a blueprint for others to heed, the Auburn system secured the gold standard for any institutional innovation. It moved from the experimental margin to the practical center and displaced, by means of its triumph, other conceivable ways of doing things. In short, it made the prison *necessary*.

By conceding necessity, Lewis's sorcerer's-apprentice account of how American prisons went so catastrophically awry ends up, albeit in a roundabout way, a brief in the prison's defense. Lewis laments the state of prisons in his own era, but his abiding faith in the prison's capacity to do useful social work is in no way shaken. To the contrary, Lewis simply hoped to replace bad, dehumanizing prisons with good, reformative ones. Toward this end, the way forward for Lewis lay in the past. Like a good constitutional originalist or religious restorationist, the key to making bad prisons good was to reclaim, enact, and perfect the founders' curious vision.

Slavery by Another Name

For worse and for better, our illusions are different than Lewis's. Decades into the social and moral catastrophe of mass incarceration, we are witnessing the "rebirth" of the modern prison. Attuned to how prisons prey on poor people and people of color, today's historians, in reconstructing the way prisons acquired their necessity, tend to look not to the post–Revolutionary War North but to the postbellum South. And rather than good-faith efforts to alleviate public miseries, what scholars like Mary Ellen Curtin, Rebecca McLennan, and Sarah Haley have found instead are racialized regimes of social control engineered to preserve racial caste and exploit stocks of unfree labor.[67]

With the rapturous reception of Ava DuVernay's 2016 documentary titled *13th*, this history has given rise to a movement narrative.[68] As the eponymous amendment reads, "Neither slavery nor involuntary servitude, except as a punishment for crime whereof the party shall have been duly convicted, shall exist within the United States, or any place subject to their jurisdiction." The Thirteenth Amendment may have freed the slaves, but by mandating involuntary servitude as punishment for convicted criminals, it preserved a vital "loophole." Emancipation's counter-reformation came in a wave of laws that punished petty crimes like loitering and drunkenness. By 1865 all but two southern states had outlawed vagrancy, and they did so in a manner so willfully ill-defined that, in practice, any Black person not under the direct supervision of a white man could, without any additional cause, find themselves subject to arrest. As Douglas Blackmon put it in *Slavery by Another Name*, the book that would win him the 2009 Pulitzer Prize, "Beginning in the late 1860s, and accelerating after the return of white political control in 1877, every southern state enacted an array of interlocking laws essentially intended to criminalize Black life."[69] Less a case of righteous intentions gone awry, prisons have become more like white supremacy successfully preserved. Rendered in this way, prisons retain their aura of necessity, but not one we should any longer be willing to countenance.

Lewis's history of the prison served a reformist project well, but the new revisionism is better for smashing. What if instead of conceding necessity—and by extension, incarceration in perpetuity—we approached the modern prison for what it actually is: a historically contingent thing that emerged under certain historical conditions, will exist for a time, and will one day vanish? From such a starting point, what might criticisms of mass incarceration look like? How far might correlative policy prescriptions go?

Michelle Alexander's *The New Jim Crow*, which Cornel West accurately blurbed as "a secular bible for a new social movement," has turned a lot of people on to the horrors of mass incarceration. The mass mobilization against the "New Jim Crow" is an overwhelmingly positive development, but political frames have material consequences. Inasmuch as *white* Americans are incarcerated at four times the rate of French people and five times that of Germans, anti-Black racism is clearly only part of the mass-incarceration story.[70] But if there is *any* truth to the allegation of imprisonment being slavery by another name, and if there is *any* truth to mass incarceration being the New Jim Crow (and on each count we believe that there is *ample* truth), then ending mass incarceration—*really* ending mass incarceration—by all rights demands not reforms to ameliorate prisons, but rather a social movement to abolish imprisonment altogether.

Though the logical extension of the New Jim Crow argument is prison abolition, it is very difficult for most of its proponents to see this. So long as prisons remain necessary, the abolition of prisons remains impossible.

Lurching beyond Impossibility

That which is possible in the present is substantially dictated by the options history has preserved for us. At the same time, the past, as it is imagined, is to some extent a projection of the present and of what we collectively take for granted. Consider the civil rights movement. Is it at all surprising that during the era of mass incarceration, civil rights became a story of individual aspiration, of fantasy as strategy, and of prayer as will? This, as it has come down to us, was King's dream, and this, in faint echo, was Obama's hope. Dreams and hope are beautiful things, and they offer both succor and inspiration. But inasmuch as they primarily represent work a person does on oneself (and secondarily imply that it takes a messianic figure to effect history), dreaming and hoping invariably prove little match for the monumental institutional forces that have sustained mass incarceration.

But properly conceived, the civil rights movement belongs to another tradition, too, one with a decidedly different mood and spirit. This tradition is collectivist, confrontational, militant, and activist. This tradition is abolitionism. With the post–civil rights era beatification of King as a civic saint, the civil rights movement's abolitionist tendencies were separated out and shunned as Black Power. But as is its wont, the repressed is making its comeback. After generations in the relative shadows, John Brown, Harriet Tubman, and Denmark Vesey are once more American luminaries. It is worth noting which strain of abolitionism is being revived. Abolitionists in ascension today are not those who might be counted on to play nice at a fundraising gala. In movies, in scholarship, and in conversations on Twitter, attention is being paid to the radicals, the ones for whom moral clarity eventually made violence a necessary means.[71]

The appeal of an abolitionist politics these days is not just because of the depth and scope of the injustices and perils we confront, but also because of a gathering understanding that our civic institutions as they are presently constituted are wholly incapable of doing anything to fix them. In 2008 progressives and moderates elected Barack Obama with the hope that, as president, this charismatic but conciliatory man might be able to wring from a broken political system substantive victories. In the Affordable Care Act, arguably he delivered, but that policy, one originally designed by a conservative think tank, required a senatorial supermajority and years of wrangling. In the wake of the Sandy Hook massacre, when over 90% of Americans favored modest new gun control measures, Congress was unable to pass even the most meager of reforms.[72] With the Senate, House, and Electoral College skewed toward older, rural white voters and a conservative Supreme Court installed by minority rule, achieving meaningful social change through institutional means is, for the foreseeable future, also—to work our dominant theme—an impossibility. What endemic racial, economic, and gender injustices call into relief, the gathering climate crisis lights up in neon. Politics as usual cannot deliver justice and cannot forestall ecological catastrophe.

Meanwhile, at the margins of these ossified political procedures, at the local level, far more hopeful and vibrant activities are taking place. Elected officials and mass media may have chided Occupy Wall Street and Black Lives Matter for their lack of concrete policy prescriptions, but in this refusal to participate (what Bernard Harcourt has called "political disobedience") lies an alternative engine for effecting social change.[73] The reasoning runs like this: When incremental change through existing means becomes impossible, why not embrace a mobilizing vision for radical change whose realization would require nothing short of a popular uprising? Bernie Sanders's 2016 campaign for president manifested some of this insurrectionary spirit, but it was beaten back. Both within and beyond the bounds of party politics, the collective marshaling of a democratic will toward social transformations prejudged as impossible represents our last and only hope. This is the spirit of abolition.

Abolitionist dreams begin where impossibility leaves off. As agents of the most transformative social movement in our country's history, the nineteenth-century abolitionists are also an enduring, if malleable, archetype. As Andrew Delbanco ambivalently characterized them in his 2012 book *The Abolitionist Imagination*, abolitionists represent "a recurrent American phenomenon: a determined minority sets out, in the face of long odds, to rid the world of what it regards as a patent and entrenched evil."[74] In a fallen world soaked through with evil, moral absolutism becomes the only acceptable response. As incarcerated journalist Mumia Abu-Jamal puts it, "Abolitionists are, simply put, those beings who look out upon their time and say, 'No.' "[75] Or as radical criminologist Vincenzo Ruggiero has glossed it, abolition is "a flag under which ships of varying sizes sail carrying varying quantities of explosives."[76] Absolutism may fuel abolitionists' imagination, but this will to negation—for nothing burns hotter than negation—drives abolitionists' passion. The will to abolish is what comes forth when pessimism about the possibility for effecting justice hits rock bottom and careens back up in the form of righteous fury. Like Kierkegaard's knight of faith who must first pass through infinite resignation, abolitionism is both the abandonment of hope and its weaponization. In ways that can only be read as dangerous, abolitionism is both apocalyptic and messianic. It is the struggle of good against evil, and though it acknowledges that death will almost surely take you and me before the struggle is won, it is unyielding in its sense of urgency. As Delbanco puts it, abolitionism "identifies a heinous evil and wants to eradicate it—not tomorrow, not next year, but now."[77] In its moralizing heat, its revivalist alacrity, and its mulish refusal to accept the fallen world as finished, abolitionism necessarily resonates in a *religious* key.[78]

But what makes the abolitionists the best of all possible archetypes is what happens next: ever so slowly, they grow their strength. In ink and in person, they organize and fight, winning hearts and minds. They contest elections and sponsor legislation. They take over existing institutions and found new institutions. Soon, what was unthinkable is no longer quite so unthinkable. Eventually, they win.

To end mass incarceration, an abolitionist horizon is necessary. Whereas reform begins with the essentially secular stuff of data and policy, abolitionism plumbs a deeper, more soulful well. Whereas the call to "end mass incarceration" is merely quantitative (*mass*), the call to abolish prisons is qualitative—and therefore inherently fierce. If prison reform requires new policy proposals, prison abolition necessitates fundamental changes in the ways we understand transgression and atonement, collective responsibility and individual entitlement, justice and injustice. Succumbing from the start to the indigenous discourses of mass incarceration, reform invariably talks about what to do with dangerous men. At its most progressive, reform aspires to improve conditions, rehabilitate offenders, reduce recidivism, and shrink prison populations—all the while conceding that "public safety," a notion deeply entwined with the logic of mass incarceration, is the overriding concern. Abolitionism refuses these languages and instead insists on principles, on absolutes, on truths—and sets about willing these truths onto a recalcitrant world.

As activist-scholar Ruth Wilson Gilmore characterizes the abolitionist attitude: "Abolition is a form of consciousness. A dynamic aimed toward unfinished liberation requires not inclusion in this system, but the collapse of racial capitalism and the emergence of a new way of being in the world."[79] The racial critique of white supremacy is also an economic critique: of capitalism. For Gilmore, "racial capitalism" does more work than simply diagnosing the central role of slavery in the formation of capitalism in America.[80] Rather, she describes how "race-thinking" has haunted capitalism from the beginning and has shaped the ways that "those with power organize vulnerability" so as to create "sacrificeable populations."[81]

Abolitionist Law Center legal director Bret Grote strikes similar chords.[82] According to Grote, "For it to be coherent and successful, modern abolitionism must also be an anti-capitalist movement."[83] Diagnostically, this entails "the recognition of the historical and institutional sources of this system's power," which means seeing the United States as a "settler colonial society, a slave society, and a hetero-patriarchal society." Framed as such, the law is revealed to be "just another weapon wielded against the powerless." Echoing Gilmore's talk of sacrificeable populations, Grote distinguishes abolitionist politics "from the common liberal trope that the problem is a lack of distribution of rights. Disparities of power are inherent in the system; they are the basis of the system." There is no "reforming" away that which is endemic. For justice to be, systems that guarantee prosperity for some at the direct expense of others must be abolished.

As should be abundantly clear, by "the system," today's prison abolitionists are not referring exclusively to the criminal justice system. Rather, as these activists and organizers are the first to concede, the mass movement that abolishes prisons must also reshape how we educate our children, secure our communities, care for our vulnerable, protect our commons, and—if successfully internationalized—save the planet from ecological collapse. But the spearhead is the struggle against the criminal justice system, or, more concretely, what, in a nod to President Eisenhower's admonition against creeping perpetual militarism, Angela Davis dubbed "the prison industrial complex."[84] Primarily material and repressive in nature, a public and private network of buyers and sellers, managers and workers, the complex also stretches into the realms of ideology and psychology. For Grote, the prison industrial complex is the ensemble of institutions that are "essential to the contemporary US imperialist mode, essential to its management and its psychology. It is the blunt force that divides the population against itself." Within and against this system, prison abolition, for Grote, is "a transcendent ideal that is aspired to but not yet embodied," "an integrated unleashing of many types of liberation." It is also "a practice of struggle," and the concerted pursuit of "strategic objectives that will reduce the capacity of the state to perpetuate violence."[85]

In the score of "Abolition Statements" that in 2015 launched the journal *Abolition: A Journal of Insurgent Politics*, religion is on the one hand conspicuously absent.[86] None of the statements refer to God, and only one was written by someone affiliated with a religious institution. At the same time, however, in a way that is not merely analogical, these abolition statements are testimonies. In form and in spirit, they evince abolitionism's ethos, which even in its dominant secular idioms calls to mind some of the best American religious stuff: the Christian stubbornness to not accept the world as given, the will toward radical social transformation, and a form of individual redemption bound up in collective redemption. Nowhere does this spirit shine through with greater clarity and beauty than in the abolition statement offered by philosopher Lisa Guenther, who writes:

> Abolition is both a negative process of dismantling oppressive structures and a positive process of imagining, creating, and sustaining the sort of relationships, practices, and institutions that would make oppressive structures obsolete. Abolition is not a *telos*, if by *telos* one means the end of a process that is eventually completed, once and for all. It is not an eschaton, if by eschaton one means a redemptive end-state beyond history and politics. But there may be a sense of weak messianism, an eschatological opening to the otherwise in the midst of the everyday, that expresses the ethical and political temporality of abolition. These are the moments in which another world becomes possible: beyond prisons, beyond slavery, beyond white supremacy. They are the hinges on which social movements turn, the point when something clicks: I get it. Nothing can be the same again. We have work to do.[87]

Weak messianism. Whereas a strong messianism would place its faith in a prophet to come and redeem us, and sentence us to vigilant time-passing in the meanwhile, a weak messianism harbors no such hope for outside deliverance. In those moments of collective ethical growth in which another world becomes possible, we pledge ourselves to one another and to the collective duty of bringing that world into being. Abolitionist faith is the faith that together, in time, we will radically reshape the world in the image of true, divine justice. Whether this faith be conceived of as religious or secular, it is in this collective faith that the daily struggle continues.

Practicing Abolition

By need and by design, prison abolition cannot only be about destroying what we have. It must also be about collectively imagining what will follow after, and experimenting in the present with those possibilities. We have practice in picturing prisons laid to rubble (e.g., storming the Bastille)—it is what comes next that so boggles the mind. "Why should it be so difficult to imagine alternatives to our current system of incarceration?" Angela Davis asks in *Are Prisons Obsolete?* This difficulty is the crown jewel of mass incarceration as a cultural edifice. Within the rules of polite conversation, the burden is invariably placed on the prison abolitionist to answer the question: What are we to do with the bad and dangerous men? The genealogical response that calls attention to the curious way that the what-are-we-to-do-with-the-bad-men problem is the problem that American politics is *always* seeking to answer, and invariably answers with some version of state violence, may well land and resonate, but it does not displace the question. To qualify as credible, the would-be abolitionist is expected to offer some sort of techno-utopian alternative to incarceration. For Davis, inasmuch as this alternative is sure to be made in the image of the modern prison, wonkishness of this sort is a temptation to be resisted. Instead of looking for "one single alternative system of punishment that would occupy the same footprint as the prison system," according to Davis, we must

> imagine a constellation of alternative strategies and institutions, with the ultimate aim of removing the prison from the social and ideological landscape of our society. In other words, we would not be looking for prisonlike substitutes for the prison, such as house arrest safeguarded by electronic surveillance bracelets. Rather, positing decarceration as our overarching strategy, we would try to envision a continuum of alternatives to imprisonment—demilitarization of schools, revitalization of education at all levels, a health system that provides free physical and mental care for all, and a justice system based on reparations and reconciliation rather than retribution and vengeance.[88]

Abolition necessitates both the destruction of the institutional networks that undergird and are in turn sustained by millions of encaged people, and the generation of new social institutions that enable people and communities to flourish. After W. E. B. Du Bois's characterization of the post-emancipation politics of Radical Reconstruction, Davis and others use the term "abolition democracy" to describe this creative institutional work.[89]

None of this is remotely "academic" in the pejorative sense of the term. In 1998 Davis was part of the group that founded Critical Resistance. Based in Oakland with satellite offices around the country, Critical Resistance has been steadily building a coalition for prison abolition. Because mass incarceration has been driven by the lucrative prison building boom—what

Ruth Wilson Gilmore dubbed, in California's trendsetting case, the "golden gulag"—the central front of the Critical Resistance strategy is to stop new prisons from being built. Only three years after it was launched, a coalition that included Critical Resistance used an adverse environmental impact report to scuttle a $335 million prison project in Delano, California.[90]

If this kind of effort represented a dissident vanguard in the 1990s, it is becoming increasingly common today. In Madison, Wisconsin, a coalition led by Black youths demanding community control of police and "the human right to housing, food, education, and health care" successfully blocked the city from building a new jail.[91] In Philadelphia, along with groups led by incarcerated and formerly incarcerated individuals like Fight for Lifers and the Coalition to Abolish Death By Incarceration (CADBI), prison abolitionists were instrumental in the 2017 election of radical reformer Larry Krasner as Philadelphia's district attorney—a seismic victory which has spawned a national wave of DA candidates committed to decarceration.[92] Up the road in New York City, drawing energy from the high-profile tragedy of Kalief Browder, who, taken to Rikers Island at sixteen for a stolen backpack and unable to make bail, was tortured for years with beatings and solitary confinement, and subsequently killed himself, a broad-based coalition led by the formerly incarcerated organizers of Just Leadership USA pushed to #CloseRikers.[93] In February 2016, the *New York Times* editorial board endorsed this plan, and a year later, so did Mayor Bill de Blasio.[94] What—if anything—will replace Rikers when it closes remains the pivotal question. Against more conservative interests, the No New Jails NYC collective is fighting for the abolitionist outcome. Mass incarceration is a problem best confronted locally, and via grassroots efforts in communities across the country, organized prison abolitionists are achieving real wins. With each struggle, abolitionist politics is pushing further into the mainstream.[95]

As abolitionist organizers work to dismantle existing systems of policing and punishment, they are simultaneously experimenting with possible futures. The impulse to give up on the state and seek instead to effect justice ourselves may well have a whiff of neoliberal despair about it, but as an anarchist and a Republican would both agree, it is also plainly the stuff from which healthy communities are made. Some organizers build abolitionist futures by reclaiming the abolition spirit that once pervaded restorative justice.[96] Under the banner of restorative justice—or better, "transformative justice," since in communities broken by systematic injustices there is no prior justice to "restore"—practitioners work to decenter the bad men who must be punished and focus instead on the inflicted harms that require healing. Whereas defenders of the criminal justice system *claim* to care about victims, transformative justice is, its proponents claim, the system better geared for making whole those who have been hurt—by trading a system built to respond to the problem of human evil for one built to address human suffering. Personal accountability isn't abandoned in the transformative-justice framework; it is rather channeled away from punishment and toward the common good. While in standard issue American justice, what those who have been harmed are offered is the spectacle of the offender's suffering, in a transformative-justice framework, the attempt is to afford those who have been harmed with the opportunity for real healing. Meanwhile, finding themselves nurtured rather than cast out, offenders are empowered to become agents of transformation in their communities.[97]

In Chicago, which is a hotbed for abolitionist organizing, Project NIA, an abolitionist organization dedicated to ending youth incarceration, convenes talking circles—modeled on Native American peace circles—where offenders and victims, alone or in combination, gather with their families and communities.[98] Everyone is endowed the same right to speak, and decisions are all made by consensus. In these circles, participants receive support, resolve conflicts, and seek solutions to communal problems. In the course of these deliberations and their attendant stipulations, offenders are reintegrated into their communities. Though Project NIA currently operates its talking circles independent of Chicago's justice system, it is open to its talking circle becoming a diversion option for area children committed by the court to youth facilities.[99]

Closing jails and empowering communities to engage in restorative practices are examples of what Mariame Kaba, Project NIA's founder, calls a "non-reformist reform."[100] In contrast to reformist reforms that actually serve to strengthen the carceral state—police body cameras are a good example—non-reformist reforms try, in ways small and not so small, to heal individuals and communities and to transform the world. For Kaba, the challenge is to discern "[h]ow we create the conditions for a world without prisons, policing and surveillance while at the same time eradicating interpersonal violence." Abolitionism, then, is "a practice of creating new structures that will allow people to feel safe, have their needs met, on our way toward an abolitionist end."[101]

From building coalitions to stop new prisons, to community bail funds, to pushes to elect district attorneys dedicated to shirking the system, prison

abolitionists working locally have long been central to efforts to improve individual lives and push back against the systemic injustices that are articulated in crime, policing, and punishment. As Kaba, Dan Berger, and David
Stein argued in *Jacobin*, "For more than thirty years, abolitionists have been
at the forefront of . . . [vital] campaigns and coalitions . . . : parole for those
convicted of violent offenses, decriminalization of drug use, sentencing
reductions, better conditions for imprisoned people, an end to mass surveillance, and fewer people in prison."[102] And the momentum is building.[103]

Should incarcerated people be tortured with solitary confinement? Should
poor mothers languish in jail simply because they can't make bail? Should the
obligation of a district attorney be to put as many people in prison for as long
as possible? If you answered "no" to these questions, and feel impelled to do
something about it, then prison abolition is the best available stance. In all
likelihood, it *is* the stance of those at the forefront of these struggles in your
community. Whether you call yourself an abolitionist or not matters little. So
long as you are committed to ridding your community of systemic forms of
state violence—committed not merely to ameliorating these abominations,
but to stamping them out and replacing them with practices and institutions
more substantively committed to human thriving—then you are already allied with the abolitionist struggle.

As we have argued, the righteous unreasonableness of the abolitionist
stance has—even in its avowedly secular expressions—resounds in the key of
religion. This revivalist spirit is already manifest in the emergent movement
to abolish prisons. But as we hope to demonstrate in this book's final chapter,
prison abolitionists have much to gain from drawing more explicitly on the potent trove of religious resources that American culture places on offer. This is
true from a movement-building perspective, it is true for ritualizing solidarity,
and it is especially true to the degree that the realization of abolition democracy necessitates the wholesale reconceptualization of justice. Just as prison in
America has always been a strangely religious enterprise, abolitionisms past
have drawn extensively on Americans' ideas, practices, and feelings to conjure
a vision of justice that only a higher power could deliver.

To move forward, we must look back. Part of how we come to have so
many people living in cages is that the abolitionist impulse in American religion has been concertedly repressed. How has this repression been effected?
What precisely has been repressed? What remains unvanquished? In pursuit
of these dormant potentialities, these half-buried explosives, we turn next to
the religious histories of mass incarceration.

Notes

1. *Morales v. Schmidt*, 340 F. Supp. 548–549 (W.D. Wis. 1972).

2. For a critical edition, see *The Kerner Report: The National Advisory Commission on Civil Disorders*, with an introduction by Julian E. Zelizer (Princeton, NJ: Princeton University Press, 2016).

3. See Karl Menninnger, *The Crime of Punishment* (New York: Viking Press, 1968); Nigel Walker, *Sentencing in Rational Society* (New York: Penguin, 1969); Richard Harris, *The Fear of Crime* (Westport, CT: Praeger Publishers, 1969); Ramsey Clark, *Crime in America* (New York: Simon and Schuster, 1970); and Jessica Mitford, *Kind and Usual Punishment: The Prison Business* (New York: Knopf, 1973).

4. On the Stanford Prison Experiment, see Phillip Zimbardo, *The Lucifer Effect: How Good People Turn Evil* (New York: Random House, 2008). We note the experiment for its cultural significance, not necessarily as an endorsement of its claims, and certainly not as an endorsement of its methodology.

5. Mitford, *Kind and Usual Punishment*, 71.

6. On the Attica uprising, see Tom Wicker, *A Time to Die: The Attica Prison Revolt* (Chicago: Haymarket Books, 2011); and Heather Ann Thompson, *Blood in the Water: The Attica Prison Uprising of 1971 and Its Legacy* (New York: Pantheon Books, 2016). For an abolitionist critique of *Blood in the Water*, see Orisanmi Burton, "Diluting Radical History: *Blood in the Water* and the Politics of Erasure," *Abolition Journal* (January 26, 2017), https://abolitionjournal.org/diluting-radical-history-blood-in-the-water-and-the-politics-of-erasure/. On the era of prison uprisings more generally, see Dan Berger, *Captive Nation: Black Prison Organizing in the Civil Rights Era* (Chapel Hill: University of North Carolina Press, 2016).

7. David J. Rothman, *The Discovery of the Asylum: Social Order and Disorder in the New Republic* (Boston: Little, Brown, 1971), 295.

8. William G. Nagel, *The New Red Barn: A Critical Look at the Modern American Prison* (New York: Walker, 1973).

9. National Council on Crime and Delinquency, "Institutional Construction: A Policy Statement," *Crime and Delinquency* 18 (1972), 331; National Advisory Commission on Criminal Justice Standards and Goals, *Task Force Report on Corrections* (Washington, DC: Government Printing Office, 1973), 597.

10. Emmanuel Margolis, "No More Prison Reform," *Connecticut Bar Journal* 46, no. 3 (September 1972), 451; "Emanuel Margolis, Civil Rights Lawyer, Dies," *Westport News* (August 18, 2011), http://www.westport-news.com/news/article/Emanuel-Margolis-civil-rights-lawyer-dies-2108506.php.

11. Margolis, "No More Prison Reform," 452.

12. Associated Press, "Legislator Took Turn as Prisoner," *Indiana Gazette* (February 17, 1972), 28; William Cockerham, "McKinney 'Jailed,' Won't Forget 2 Days," *Hartford Courant* (February 17, 1972), 12A. As Cockerham reports, McKinney's response was to advocate for more funding for prisons, with the goal of turning incarcerated men and women into "taxpayers." The Haddam jail where McKinney was "jailed" was regularly used for giving judges, lawyers, and all new correctional officers a

prison experience. See Lawrence Fellows, "Prison Is 'Experienced' by 21 Probation Officers," *New York Times* (January 16, 1973), 43; Gordon S. Bates, *The Connecticut Prison Association and the Search for Reformatory Justice* (Middletown, CT: Wesleyan University Press, 2017), 289.

13. "How Many Lives," *off our backs: A Women's News Journal* 2, no. 1 (September 1971), http://www.usprisonculture.com/blog/wp-content/uploads/2013/05/offbacksabolition.pdf. As disseminated by Mariame Kaba, "When Prison Abolition Was a Feminist Concern . . . ," *Prison Culture* (May 13, 2013), http://www.usprisonculture.com/blog/2013/05/13/when-prison-abolition-was-a-feminist-concern/

14. "How Many Lives," *off our backs: A Women's News Journal* 2, no. 1 (September 1971), http://www.usprisonculture.com/blog/wp-content/uploads/2013/05/offbacksabolition.pdf.

15. Angela Y. Davis, "Speech Delivered at the Embassy Auditorium" (June 9, 1972), http://americanradioworks.publicradio.org/features/blackspeech/adavis.html.

16. In the 1980s the office would have its mandate altered to include a particular focus on racial bias in the juvenile justice system, and in the 1990s it worked to promote the development of restorative justice frameworks for juvenile justice. Office of Juvenile Justice and Delinquency Prevention website, https://www.ojjdp.gov/about/legislation.html.

17. Thomas Mathiesen, *The Politics of Abolition* (New York: Wiley, 1974), brings together texts published in Norwegian in 1971 and 1973.

18. Sam Roberts, "Jerome G. Miller, 83, Dies; Reshaped Juvenile Justice," *New York Times* (August 15, 2015), A23; Jerome G. Miller, *Last One over the Wall: The Massachusetts Experiment in Closing Reform Schools* (Columbus: Ohio State University Press, 1991).

19. William G. Nagel, "A Statement on Behalf of a Moratorium on Prison Construction," *Law and Psychology Review* 31 (1977), 32.

20. Orlando Faulkland Lewis, *The Development of American Prisons and Prison Customs, 1776–1845: With Special Reference to Early Institutions in the State of New York* (New York: Prison Association of New York, 1922), 7.

21. The American Correctional Association, the organization that Lewis headed, has "championed the cause of corrections and correctional effectiveness" for going on 150 years, and it now doubles both as an accrediting agency for correctional facilities and as a trade association. http://www.aca.org/ACA_Prod_IMIS/ACA_Member/About_Us/Our_History/ACA_Member/AboutUs/AboutUs_Home.aspx?hkey=0c9cb058-e3d5-4bb0-ba7c-be29f9b34380.

22. Ibid., 7.

23. For a breakdown of all those incarcerated in the United States, see Peter Wagner and Wendy Sawyer, *Mass Incarceration: The Whole Pie 2019*, Prison Policy Initiative (March 19, 2019), https://www.prisonpolicy.org/reports/pie2019.html.

24. See https://www.charleskochinstitute.org/issue-areas/criminal-justice-policing-reform/. For a critical take, see Michelle Chen, "Beware of Big Philanthropy's New Enthusiasm for Criminal Justice Reform," *The Nation* (March 16, 2018), https://www.thenation.com/article/beware-of-big-philanthropys-new-enthusiasm-for-criminal-justice-reform/.

25. For race numbers and nonviolent drug crime numbers, see E. Ann Carson, "Bureau of Justice Statistics (BJS)—Prisoners in 2013," Bureau of Justice Statistics (September 16, 2014), http://www.bjs.gov/content/pub/pdf/p13.pdf. The best available bail number is an estimate. See Ram Subramanian et al., "Incarceration's Front Door," *Vera* (February 2015), http://archive.vera.org/sites/default/files/resources/downloads/incarcerations-front-door-report.pdf.

26. See the Sentencing Project, "Trends in U.S. Corrections" (December 15, 2015), http://sentencingproject.org/wp-content/uploads/2016/01/Trends-in-US-Corrections.pdf. For international rates, see "Highest to Lowest—Prison Population Total," http://www.prisonstudies.org/highest-to-lowest/prison-population-total .

27. To its credit, 2018's modestly-dubbed "First Step Act" made no claim to be "ending mass incarceration." For critique of the legislation, see Dan Berger, "What the Latest Bipartisan Prison Reform Gets Wrong and Why It Matters," *Truthout* (November 16, 2018), https://truthout.org/articles/what-the-latest-bipartisan-prison-reform-gets-wrong-and-why-it-matters/. On its (non)-implementation, see Justin George, "First Step Act Comes Up Short in Trump's 2020 Budget," *The Marshall Project* (March 12, 2019), https://www.themarshallproject.org/2019/03/12/first-step-act-comes-up-short-in-trump-s-2020-budget.

28. Body cameras for law enforcement is one site where recent prison reform efforts may well have a negative net effect. See Chad Marlow and Jay Stanley, "Should We Reassess Police Body Cameras Based on Latest Study?" ACLU blog (November 20, 2017), https://www.aclu.org/blog/privacy-technology/surveillance-technologies/should-we-reassess-police-body-cameras-based. For the DC study, see http://bwc.thelab.dc.gov/#home. California's 2018 ending of cash bail but replacing it with risk-assessment metrics is potentially another example of reforms that reconfigure rather than shrink the carceral state. See Jeremy B. White, "California Ended Cash Bail. Why Are So Many Reformers Unhappy About It?" (August 29, 2018), https://www.politico.com/magazine/story/2018/08/29/california-abolish-cash-bail-reformers-unhappy-219618.

29. For a complementary argument, see Marie Gottschalk, "The Folly of Neoliberal Prison Reform," *Boston Review* (June 8, 2015), http://bostonreview.net/books-ideas/marie-gottschalk-neoliberal-prison-reform-caught. For an alternative quantification of the problem in service of a brief for radical decarceral reform, see Nazgol Ghandnoosh, "Can We Wait 75 Years to Cut the Prison Population in Half?" *The Sentencing Project* (March 8, 2018), https://www.sentencingproject.org/publications/can-wait-75-years-cut-prison-population-half/.

30. See Nietzsche's *Genealogy of Morals*, first essay, and Foucault's *History of Sexuality*, Volume I.

31. "People know what they do; they frequently know why they do what they do; but what they don't know is what what they do does." Michel Foucault, *The Birth of the Clinic: An Archaeology of Medical Perception* (London: Routledge, 1989), xvii. In relation to the study of religion, see Andrea Sun-Mee Jones, "What the Doing Does: Religious Practice and the Problem of Meaning," *Journal for Cultural and Religious Theory* 6, no. 1 (2004), 86–107.

32. See The Sentencing Project, "Incarcerated Women and Girls" (November 30, 2015), http://www.sentencingproject.org/wp-content/uploads/2016/02/Incarcerated-Women-and-Girls.pdf.

33. Ta-Nehisi Coates, *Between the World and Me* (New York: Spiegel & Grau, 2015), 11.

34. "California Lawmakers Pass Bill Inspired by Brock Turner Case," CNN (August 30, 2016), http://www.cnn.com/2016/08/29/politics/california-mandatory-prison-unconscious-intoxicated-brock-turner/index.html. In June 2018, after a highly misguided movement engineered by Stanford law professor Michele Dauber, Judge Aaron Persky was successfully recalled. For why this is bad, see John Pfaff, "California Ousts an Elected Judge. Everybody Loses," *Washington Post* (June 13, 2018), https://www.washingtonpost.com/news/posteverything/wp/2018/06/13/california-ousts-a-judge-everybody-loses/?utm_term=.800d66e5bfe5.

35. Victoria Law, "Against Carceral Feminism," *Jacobin* (January 11, 2017), https://www.jacobinmag.com/2014/10/against-carceral-feminism/. Toward an anti-carceral feminism, see also Beth Richie, *Arrested Justice: Black Women, Violence, and America's Prison Nation* (New York: NYU Press, 2012); Sarah Schulman, *Conflict Is Not Abuse: Overstating Harm, Community Responsibility, and the Duty of Repair* (Vancouver, BC: Arsenal Pulp Press, 2016); and Emily Thuma, *All Our Trials: Prisons, Policing, and the Feminist Fight to End Violence* (Champaign: University of Illinois Press, 2019).

36. *Payne v. Tennessee*, 501 U.S. 808 (1991).

37. Austin Reed, *The Life and Adventures of a Haunted Convict*, ed. Caleb Smith (New York: Random House, 2016), xvii. For a complementary abolitionist framing of Austin Reed's memoir, see Joy James, "The Roots of Black Incarceration" *Boston Review* (March 22, 2016), http://bostonreview.net/books-ideas/joy-james-austin-reed-life-adventures-haunted-convict.

38. Reed, *Life and Adventures*, 157.

39. Reed, *Life and Adventures*, 158.

40. An emerging consensus holds long-term solitary confinement to be torture. See, for example, Atul Gawande, "Hellhole," *New Yorker* (March 30, 2009); and "Special Rapporteur on Torture Tells Third Committee Use of Prolonged Solitary Confinement on Rise, Calls for Global Ban on Practice," UN press release (October 18, 2011), http://www.un.org/press/en/2011/gashc4014.doc.htm. For a philosophical consideration, see Lisa Guenther, *Solitary Confinement: Social Death and its Alternatives* (Minneapolis: University of Minnesota Press, 2013).

41. Reed, *Life and Adventures*, 159. On the ambivalence of the prison chaplain's role, see also Winnifred Fallers Sullivan, *A Ministry of Presence: Chaplaincy, Spiritual Care, and the Law* (Chicago: University of Chicago Press, 2014).

42. See Joshua Dubler, *Down in the Chapel: Religious Life in an American Prison* (New York: Farrar, Straus & Giroux, 2013).

43. Michel Foucault, *Discipline and Punish: The Birth of the Prison* (New York: Vintage, 1995), 195–230.

44. See especially Marcel Gauchet, *Disenchantment of the World* (Princeton, NJ: Princeton University Press, 1999); Charles Taylor, *A Secular Age* (Cambridge,

MA: Belknap Press of Harvard University Press, 2007); Michael Allen Gillespie, *The Theological Origins of Modernity* (Chicago: University of Chicago Press, 2008); and Brad Gregory, *The Unintended Reformation: How a Religious Revolution Secularized Society* (Cambridge, MA: Belknap Press of Harvard University Press, 2012).

45. Carl Schmitt, *Political Theology: Four Chapters on the Concept of Sovereignty* (Chicago: University of Chicago Press, 2005).

46. See, for example, Thomas Dumm, *Democracy and Punishment* (Madison: University of Wisconsin Press, 1987); Foucault, *Discipline and Punish*; and Rothman, *Discovery of the Asylum.*

47. Alexis de Tocqueville, *Democracy in America and Two Essays on America*, ed. Isaac Kramnick, trans. Gerald Bevan (London: Penguin Classics, 2003), 498–503, 510–519. On the role historically of Protestant religion in American public life, see, for example, Sacvan Berkovitch, *The Puritan Origins of the American Self* (New Haven, CT: Yale University Press, 1975); Tracy Fessenden, *Culture and Redemption: Religion, the Secular, and American Literature* (Princeton, NJ: Princeton University Press, 2007); and David Sehat, *The Myth of American Religious Freedom* (New York: Oxford University Press, 2011).

48. See Karl Marx, "A Contribution to the Critique of Hegel's Philosophy of Right," in *Marx: Early Political Writings* (Cambridge: Cambridge University Press, 1994), 57–70. On the broader point, see, for example, Anne-Marie Cusac, *Cruel and Unusual: The Culture of Punishment in America* (New Haven, CT: Yale University Press, 2009); and Dumm, *Democracy and Punishment.*

49. Jennifer Graber, *The Furnace of Affliction: Prisons and Religion in Antebellum America* (Chapel Hill: University of North Carolina Press, 2011), 5.

50. On the Philadelphia and Auburn models, see Adam Jay Hirsch, *The Rise of the Penitentiary: Prisons and Punishment in Early America* (New Haven, CT: Yale University Press, 1992); Lewis, *The Development of American Prisons*; and Rebecca McLennan, *The Crisis of Imprisonment: Protest, Politics, and the Making of the American Penal State, 1776-1941* (New York: Cambridge University Press, 2008), 1–86.

51. Graber, *The Furnace of Affliction*, 6.

52. Ibid., 183.

53. Ibid., 47.

54. See Nathan Hatch, *The Democratization of American Christianity* (New Haven, CT: Yale University Press, 1991). For the canonical Marxistist account, read Paul Johnson, *A Shopkeeper's Millennium: Society and Revivals in Rochester, New York, 1815-1837* (New York: Hill and Wang, 2004).

55. Graber, *The Furnace of Affliction*, 91.

56. Lewis, *The Development of American Prisons and Prison Customs*, 16.

57. Ibid., 22.

58. Ibid., 26.

59. See Norman Johnson, Kenneth Finkel, and Jeffrey Cohen, *Eastern State Penitentiary: Crucible of Good Intentions* (Philadelphia: Philadelphia Museum of Art, 1994); and Jennifer Janofsky, "Hopelessly Hardened: The Complexities of Penitentiary

Discipline at Philadelphia's Eastern State Penitentiary," in *Buried Lives: Incarceration in Early America*, ed. Michelle Tarter and Richard Bell (Athens, GA: University of Georgia Press, 2012), 106–123.

60. Lewis, *The Development of American Prisons and Prison Customs*, 41.

61. Ibid., 80.

62. Ibid., 81.

63. Ibid., 78.

64. Ibid., 87.

65. Ibid., 78.

66. Ibid., 8.

67. See Mary Ellen Curtin, *Black Prisoners and Their World, Alabama, 1865–1900* (Charlottesville: University of Virginia Press, 2000); Sarah Haley, *No Mercy Here: Gender, Punishment, and the Making of Jim Crow Modernity* (Chapel Hill: University of North Carolina Press, 2016); and McLennan, *The Crisis of Imprisonment*. McLennan's volume focuses on the North and South alike. On the antebellum pre-history of the exclusions of incarcerated people under the Thirteenth *and* Fourteenth Amendments, see chapter 2.

68. For scholarly assessments of *13th*, see the excellent discussion of the film by Dan Berger, Patrick Rael, and Dennis Childs at the African American Intellectual History Society's website: http://www.aaihs.org/mass-incarceration-and-its-mystification-a-review-of-the-13th/, http://www.aaihs.org/demystifying-the-13th-amendment-and-its-impact-on-mass-incarceration/, and http://www.aaihs.org/slavery-the-13th-amendment-and-mass-incarceration-a-response-to-patrick-rael/.

69. Douglas Blackmon, *Slavery by Another Name: The Re-enslavement of Black Americans from the Civil War to World War II* (New York: Anchor Books, 2009). To track this story into the prelude to mass incarceration, see Risa Golubuff, *Vagrant Nation: Police Power, Constitutional Change, and the Making of the 1960s* (Oxford: Oxford University Press, 2016).

70. On white incarceration rates and other visual data, see German Lopez, "Mass Incarceration in America Explained in 22 Graphs and Charts," *Vox* (October 11, 2016), https://www.vox.com/2015/7/13/8913297/mass-incarceration-maps-charts.

71. While it eventually played to mixed reviews, the $17.5 million Fox Searchlight paid Nate Parker to acquire *Birth of a Nation*, Parker's Nat Turner biopic, would seem to evidence the emergence of an appetite for abolitionist iconography.

72. Jon C. Rogowski and Patrick D. Tucker, "Critical Events and Attitude Change: Support for Gun Control after Mass Shootings," *Political Science Research and Methods* (May 23, 2008). Full text available at https://scholar.harvard.edu/files/rogowski/files/mass-shootings-attitudes.pdf.

73. See W. J. T. Mitchell, Bernard E. Harcourt, and Michael Taussig, *Occupy: Three Inquiries in Disobedience* (Chicago: University of Chicago Press, 2013), 45–92.

74. Andrew Delbanco et al., *The Abolitionist Imagination* (Cambridge, MA: Harvard University Press, 2012), 3. For a complementary study of a figure not always included under the abolitionist umbrella, see Gary Dorrien, *The New Abolition: W. E. B. DuBois and the Black Social Gospel* (New Haven, CT: Yale University Press, 2015). For

thinking through the tricky ethics of the abolitionist imagination, see Ted A. Smith, *Weird John Brown: Divine Violence and the Limits of Ethics* (Palo Alto, CA: Stanford University Press, 2014).

75. Mumia Abu-Jamal, "Long Live John Africa!," *Abolition Journal* (June 17, 2015), https://abolitionjournal.org/mumia-abu-jamal-long-live-john-africa/.

76. Vincenzo Ruggiero, *Penal Abolitionism* (New York: Oxford University Press, 2010), 1.

77. Delbanco, *The Abolitionist Imagination*, 23.

78. American abolitionism has its roots in Christianity, but abolitionism also, of course, shares revolutionary instincts with Marxism, a tradition animated by a similar fury at the world for what it fails to be and the consequent insistence on the abolition of the existing social order. For these reasons, we were not entirely surprised to learn that abolitionist luminary Ruth Wilson Gilmore grew up in a politically engaged liberal Protestant church. See Rachel Kushner, "Is Prison Necessary? Ruth Wilson Gilmore might change your mind," *New York Times Magazine* (April 17, 2019), https://www.nytimes.com/2019/04/17/magazine/prison-abolition-ruth-wilson-gilmore.html. On the dovetailing of Marxism and Black Christianity, see Cornel West, *Prophesy Deliverance* (Louisville, KY: Westminster John Knox Press, 2002), 95–130.

79. Public talk, New School for Social Research, New York City (September 16, 2016).

80. For the new scholarship on slavery and capitalism, see, e.g., Edward Baptist, *The Half Has Never Been Told: Slavery and the Making of American Capitalism* (New York: Basic Books, 2014); Sven Beckert, *Empire of Cotton: A Global History* (New York: Vintage, 2015); and Ned and Constance Sublette, *The American Slave Coast: A History of the Slave-Breeding Industry* (Chicago: Chicago Review Press, 2015).

81. Gilmore, Public Talk. On the category of racial capitalism, see Cedric Robinson, *Black Marxism: The Making of the Black Radical Tradition* (Chapel Hill: University of North Carolina Press, 2000); and Robin D. G. Kelley, "What Did Cedric Robinson Mean by Racial Capitalism?," *Boston Review* (January 12, 2017), http://bostonreview.net/race/robin-d-g-kelley-what-did-cedric-robinson-mean-racial-capitalism.

82. The Abolitionist Law Center is a Pittsburgh-based law firm that does extraordinary work advocating and litigating on behalf of people incarcerated in the commonwealth of Pennsylvania. See https://abolitionistlawcenter.org/.

83. Personal Interview, May 5, 2016.

84. Angela Y. Davis, "Masked Racism: Reflections on the Prison Industrial Complex," *Colorlines* (September 10, 1998), https://www.colorlines.com/articles/masked-racism-reflections-prison-industrial-complex.

85. Personal Interview.

86. See https://abolitionjournal.org/category/abolitionstatements/.

87. Lisa Guenther, "These Are the Moments in Which Another World Becomes Possible: Lisa Guenther on Abolition," *Abolition Journal* (July 10, 2015), https://abolitionjournal.org/lisa-guenther-abolition-statement/. "Weak messianism" is a concept Guenther takes from Walter Benjamin. In the summer of 2016 we published a brief short piece in *Abolition Journal* titled "Mass Incarceration Is Religious (and So Is Abolition): A Provocation," https://abolitionjournal.org/mass-incarceration-is-religious-and-so-is-abolition/. While to date *Abolition Journal*'s explicit religion

content has been relatively thin, scholars of religion Ashon Crawley and Roberto Sirvent are presently editing a special issue on religion and spirituality.

88. Angela Davis, *Are Prisons Obsolete?* (New York: Seven Stories Press, 2003), 107.

89. See Angela Davis, *Abolition Democracy: Beyond Empire, Prisons, and Torture* (New York: Seven Stories Press 2005); George Lipsitz, "Abolition Democracy and Global Justice," *Comparative American Studies: An International Journal* 2 (2004), 271–286; and Allegra M. McLeod, "Envisioning Abolition Democracy," 32 Harv. L. Rev. 1613 (2019).

90. For the history of Critical Resistance, see The CR10 Publications Collective, *Abolition Now!: Ten Years of Strategy and Struggle Against the Prison Industrial Complex* (Oakland, CA: AK Press, 2008). For concrete resources, see CR's abolitionist toolkit, http://criticalresistance.org/resources/the-abolitionist-toolkit/.

91. Young Gifted and Black Coalition, "Who We Are," http://ygbcoalition.org/who-we-are.

92. On the role of the prosecutor in the expansion and perpetuation of mass incarceration, see John Pfaff, *Locked In: The True Causes of Mass Incarceration and How to Achieve Real Reform* (New York: Basic Books, 2017). For a first-draft history of Larry Krasner's first year in office, see Ben Austen, "In Philadelphia, A Progressive D.A. Tests the Power—and Learns the Limits—of His Office," *New York Times Magazine* (October 30, 2018), https://www.nytimes.com/2018/10/30/magazine/larry-krasner-philadelphia-district-attorney-progressive.html. Some would reasonably contest whether electing a reformist district attorney falls within an abolitionist politics. We have chosen to group the coalition that elected Larry Krasner under the abolitionist umbrella as much for its energy and for how it defied—and shifted—what had seemed possible as for his administration's concrete yields. For a productively skeptical assessment of Krasner and the hope posed by "progressive prosecutors" more broadly, see Alex Karakatsanis, "The Punishment Bureaucracy: How to Think About 'Criminal Justice Reform'" *Yale Law Journal* (March 28, 2019), https://www.yalelawjournal.org/forum/the-punishment-bureaucracy.

93. See Jennifer Gonnerman, "Before the Law," *New Yorker* (October 6, 2014); and Gonnerman, "Kalief Browder, 1993–2015," *New Yorker* (June 7, 2015).

94. See Editorial Board, "Imagining a Rikers Island with No Jail," *New York Times* (February 24, 2016), http://www.nytimes.com/2016/02/24/opinion/imagining-a-rikers-island-with-no-jail.html; and http://www.closerikers.org/. With respect to Rikers, the devil remains in the details, and though Mayor de Blasio's plan would shrink New York City's jail population in half, organizers are opposing the new "community" jails proposed for the boroughs; see Amy Plitt, "City Unveils Plans for 4 Borough-Based Prisons as Part of Rikers Island Closure," *Curbed New York* (August 15, 2018), https://ny.curbed.com/2018/8/15/17693002/rikers-island-new-york-shutdown-new-jails; Raven Rakia and Ashoka Jegree, "How the Push to Close Rikers went from No Jails to New Jails," *TheAppeal.com* (May 29, 2018), https://theappeal.org/how-the-push-to-close-rikers-went-from-no-jails-to-new-jails/; and https://nonewjails.nyc/. As of this writing, the struggle continues.

95. On the significance of locality in thinking about and confronting mass incarceration, see Mona Lynch, "Mass Incarceration, Legal Change, and Locale: Understanding and Remediating American Penal Overindulgence," *Criminology and Public Policy* 10, no. 3 (2011), 673–698.

96. We discuss the emergence and evolution of restorative justice in chapter 3.

97. For primers and resources on restorative and transformative justice, see John Braithwaite, *Restorative Justice and Responsive Regulation* (New York: Oxford University Press, 2002); Danielle Sered, *Until We Reckon: Violence, Mass Incarceration, and a Road to Repair* (New York: The New Press, 2019); Howard Zehr, *The Little Book of Restorative Justice* (Brattleboro VT: Good Books, 2002); and Generation 5, "Toward Transformative Justice: A Liberatory Approach to Child Sexual Abuse and other forms of Intimate and Community Violence & a Call to Action for the Left and the Sexual and Domestic Violence Sectors," (June 2007), http://www.generationfive.org/wp-content/uploads/2013/07/G5_Toward_ Transformative_Justice-Document.pdf. For critiques of restorative justice, see Laura Nader, "Coercive Harmony: The Political Economy of Legal Models," *Kroeber Anthropological Society Papers* 92 (2005), 7–22; and Paul Takagi and Gregory Shank, "Critique of Restorative Justice," *Social Justice* 31, no. 3 (2004), 147–163.

98. On abolitionist organizing in Chicago and what it means for the abolitionist conception of justice, see Allegra M. McLeod, "Envisioning Abolition Democracy," *Harvard Law Review* 132 (2019), 1613–1649.

99. Such experiments are always at risk of co-optation. As Kaba discovered, once the Chicago PD had been afforded the ability to divert young people who had been arrested, they began to arrest people they previously would have left alone. Observing this expansionist trend, Project NIA began to approach potential participants directly, thereby cultivating a means of doing justice that was not dependent on systems of state violence.

100. The category of "non-reformist reforms" was developed by French social theorist André Gorz in his book, *Strategy for Labor* (Boston: Beacon Press; 2000). For thinking about the broader aspects of this category, as in the case of Universal Basic Income, see Peter Frase, "Curious Utopias," *Jacobin* (May 14, 2013), https://www. jacobinmag.com/2013/05/curious-utopias/.

101. Mariame Kaba, public talk, New School for Social Research, New York City (September 16, 2016). Abolitionist organizer Jason Lydon employs the following seven criteria to assess whether a proposed reform is indeed abolitionist: (1) Will this reform put more power in the hands of prisoners or people affected by the carceral system? (2) Will this policy change create an opportunity for prison officials to request more financial resources that would expand the carceral system? (3) Is this a reform that will create a system that will need to be abolished later in the struggle to rid the world of prisons and jails? (4) Have prisoners made a specific request for this policy change? If yes, are you in direct relationship with these prisoners? If no, why is this the policy change you are working on at this moment? (5) How does this reform fit in with larger movements led by those most affected by the violence of the carceral system (specifically Black people, im/migrants, LGBTQ

people, disabled people)? (6) Is this an incremental change that policy-makers will be able to use to claim they made a difference and avoid taking the next step (e.g., limiting/regulating solitary confinement rather than abolishing it)? (7) Does this reform require you to rely on demonizing some criminalized people while securing changes for others? (Personal e-mail.)

102. Dan Berger, Mariame Kaba, and David Stein, "What Abolitionists Do," *Jacobin* (August 8, 2017), https://www.jacobinmag.com/2017/08/prison-abolition-reform-mass-incarceration. On community bail funds, see Smart Decarceration Initiative, "National Survey of Community Bail Funds: Report to the Community" (April 2017), https://advancingjustice.wustl.edu/Documents/Bail_Fund%20Report_Final_071417.pdf.

103. Evidence of the mainstreaming of abolitionist politics includes the 2017 endorsement of prison and police abolition by the Democratic Socialists of America's National Political Committee: "Abolish Police and Prisons" https://medium.com/@DSA_Praxis/abolish-police-and-prisons-fa263c44b3cb; and the 2018 *Nation* cover: John Washington, "What is Prison Abolition?" *The Nation* (July 31, 2018), https://www.thenation.com/article/what-is-prison-abolition. For a proposed abolitionist turn in the study of criminal law see Dorothy E. Roberts, "Democratizing Criminal Law as an Abolitionist Project," *Northwestern University Law Review* 111, no. 6 (2017), 1597–1607; for some of the first fruits of this turn see the 2019 *Harvard Law Review* symposium featuring contributions by Patrisse Cullors, Angel E. Sanchez, and Allegra M. McLoud, https://harvardlawreview.org/topics/prison-abolition/, (April 10, 2019).

Adjacent to the movement to abolish prisons are those pushing to abolish the police. See Tracey L. Meares, "Policing: A Public Good Gone Bad," *Boston Review* (August 1, 2017), https://bostonreview.net/law-justice/tracey-l-meares-policing-public-good-gone-bad; and Alex S. Vitale, *The End of Policing* (New York: Verso, 2017). In the Trump era, an abolitionist frame is also productively being brought to bear on the Immigration and Customs Enforcement (ICE), which is directly responsible for the caging and deaths of immigrant children. See Sean McElwee, "It's Time to Abolish ICE," *The Nation* (March 9, 2018), https://www.thenation.com/article/its-time-to-abolish-ice/.

2

The Political Theology
of Mass Incarceration

On November 26, 1960, Martin Luther King Jr. stood in front of a live audience in a New York City television studio. At the podium across from him was James J. Kilpatrick, editor of the *Richmond News Leader*, author, and public intellectual. Kilpatrick was the serious, learned, respectable face of segregation. For political moderates in the studio and watching at home, Kilpatrick was a portrait of civility and reasonableness—quite the opposite of the goons in white robes and hoods.

Kilpatrick was nervous. In April he had appeared on television with King and several others, and it had gone badly. This time, however, it would only be King and Kilpatrick, and each would have plenty of time to speak his piece. The studio audience was a mix of civil rights supporters and opponents, along with mayors from around the country who happened to be in town for a convention.[1]

The debate was not a success for King. Ella Baker was in Atlanta at a meeting of the nascent Student Nonviolent Coordinating Committee (SNCC), and she concluded that King was "no match" for Kilpatrick. "The students were sitting there in front of the TV, waiting for him to 'take care' of Kilpatrick. Finally, some got up and walked away."[2] It might be tempting to attribute the civil rights icon's unpersuasive performance to the venue. King captivated audiences with his oratory, but he was a preacher: he excelled at monologue, not dialogue. This, however, was not the main problem. As King himself was the first to concede, his arguments had not worked; they had not persuaded—and in future speeches, he would change them.[3] Put another way, the problem was not so much King's arguments as what appeared to be his lack of arguments. In contrast to Kilpatrick, who with sober reason argued for the vital importance of following the law and the disastrous consequences of the rule of law's erosion, King relied instead on an abstract-sounding "moral law." What was this mysterious thing, "moral law"? Where exactly was it? What was its significance in the real world?

King's moral law had ancient roots and modern religious and secular resonances. In speaking this language, King evoked both the natural law of medieval Christian luminaries Augustine of Hippo and Thomas Aquinas and the Declaration of Independence's "Laws of Nature and of Nature's God."[4] For King, "moral law" was an appeal to sacred principles that should guide life in the world. Human beings have access to these principles through reflection on human nature, and specifically on the image of God imprinted on human nature.[5] We can catch sidelong glimpses of divine justice, and we should allow it to guide our lives, individually and collectively. The laws passed by legislators do not have the last word: moral law, reflecting divine justice, trumps the laws of the land. Not too long before, this notion of moral law was second nature to the American public and was integral to the stories that American statesmen publicly told about the country's promise and mission, but now it rang hollow. Civil religion was changing under King's feet. It was not King's style but his theology that did not catch.

The proximate cause of the King-Kilpatrick debate was the sit-in movement, which during the summer months had exploded throughout the South. King was a vocal defender of the students' actions. As a practice of nonviolence and as a political tactic, sit-ins were intended to bring about a better democracy, a democracy that would finally put into practice the principle that all men are created equal. In King's view, this equality was a sacred principle, an aspect of divine justice. To enact this sacred principle in the world, the demonstrators were tapping into a "moral sense" inherent in all humans. Those who witnessed the sit-ins would realize the injustice of segregation and would take consequent actions against segregation. As the civil rights icon put it, the sit-ins were "crusades" seeking "conversion." By leveraging the human conscience, a conscience present in oppressed and oppressor alike, activists would be able to achieve revolutionary-grade change without the use of violence. Democratic ideals inhered in the students' ends, in their means, and in the bridge that spanned them. The students showed respect for the law by trying to make the law better, bringing it "in line with the moral law of the universe."[6]

Kilpatrick saw things differently. From the white southerner's perspective, the sit-in demonstrations were essentially about law-breaking. As much as King would have liked to paint a picture of angelic youths singing hymns in Woolworth's, in reality, Kilpatrick asserted, the demonstrations approached and sometimes reached violence. Like all instances of criminal trespass, sit-ins resulted in "riot and disorder." This is the centerpiece of the segregationist argument, and it would become, a few years later, a leitmotif in American political rhetoric: "law and order" as opposed to "riot and disorder." To Kilpatrick's charge that the sit-ins brought "riot and disorder," King responded that if such disorder existed it was brought about by defenders of segregation; the protesters were trained and disciplined. Yet King's words were little match for the images of force and violence broadcast across the country from the demonstrations. The power of these images overwhelmed any attempt to isolate their cause.[7]

King's argument—that human nature, made in the image of God, affords insight into the sacred principles of justice not yet manifest in the laws of the world—was secularized and individualized by Kilpatrick. Where access to moral law, for King, involved a disciplined process of discernment, Kilpatrick reduced moral law to personal choice. King himself flirted with a complementary secularization when he glossed his argument as a simple appeal to "conscience" and omitted reference to God or to the Christian natural-law tradition. But when pressed to elaborate, King appealed to "the insights of the ages through saints and prophets." For King, that is, history and tradition provided resources for honing our own moral instincts, thereby helping us to discern what the higher law is.[8] None of this made sense to Kilpatrick. In Kilpatrick's view, King was arguing that we should be able to choose which laws to follow and which laws we can ignore because we feel they are wrong. Whether we feel that they are wrong simply because we find them burdensome or because we believe that God says they are wrong does not matter: that is private business, not public business. Likewise, religion is private business, not public business. The way we can all live together, each with their own religious convictions, is to follow religiously neutral laws—that is, to follow American laws. Those who chose to break the law would rightly bear the consequences of this choice. Convictions about higher laws, about justice prescribed by God, are convictions that should be confined to the individual's heart; they do not supersede state law.

Kilpatrick conceded the importance of equality in matters of voting and education, but he argued that eating arrangements did not have the same magnitude of importance. As a marginal site for the principle of equality, lunch counters fell to the jurisdiction of another American ideal. That ideal was the right to private property. The owners of department stores ought to be able to use their property as they like, to serve whomever they like at their establishments. The rule of law protects private property. King conceded that property rights were "sacred," but he charged that the supposedly private property of the department store lunch counters was in fact a mix of private and public, privately owned but publicly supported. Kilpatrick pushed back, asking whether the right to boycott, which King clearly supported, might be analogous to the right of a store owner to decide which customers to serve. Time ran out before King could respond.

Understanding Kilpatrick's reasoning, and why it carried the day, goes a long way in helping understand the pivot between the civil rights era and the ascendant conservative epoch that was nipping at its heels—a legal, institutional, and cultural logic forged at the nexus of economics, politics, race, and religion, in which, more than half a century later, we remain collectively entrenched. Kilpatrick's move, in short, was to uncouple justice and law, to stop talking about justice because it is a private matter, and to link law with private property. Put another way: Kilpatrick was conflating justice and law, linking them with private property, and discarding the sense of justice as a higher ideal. Under this logic, "law and order" became trump and beacon, and the "free market"—with its attendant mandate to business owners to conduct business however they pleased—was endowed with quasi-holy attributes. The King-Kilpatrick debate took place just as one configuration of religious and political concepts, one political theology, was being eclipsed by another, with the two engines of American history fueling the change: the problem of race and the problem of the free market. Just a few years earlier, the debate would have looked quite different, with segregationists defending the right to civil disobedience—specifically, the right to ignore the Supreme Court's school integration rulings. To justify their civil disobedience, segregationists appealed to a moral law and to higher ideals of justice as well: it was an idiom potentially persuasive to the American public.[9] By the 1960s, justice and moral law were no longer central to the political vocabulary of the left, surpassed at first by revolutionary fervor, then domesticated into the more docile language of human rights.[10]

These tremors register a major reconfiguration of the American religious landscape. Beginning around 1960, mainline Protestants rapidly lost influence in American culture and politics. Thereafter, evangelicals consolidated their institutional sway.[11] King and Kilpatrick may seem odd figures to mark this transformation. The prophetic style of African American Christianity that King represented contrasted sharply with, and challenged, the comfortable white Protestantism exemplified by public theologians like Reinhold Niebuhr and Paul Tillich.[12] Though somewhat hard to imagine now, up through the early days of television, American public discourse prominently featured liberal theologians speaking out on political issues, and even secular intellectuals, such as John Dewey, spoke in a religious idiom. Civil rights preachers challenged this status quo using an emotive, rhetorically powerful style that surprised and excited white liberal Protestants. While the anti-segregation message of civil rights preachers ran ahead of the commitments of many liberal Protestant lay people, it was largely aligned with the views of white Protestant elites.[13] As much as it represented a departure in tone and emphasis, the civil rights vocabulary of love and justice toed closely to the familiar theological vocabulary—a vocabulary in which liberal Protestant elites were trained, and which was increasingly the language of the laity as well. Navigating the lane that Niebuhr and Tillich had carved out, King quickly became a Protestant saint, and his vision of a "beloved community" became the way that social justice was framed in many Protestant denominations.[14]

Kilpatrick, by contrast, had no patience for abstract Christian ideals of love and justice. He came from a family of agnostics and had little personal interest in religion. According to his biographer, Kilpatrick "found spiritual order in two unrelated sources: the Constitution and baseball."[15] To which we would add a third: the law. For Kilpatrick, the law was sacred, not because it was God-given, but because it was the law. He was a secularizer, re-describing King's noble-sounding love ethic as a "principle of togetherness"—one that would, he cautioned, result in "intimate race mixing" and the eventual obliteration of race altogether. By re-describing religious belief as personal choice ("everyone has the right to decide for himself"), Kilpatrick effectively subjected it to market logic while clipping off those aspects of religion that would impede market functioning. Personal faith and obedience to God were virtues to be celebrated. To the extent that they impeded the functioning of the free market, however, religious histories, traditions, and commitments needed to be set aside.

Kilpatrick's apparent success in the debate marks more than merely a chapter in the secularization of American culture. In fact, Kilpatrick's vision was ascendant not only for secularists, but also, perhaps even more importantly, for evangelicals. Strange as it may seem from a theological perspective, Kilpatrick's victory gestures at how secularism and evangelicalism rose together. Acting antagonistically, in the coming era, the two movements would consume and displace the liberal Protestantism that had reigned hegemonic.

Evangelicalism has a long history in the United States, and it is at the origins of denominations now central to the liberal Protestant "mainline."[16] During the first quarter of the twentieth century, evangelicalism surged and eagerly took on liberal Protestant elites. After their public rebuke in the Scopes "Monkey Trial," evangelicals temporarily left the stage of American public life. Liberals celebrated, but their smug sense of triumph proved to be a time bomb. Out of the spotlight, in churches and in para-church organizations, the evangelical movement regrouped and organized. In the final third of the twentieth century, evangelicals returned in force to the public stage and quickly moved from the margins of American public life to the center.[17] This emergence brought with it a massive shift in the realms of American culture. Within this framework—a framework that predominates still—the locus of religion is the self. As faith, as "personal relationship," religion is preeminently a matter between oneself and one's God. Forward-looking progress no longer motivated projects; the individual would enter the City of God in the afterlife.[18] Religious ethics, then, become primarily personal, not social. What matters is personal piety, and ultimately, personal salvation. If religious ethics are to motivate politics, it is a politics that commends personal morality and proscribes behaviors deemed to be immoral, not a politics that is aspiring to struggle collectively toward a beloved community, to model the social world on the Kingdom of God.[19] At day's end, religious faith is a vertical relation: the function of religious community is to strengthen the tie that binds the heart of a man to his maker.[20]

Though diametrically opposed to the believer's (and nonbeliever's) standpoint, in their foregrounding of the self and their marginalization of the collective, evangelical faith and secularist self-actualization share a good deal of cultural DNA, perhaps nowhere more so than in relation to justice. Secularists and evangelicals share a worldview that reduces justice to the proper operation of the law. For both groups, in spite of their divergent theological horizons, the meaning of justice is confined to modifying a system for the management of law-breakers: the criminal justice system. Were justice to be regarded as more than the law, worries the secularist, sectarian religious values could be imposed on the pluralistic public. For the evangelical, meanwhile, one must give unto Caesar what is Caesar's, following the laws of this world and ceding the meaning of justice to secular authorities. In the case of evangelicalism, state law is a subordinate sphere, but a more or less sovereign sphere. In the case of secularism, state law is the only sphere. The evangelical anxiety about secularism, expressed so vociferously in the 1980s and 1990s, is perhaps, then, an anxiety of influence. It is an anxiety that also suggests just how obsolete liberal Protestantism was, and how dogmatically secular American elites had become.

In their heyday, liberal Protestants were forward-looking and socio-logically ambitious. For the liberal Protestant, justice, as affirmed by God, couldn't so easily be translated to worldly terms, and the relationship between following the law and enacting justice was not so simple. Discernment through reflection on the "saints and prophets," one's own God-given moral intuitions, and the insights of the sciences and humanities were required in order to know how to push existing political and social arrangements in the direction of justice.[21] In the twentieth-century liberal Protestant imagination, there was little possibility that divine justice would finally be achieved on earth, but the effort to bring American justice closer to God's law, even incrementally, was the citizen's highest calling. Moreover, from this Protestant perspective, articulated by King and others, there were not a finite set of injustices to be rectified. Rather, there were uncountable systematic, interconnected, intractable injustices being ever abetted by new forms of injustice—all of which must be combatted simultaneously.

Evangelicals tend to be oriented differently. While they are no less exceptionalist about America, their exceptionalism is rooted in the idea of the United States as being a Christian nation. For philosophical and historical reasons, however, they tend to be somewhat more skeptical of state institutions. Whereas religious liberals seek to bend the law toward justice, many evangelicals would simply prefer for the law to leave them alone. When evangelicals do look to make and change the law, their ambition is not primarily to effect social justice, but to regulate individual morality. From this baseline, many evangelicals experienced the civil rights era's loosening of white, Protestant hegemony—what historian David Sehat has called the "moral establishment"—as a direct assault on their person, their community, and their country. If, for American evangelicals, Jesus's salvific death subjugated religious law to personal faith, attitudes toward secular law tend to be rather deferential. At the very least, state law, which had reliably protected white property from Native and formerly enslaved populations, was granted sovereignty. More frequently, the country's Christian founders are credited with deriving American law from God's law—a sacred civic order that was viciously undermined beginning in the 1950s, when the Warren Court started changing the laws. By undermining the Jim Crow order, taking prayer out of schools, and licensing sexual immorality with legalized birth control (and, eventually, abortion), "activist" judges were apostates, betrayers of American values. Their decisions would be read as evidence of aggressive social decay. These malignant state actors were violating republican citizenship, turning the nation away from God, and vitiating the divinely-sanctioned legal order of this exceptional nation.[22]

Secularism preserves liberal Protestantism's spirit but disavows its mood. Secularists retain the liberal Protestant's commitment to social justice, but by relinquishing higher law as a horizon and wedge, they tend to have a more difficult time imagining radical alternatives to the present. Their visions for social change tend to be less transformational and more reformist. Kilpatrick, standing in for both secularists and evangelicals, viewed injustices as specific malfunctions of the law in need of limited fixes so that the law could function properly—so that justice could reign. In sum, when reduced to ideal types, liberal Protestantism tended to authorize a broad vision for social and political reform; evangelicalism and secularism, by contrast, tend to limit their ethical imaginings, and to be somewhat more pessimistic—a secularist might say *realistic*—about the state's capacity to realize even these ratcheted-down ambitions.

Kilpatrick's victory over King was a bellwether of this cultural shift. The segregationist's success was caused neither by his mastery of the medium nor by the objective persuasiveness of his arguments, but rather by the alignment of Kilpatrick's arguments with his audience's expectations. The liberal Protestant moral framework that characterized the civil rights movement had reached the limit of its power and was beginning to ebb. Evangelicalism and secularism were ascending, and the moral law language King employed was rapidly losing its power to persuade. But the significance of the King-Kilpatrick debate is not just in what it shows about American religion. Its significance is also in what it has to say about American prisons. The exponential growth of the US prison population began in the years following the King-Kilpatrick debate. In our view, changes in religious ideas about law and justice anticipated our current era of mass incarceration. This shift in consciousness provided an essential condition for mass incarceration's emergence. If not, in a simple sense, mass incarceration's "cause," without this religious shift, the carceral logics that justify and help us make sense of mass incarceration would be, quite literally, *unthinkable*. In short, once liberal Protestant ideas gave way to evangelical-secularist ideas in the American public imagination, once justice was equated with law and order, calls for justice became calls for more law enforcement and punishment. Inasmuch as an "unjust criminal justice system" is for most an oxymoron, the dominant culture has no vocabulary to talk about the injustice of policing practices and imprisonment. And for those who *do* criticize, the change that is imagined generally peaks with a vision of law enforcement being more fair.

The law-and-order framework is not unique to the era of mass incarceration. In a broad sense, it is as old—at least—as private property. Nor, as an analytic matter, can the power the law-and-order framework wielded among white evangelicals in the second half of the twentieth century be disaggregated from the fact that, in America, the law—as instantiated in state violence especially—is reliably aligned with white supremacy. Race and capitalism, that is to say, matter irreducibly. But by thinking religion into the stories we tell about mass incarceration, we may shed additional light on how the law-and-order framework of the post–civil rights era came to engulf—from horizon to horizon, and with catastrophic consequences— how Americans think and pursue justice.

The Higher Law Era

Robert Bellah began his landmark analysis of America's "civil religion" with excerpts from John F. Kennedy's inauguration speech.[23] In Kennedy's words, in the three times he invokes God in particular, Bellah draws out evidence of shared quasi-religious commitments at the heart of American political culture. Our project is somewhat different. Where Bellah sees commonality, we see contestation. The King-Kilpatrick debate marks a significant moment in this history of contestation. In the preceding era, American political rhetoric appealed to higher ideals of justice toward which the law should be transformed; afterward, politicians identified justice with law and order, leaving little remaining to leverage against the injustices of domestic state surveillance, violence, and confinement. In its details, this story is, of course, not so straightforward, and at each moment competing ideals and vocabularies overlapped. Tracking these complexities demonstrates how our current political configurations are far from necessary. Alternative paths could have been taken, and we may collectively decide to take them still. As we see in Kilpatrick's defeat of King, today's emergent position may foretell tomorrow's new consensus. The struggle for the soul of the American republic is not over yet.

A perhaps irresolvable tension in the struggle over American political culture is that between conceptions of justice identified with law (or the state) and conceptions of higher justice. From the standpoint of the present, where 2.3 million live in cages, the desiccated conception of justice of the statist orientation comes to seem almost natural. That America's political elites ever thought and spoke differently comes as something of a surprise.

Even, and especially, in its function as civil liturgy, political oratory provides no clear window into American religion or politics. As a mode of speech—and as an attendant archive—it is at once tactical and idiosyncratic. But in the words of presidents and presidential candidates, we can track the surges and drifts of public sentiment, the ideas and feelings that public policy reflects and shapes—ideas and feelings that, in the United States anyhow, are inextricably enmeshed in religious tropes and affects. An analysis of the legislative process or the specific public debates that produced certain legislation would purport to offer a clearer causal story, but it is not the story we tell in the pages to follow. Such a causal story rests on the pragmatic assumption that if we just look closely enough at actors' actions, their true motivations will be revealed. We are skeptical of such a clean account. As we see it, by contrast, the history of public policy is rife with contingencies.[24] Not by the will of great men, nor by any sort of ingrained national character, were the public institutions we find ourselves within in any way foreordained. Nonetheless, by looking at presidential rhetoric, we are afforded a window into the religious worlds of American publics. These sources shed light on what Americans claim to believe and how they act upon those beliefs, and they showcase a set of world-making concepts with world-transforming power.

At the beginning of our story, American politicians, both Democrats and Republicans, regularly framed their job as moving toward—but never achieving—divine justice on earth. Consider Adlai Stevenson. A Unitarian Universalist, Stevenson was not one to invoke God all that often. However, in accepting the Democratic Party's presidential nomination in 1956, Stevenson quoted Emerson: "The highest revelation is that God is in every man." From this starting point, much like King, Stevenson urged his audience to "listen again to our hearts" and "speak again to our ideals." We have access to God within ourselves, and we can sense what the best, most just world would be like. We can check our political options against what God would want not by matching up the wording of legislation with the words of the Bible but by embracing the divine ideals beckoned by "our hearts." With the economic resources now available, in a time of prosperity, "we can do justice to our children," providing them with better educations and with a better world. This sense of justice that pulls us forward, and that inspires our hopes for future generations, has nothing to do with protecting private property. Quite the opposite: for Stevenson, "material things alone" cannot satisfy our "spiritual hunger," and a culture that stresses quantity at the expense of quality risks substituting the celebration of "Bigness" for the worship of God.[25]

Stevenson's Republican opponent, Dwight Eisenhower, a Presbyterian who would vanquish him in both his presidential runs, was much more explicit about his worship of God and his desire to advance God's justice on earth. Before the assembled throngs, Eisenhower began his first inaugural address with a prayer. The new president petitioned God for "the power to discern clearly right from wrong," and he further asked God to "allow all our words and actions to be governed thereby, and by the laws of this land." Note the two categories in play here. For Eisenhower, the justice given by God is clearly a different thing from American laws. Eisenhower distinguishes the two and prioritizes the former. Addressed only obliquely by Eisenhower is what happens if and when God-given justice and American law come into conflict. This potential tension is all the more acute given Eisenhower's next line: "Especially we pray that our concern shall be for all the people regardless of station, race, or calling." The intimation is hard to miss. Particularly in matters of race, Eisenhower seems to be saying, we should open ourselves to our God-given capacity to see justice, and to make America more just—up to and including when that means changing the laws of the land. Eisenhower's political theology in this regard forces his hand. When laws are fair and just, they reflect discernment of the divine. When laws fail to properly distinguish between right and wrong, they do not.[26] When laws fail, we are obligated by God, and by the divine force within us, to do better. It is a truism to say that in America, religion and politics are enmeshed, but for Eisenhower, religion provides politics with its imperative.

No less theological was Eisenhower's conceptualization of freedom. As was true for other American politicians of his time, freedom, for Eisenhower, was first and foremost that which distinguished democracy from Communism, and the United States from the Soviet Union. The Cold War pitted good against evil in a cosmic struggle, and as proofed by the atheism of the Communists, God was manifestly on the American side. This alignment offered providential assurance. Yes, the fate of the world teetered in the balance, but freedom, and its earthly vessel, the United States of America, would eventually triumph. Not merely by association was freedom tethered to God. For Eisenhower, freedom is—pursuant to the ancient Christian paradox—the freedom to obey God's law. As Eisenhower put it, "At such a time in history, we who are free must proclaim anew our faith. This faith is the abiding creed of our fathers. It is our faith in the deathless dignity of man, governed by eternal moral and natural laws." As individuals and as a collective, an unshakable, uncompromising commitment to human dignity is what distinguishes the free from the unfree. This dignity comes from being created in God's image, and it brings with it, for each individual, the capacity to judge and the capacity to advance justice. While Eisenhower never mentions Jesus Christ, he takes faith in human dignity—a faith essential to democracy—as the core message of Christianity.

In assessing Eisenhower's liberal Protestant notion of freedom, it is also crucial to point out what it is not. It is not the freedom of the free market. Although Eisenhower does include "free labor and capital" within its scope, the neoliberal freedom to which we have become collectively attuned, where freedom is collapsed into the proper functioning of capitalism, is not yet evident. Quite the contrary. In 1957 Eisenhower declared that "mankind has entered upon an historic struggle for a new freedom; freedom from grinding poverty." The pursuit of this freedom was part of the larger pursuit of justice. Eradicating poverty was part and parcel of erecting "a peace with justice in a world where moral law prevails." In the postwar period, a mood of optimism and reformism that had periodically shaped American politics from its inception reached its apotheosis.

With or without God's shaping hand, advances in the natural and social sciences made it seem as though America was on a swift path to justice. As Eisenhower's successor would declare, humans now have the capacity to abolish poverty and to struggle against disease and war. To do so, President Kennedy asserted, we ask God's help, but we are also aware that "on earth God's work must truly be our own." In other words, the movement toward a more just nation and world, a nation and a world more in line with the moral law (a term Kennedy likely avoided for its unwanted Catholic associations), is one that we humans participate in with God's sanction. We do not turn our laws into God's, and we do not take the city of God to be other-worldly; we take belief in God to be informing our worldly struggles and motivating our public policy.[27] During the 1950s, whether Republican or Democrat, right or left, American political rhetoric about social justice shared this higher aspiration.

As far as prisons were concerned, meanwhile, as the Cold War began to heat up, the figure of the prisoner became ever more prominent in service of the principles of American-style freedom. As theorized by Hannah Arendt in *The Origins of Totalitarianism*, in 1951, and as illustrated by the 1963 reception of Alexander Solzhenitsyn's *One Day in the Life of Ivan Denisovich*, the prison became the paradigmatic institution of totalitarian governance, and the prisoner became the totalitarian state's archetypal citizen.[28] That which in the Gulag was rendered explicit was, throughout a totalitarian regime, the ordinary state of affairs: rigid conformity to the dictates of the state. In the Cold War rubric, the Soviet regime of brutal and claustrophobic state violence represented law without freedom, life without human dignity. Unfree to exercise their individual sovereignty, Soviet citizens were closed off to justice. In Moscow, only marginally less so than in the Gulag, citizens were purportedly forced to mute their voices and suppress their judgments. In a totalitarian state, where human flourishing is made impossible, all citizens are essentially prisoners. Endowed inviolably with the sacred freedoms of religion, expression, and assembly, American citizens, by contrast, were thought to be everything their Soviet counterparts were not.[29] As far as justice was concerned, the prisoners that mattered were largely elsewhere. As Americans, we were naturally positioned on the prisoner's side.

Law-and-Order Politics

Whether focused on race, capital, or party politics, the stories scholars tell about how and why mass incarceration happened invariably touch down in what, in our version of the story, too, is a decisive historical moment: the once doomed but posthumously triumphant presidential campaign of Barry Goldwater.[30] Ground zero is July 16, 1964. On that day, Goldwater delivered his acceptance speech at the Republican National Convention, in San Francisco. It was this speech that introduced the phrase "law and order" into the American political vocabulary. As was true of Kilpatrick, from a religious standpoint, Goldwater was an odd standard-bearer. Jewish and Episcopalian in background, Goldwater was a secularist, and yet he was a secularist who enchanted evangelicals, who mobilized massive grassroots support for his candidacy. Previously disparate conservative Christian forces in the South and in the southern diaspora, in California and the Southwest, formed what they called an "evangelical front" to advance the "hegemony of hope," which Goldwater represented.[31] Goldwater would lose, but as was true of his politics, his coalition portended the political and cultural alliance that would eventually triumph. Evangelicals and secularists would capture American political discourse, and mainline Protestants would be sidelined. With their eclipse, the aspirational pursuit of a higher justice would fade with them.

In Goldwater's address, the cultural logic that would come to govern the rest of the century arrives fully formed. For Goldwater, religion boils down to the pursuit of individual freedom. "God," Goldwater asserts, is "the author of freedom." Americans are to become "freedom's missionaries in a doubting world." Freedom is what we have faith in, and we must strengthen that faith. It is a faith that, Goldwater charges, his opponent, the incumbent president Lyndon Johnson, neglected. Goldwater is freedom's prophet, bringing its old message to a new generation: "We must renew freedom's mission in our own hearts and in our own homes." Freedom is God's gift, and it is exercised by the individual. Every action of the state constrains it. One must choose a side: will you stand on the side of the individual, God, and freedom, or will you stand the side of the state?

Like eighteenth-century Congregationalists and nineteenth-century evangelicals before him, Goldwater's anti-institutionalism is simultaneously political and religious. From his secularist libertarian perspective, statist liberals are the purveyors of bad religion. As purveyors of institutional structures that abnegate freedom, liberals who place their faith in the state are, structurally if not ideologically, the modern-day descendants of Jesus's Pharisees and Luther's Papists: "Those who seek absolute power, even though they seek it to do what they regard as good, are simply demanding the right to enforce their own version of heaven on earth."[32]

As a prophet for individual freedom, Goldwater is nothing less than an evangelist for secularized religion. The positive value of religion for purposes of politics is confined to the individual. As little more than a wellspring of personal virtue, religion is stripped of its communal and historical dimensions. The City of God has no place in earthly politics. Religion's place is in the heart, and its endgame is the afterlife. We are a religiously diverse nation, Goldwater asserts, but the one religious claim that unifies us is that freedom is God-given. A shared commitment to freedom is our shared civil religion. Anything more would set us on a path to "the most hellish tyrannies."[33]

But what is freedom, precisely? In his 1964 speech, Goldwater separated out the pursuit of social justice from freedom and asserted instead a narrowly economic principle. Freedom meant markets operating without impairment. This new sense of freedom did not emerge *ex nihilo*. With Communism defined in part by its state-centralized economy, freedom already correlated to a capitalist market logic, but whereas Goldwater's predecessors had seen state regulation as the handmaiden to economic freedom, Goldwater rejected such moderation as a betrayal of ideals. In classic prophetic fashion, Goldwater's call was to reclaim and restore purer forms. He was, in a sense, a capitalist revivalist. With "every action, every word, every breath, and every heart-beat," Americans needed to have a single-minded focus on freedom. Where Eisenhower's freedom was the freedom to follow God's law, Goldwater's freedom was "freedom under a government limited by laws of nature and of nature's God." Where freedom was previously made possible by constraint, freedom now becomes lack of constraint.[34] No longer did God's law furnish a shared vision for the country to pursue. Rather than spurring governmental institutions to a higher and better justice, God's law now functions as a lim-iting principle on government, which is precisely where Goldwater's secu-larist political theology wraps around to his law-and-order politics: the job of the state is to maintain social order so as to enable the free functioning of markets.[35] Freedom is secured not via the expansion and protection of civil rights, but via the protection of property and the proper enforcement of the law. Without this repressive state function, Goldwater cautions, one has freedom without order, a condition he likens to "the slavery of the prison cell." To which, with the eventual success of law-and-order politics, many were on their way.

Goldwater's advocacy of his version of freedom and his emphatic opposi-tion to civil rights for African Americans were hardly coincidental. Laws that integrated lunch counters and prohibited discrimination in housing sales were violations of the freedom that the free market demanded. Behind this reasoned opposition to civil rights was the specter of the chaos, violence, and disorder caused by the civil rights movement. From the perspective of the Goldwater Republicans, as well as some in the Johnson administration, there was little difference between well-organized, well-disciplined civil-rights protests and urban riots.[36] All were instances of Black Americans breaking the law. This law-breaking damaged business and was a threat to the social order. In his famous speech, Goldwater worried that if not "the slavery of the prison cell," freedom without order would entail "the license of the mob and the jungle." The racialized character of the "jungle" is impossible to ignore—these are Black people Goldwater is talking about.

Prior to Goldwater, crime had not been a prominent issue on the national stage. Criminal justice was almost exclusively handled at the state and local level; statutes against murder, robbery, drug dealing, and the like are prima-rily state laws. The federal government is constitutionally limited to creating laws against crimes that cross state borders or involve federal officials, and the Department of Justice had traditionally been a rather small and sleepy corner of the federal government.[37] This was beginning to change, and John F. Kennedy's appointment of his brother Bobby to the office of attorney general accelerated that change. But crime was still not an issue that national politicians spent much time talking about—until Barry Goldwater, that is. With his 1964 speech, Goldwater made crime a national concern. The Cold War was at its height, but more pressing for Goldwater than the specters of Russia and Cuba was an imminent threat much closer to home. He describes "the growing menace in our country tonight, to personal safety, to life, to limb and property, in homes, in churches, on the playgrounds, and places of business." The statistics are inadequate, but it is doubtful that crime was, in fact, rising dramatically.[38] Nonetheless, urban unrest and the scourge of illegal drugs were beginning to be a feature of the America that Americans read about in the paper and saw on television screens. Fear was rising, and Goldwater was stoking that fear. The fear may have been framed in the race-neutral language of "urban turmoil," but, as with his talk of the jungle, white anxieties about racial integration clearly served as an animating force.

Throughout his speech, Goldwater mixes violent crime with crime committed against private property, linking crime (and, implicitly, race) with his broader argument that the true meaning of freedom is free markets, and the true meaning of law is the protection of those markets. America must be a nation that "nurtures incentives and opportunity for the creative and the productive." When Goldwater does talk of the less fortunate, the "needy" and "helpless," he does not use the language of justice but rather of "human sympathy" combined with "enlightened self-interest."[39] That is, the distributed divine agency encapsulated in King's "discernment" is, for Goldwater, swapped out for Adam Smith's invisible hand. Whereas in the earlier era the political economy was overseen by God, in the new framework transcendence is excluded. Henceforth the market rules.

A month later, in Atlantic City, Goldwater's opponent, the incumbent Lyndon Johnson, accepted the Democratic Party nomination for the presidency. Just as King had opposed Kilpatrick with a grander, Godlier version of justice, so too did Johnson oppose Goldwater. Johnson won, but his victory signaled the end of an era. His administration would be the last time the mainline Protestant conception of justice would be wholeheartedly promoted in national politics. Even at this moment, in August 1964, Johnson conceded much to Goldwater. He worried aloud about violence committed in the name of civil rights activism. Referring to such activists (rioters? or sit-in strikers?), he drawled, "Those who break the law—those who create disorder—whether in the North or the South—must be caught and must be brought to justice." If Johnson aligned himself with the protesters' ends, he endorsed Goldwater's assessment of their means. "The law must be respected and violence must be stopped," he intoned. Yet Johnson also saw the president's task as that of pursuing higher ideals of justice. He offered a definition of "the true cause of freedom." It is not about free markets. It involves feeding the hungry, finding work for the unemployed, treating the sick, and educating the young. New laws would need to be enacted and new government programs created in pursuit of this true freedom.[40]

In his inaugural address, Johnson describes a covenant between America and the American people. This covenant was "conceived in justice" and "written in liberty." In other words, justice takes priority to freedom; freedom arises out of a contract to pursue justice. According to Johnson, justice is the basic promise of America. Justice is not the same as order, or as the law being executed rightly. Johnson is clear on this point, and he intentionally distances himself from Goldwater's law-and-order mantra. Rejecting Goldwater's formula as itself another version of totalitarianism, Johnson promises an America that is not "the ordered, changeless, and sterile battalion of the ants." A country where laws are merely followed and workers merely work is, for Johnson, not nearly enough. What Johnson envisions is far more dynamic. His America is a nation characterized by "the excitement of becoming—always becoming, trying, probing, falling, resting, and trying again—but always trying and always gaining." The resources of the nation are to be mobilized in the pursuit of justice. There is no clear path, no formula to apply from heaven or the social sciences. But the nation is animated by its shared commitment to that risky pursuit, by collective faith in that pursuit.[41]

Goldwater's defeat was short-lived. As the sixties became "the sixties," his brand of law-and-order politics took off. As urban uprisings proliferated, together with their potent iconography of Black youths facing off against police, Johnson appointed the Kerner Commission, composed of eleven luminaries, including senators, congressmen, the head of the Steelworkers union, and the head of the NAACP, to advise his administration on the unrest. In line with mainline Protestant conceptions of justice, and with the Johnson administration's political stance, the Kerner Commission concluded that the root causes of unrest must be addressed, not merely the symptoms.[42] The root causes included, most notably, discrimination and unemployment. To address these causes, the commission proposed renewed federal investment in housing, welfare, education, and employment, including the creation of two million new jobs in the next three years. It also proposed a focus on the local level. Municipalities should be aided in learning about the problems in their ghettos and offering the services that could respond effectively. The police should be more racially integrated, and they should focus on community policing. Force should only be used as a last resort. The rights of those arrested, even in urban uprisings, must be respected. To fund these initiatives, taxes may need to be raised. Fail to undertake these initiatives, the commission argued, and the United States would be flirting with "the destruction of basic democratic values." Disorder does not lead to justice, but neither were order and justice the same thing. Commissioners noted the grave, systematic injustices committed by American racism, and the obliviousness of most whites to these injustices. Actions needed to be taken to address "the major unfinished business of this nation." Justice required new laws and policies, and even they would not be identical with justice; new laws could set the nation on a path toward justice.[43]

Congress effectively ignored the Kerner Commission's report. Instead, it embraced a law-and-order approach closer to Goldwater's, and put federal dollars behind it. In what was then the largest law-enforcement bill in the nation's history, Congress allocated funds for state and local agencies to hire more police officers and expanded the legal powers of police, particularly in conducting wiretaps.[44] In short, while the Kerner Commission had sought to bring about justice, Congress opted instead to enforce the law. By the time the sausage had been made, justice had been reduced to law-following. The 110-page Omnibus Crime Control and Safe Streets Act of 1968 frustrated Johnson. He objected to many parts of the act, most prominently its failure to do anything to control guns or to push back against recent expansions in state surveillance. Nonetheless, as Johnson saw it, his hand was forced. "The stain of crime and the shadow of fear" in American communities was, Johnson acknowledged, an urgent matter. Concluding that the act contained "more good than bad," Johnson signed the bill into law.[45]

At the precise moment that crime emerged as a hot-button issue, the more robust, more Protestant conception of justice vanished from national politics. Johnson finished his speech marking the signing of the Omnibus Crime Bill with two appeals to justice, but both appeals affirmed Goldwater's notion of justice, in which justice meant merely following the law. Johnson called "upon every citizen in this Nation to support their local police officials with respect and with the resources necessary to enable them to do their job for justice in America." Henceforth, justice would be achieved when law is enforced properly. The second appeal Johnson made was religious—religious, but, instructively, *not* theological. "I call upon our church leaders and every parent to provide the spiritual and moral leadership necessary to make this a law-abiding Nation." Churches no longer provided moral vision for America. Their function was in their position and authority. Their task was to instill in their parishioners the moral rectitude necessary for following the law. But "the law" was now an entirely secular entity. God was gone, and gone too was the possibility of a different kind of law.

The year the Omnibus Crime Bill passed, Richard Nixon was elected president. As Nixon declared at his inauguration, the era of a moral law that challenged state law, the era of striving to enact God's justice, was over: "The laws have caught up with our conscience." There was once a time for civil disobedience, for dramatizing the mismatch between worldly laws and higher laws, but that time had passed. Bolstered by progress, the laws of America were now the expression of justice, and so, for the American citizenry, the task of justice entailed following those laws. Though nominally a Quaker, Nixon, like Goldwater and Kilpatrick, was more or less a secularist. Although not as dogmatically libertarian as Goldwater, Nixon's faith in government was limited. For Nixon, humans do image God, but that image does not impel a transformation of the world toward justice. Nixon suggests, rather, "When we listen to 'the better angels of our nature,' we find that they celebrate the simple things, the basic things—such as goodness, decency, love, kindness." On this view, the moral law, God's law, accessed through our own nature, speaks to private action, not public action. Rather than oppose good individuals to evil government, Nixon offered a vision of government joining hands with responsible individuals acting voluntarily to address social concerns. In his vision, government was not to initiate programs and mandates on its own. To be clear, Nixon did not represent a turn away from the social programs of Johnson, and even four years later he continued to list improving the environment, transportation, housing, and healthcare among his administration's goals—along with "restor[ing] respect for law." Nixon's rhetoric includes vestiges of the earlier era, vestiges of the earlier sense of justice, standing alongside justice's new meaning: "respect for law." Yet the "progress" Nixon foresaw would come about not through collective effort but by individuals taking responsibility.[46] Law had conquered justice, and collective state action was no longer the principal vehicle for engineering solutions to social problems.

The Political Theology of Mass Incarceration

The 1970s was a decade of seismic political, economic, racial, and religious transformation. On the left, the long-standing coalition that had empowered the Democratic Party to pass the New Deal and the Great Society crumbled apart. For Republicans, meanwhile, opposition to the newfound right to an abortion became a platform cornerstone, and, as expressed in Jerry Falwell's 1979 founding of the Moral Majority, leagues of evangelical parishioners came to identify as Republican Party foot soldiers. Meanwhile, Walmart went public, Keynesianism was abandoned, and Chicago school economists were given the keys to the kingdom. Liberalism waned, and neoliberalism congealed. At decade's end, the liberal idea that the task of ensuring public welfare belonged primarily to the state would be roundly repudiated. What people needed was free markets, not state interference. As it would turn out, however, for "free markets" to buttress consolidated wealth and maximize corporate profits, massive quantities of state violence would be required.[47] The law-and-order framework born in backlash to failed integration and urban unrest yielded the War on Drugs and its attendant regimes of hyper-policing and punishment, which criminalized the lives of the urban poor. In sum, over the course of the 1970s, the welfare state was reconfigured into the carceral state.[48]

Registering the epochal religious shift that was seeping into various aspects of American life, *Time* magazine would proclaim 1976 "The Year of the Evangelical," and an evangelical was finally elected to the White House. Democrat Jimmy Carter would bring to Washington a decidedly Christian sensibility, but one quite different from that of his mainline predecessors. In some ways, Carter's understanding of law and justice closely resembled that of conservative secularists Nixon, Goldwater, and Kilpatrick. Even though Carter spoke of love and justice, and of care for the weak and disadvantaged, in language reminiscent of Tillich and King, asserting that "love must be aggressively translated into simple justice," for Carter, as had been the case for Nixon, justice was far from divine. "It is time for the law to be enforced," he declared. Proper law enforcement, Carter alleged, was a precondition for all other social projects: "We cannot educate children, we cannot create harmony among our people, we cannot preserve basic human freedom unless we have an orderly society."[49]

In themes that came up often during Carter's campaign—themes that resonated especially in the wake of Watergate—respect for law was more or less interchangeable with the pursuit of justice. The costs of disorder and the pressing need for a justice under the law crystalized for Carter in one of law-and-order politics' central dramatis personae: the crime victim. Carter spoke of the "crime and lack of justice" experienced by those victimized by crime. By the phrase "lack of justice" he simply meant lack of law enforcement, for the next sentence he spoke elaborated on how this may be rectified: "Swift arrest and trial, fair and uniform punishment, should be expected by anyone who would break our laws."[50]

Like the conservative secularists, Carter was keen to acknowledge the United States' robust religious pluralism, and he touted the strength that this religious pluralism afforded. Also like them, he placed particular emphasis on the individual's dignity. Carter's belief in the sanctity of human dignity informed his key innovation in presidential rhetoric: centering the concept of human rights. In a weird echo of Goldwater's freedom, the concept of human rights is fundamentally about respecting the individual, protecting him or her from the interference of other individuals or states. In his inaugural address, Carter asserts that "our commitment to human rights must be absolute." Then Carter makes a claim about justice: we must be committed to making "our laws fair." Human rights, in its 1970s iteration, was not tied to a transformative notion of social justice, to changing the laws so that they would rectify systematic inequities.[51] Human rights were to be addressed largely in an ad hoc manner, for example in confrontations with specific actions of other nations, not by confronting the systematic and material injustices that result in human-rights violations.[52] Moreover, efforts to respect and realize human rights were almost exclusively limited to foreign lands. At home, by contrast, as informed by the Cold War confidence that respect for human rights lay at the heart of democracy, all that was required of American law was that it be enforced fairly.

God-talk made a resurgence in the oratory of Ronald Reagan. Concluding his 1980 nomination acceptance speech with a flourish, Reagan affirmed—and theologized—American exceptionalism. He asked, "Can we doubt that only a Divine Providence placed this land, this island of freedom, here as a refuge for all those people in the world who yearn to breathe freely?"[53] The former actor paused, and, feigning ambivalence, made decisively clear where he stood in the contentious debate over the place of religion in American civic life. "I'll confess that I've been a little afraid to suggest what I'm going to suggest—I'm more afraid not to—that we begin our crusade joined together in a moment of silent prayer." After a quarter of a minute of silence, he concluded, "God bless America." It was the first time a presidential nominee had uttered these words. Four years later, Reagan used the same salutation to anchor his State of the Union address. Every president since has done the same.

During the Reagan era, the push to mass incarceration was strong and unfaltering. Reagan's home state was a bellwether. In 1982, California passed Proposition 1, the New Prison Construction Bond Act of 1981. At the time, California, which hadn't built a new prison in two decades, incarcerated 28,500 people. By 1985 it would have almost 45,000 men and women behind bars. As Ruth Wilson Gilmore persuasively describes, the prison-building boom was a response to a number of economic and geopolitical shifts. But if deindustrialization and surpluses in population, land, and state capacity were, from a materialist vantage point, mass incarceration's root causes, it was in the realm of politics, and political theology, that this shift was performed and effected.[54] Fueled by racialized moral panics over drugs and street crime, politicians across the country effectively criminalized urban poverty.[55] The resurgence of presidential God-talk during the era of mass incarceration did not bring a corresponding emphasis on an as-yet-unattained divine justice. Under Reagan, rather, God provided an imprimatur, shedding legitimizing glory on the law that already exists, and authorizing state violence against those who would violate its sanctity. As Reagan put it to the National Association of Evangelicals, "Freedom prospers when religion is vibrant and the rule of law under God acknowledged."[56]

Among President Reagan's rhetorical legacies was the assimilation into the lexicon of American civil religion the epic struggles of civil rights. On November 2, 1983, with Coretta Scott King in attendance, Reagan consecrated the national holiday in honor of her martyred husband, a "man whose words and deeds in that crisis stirred our nation to the very depths of its soul." The spiritual language highlighted what the president took to be the true significance of Martin Luther King's legacy, a legacy ultimately measured less in law and governance than in national character. "Dr. King had awakened something strong and true, a sense that true justice must be colorblind." A quietly evangelical rubric, at once democratic but substantively apolitical, the notion of a national religious awakening placed the onus of collective change not in the halls of power but on—or more precisely, *inside*—ordinary Americans. As Reagan acknowledged, the Voting Rights Act of 1965 had guaranteed Black Americans' franchise, but as a sphere of activity, the law was decidedly secondary. "Most important, there was not just a change of law; there was a change of heart. The conscience of America had been touched. Across the land, people had begun to treat each other not as blacks and whites, but as fellow Americans." A change of heart from racism to an America devoid of racial distinction: for Reagan this was the legacy of Martin Luther King.[57]

Reagan's ostensibly conciliatory tone concerning King contrasted with his overtly racist dog whistles. In his infamous invocations of "welfare queens" and the "strapping young buck" blowing his food stamps on T-bone steaks, Reagan harnessed white resentment to sell the idea that welfare-state programs were redistributing hard-earned wealth to the undeserving poor. In its excesses, the welfare state had undermined the sovereignty of the people. The solution was to minimize government and unleash the goodness and glory of the private sector. As he enduringly framed it in his first inaugural address, "government is not the solution to our problem; government is the problem."[58] In fulfilling Goldwater's vision, Reagan embraced the apparent paradox: limiting government to unleash the powers of individual virtue and free markets necessitated expanding the agencies responsible for state violence. This meant building up the military abroad and expanding policing and prisons at home. As with the cosmic struggle against the Soviets, incarceration was soon to become nothing less than a sacred civic principle.

During his second year in office, Reagan made this case compellingly in his proclamation mandating "Crime Victims Week." This proclamation marked a significant moment for the decade-old victims' rights movement. It cemented its role as one of mass incarceration's most potent political forces, and it enshrined the figure of the crime victim as mass incarceration's sainted martyr. Reagan began with a lamentation. "Too often" crime victims' "pleas for justice have gone unheeded and their wounds—personal, emotional, and financial—have gone unattended." These pleas for justice were pleas for law to be enforced, for the criminal justice system to operate efficiently. In Reagan's hand, crime victims' sacred suffering served to hallow the criminal justice system. That is to say, Reagan partially resurrected justice's divine aura, but he draped it over the state's machinery of punishment:

Our commitment to criminal justice goes far deeper than our desire to punish the guilty or to deter those considering a lawless course. We must never forget that our laws represent the collective moral voice of a free society—a voice that articulates our shared beliefs about the rules of civilized behavior, and reflects our basic precept that men and women should be treated as free individuals, responsible for the consequences of their actions. When we countenance the suffering of innocent victims of crime, we thus threaten to undermine the faith of our citizens in a legal system that lies at the heart of much that is unique and precious about our Nation itself.[59]

Whatever residuum might have remained of the Quaker sense that incarceration was primarily rehabilitative found no expression in Reagan's formulation. For Reagan, punishment was about punishing the guilty and deterring others who might be tempted to do the same. But it was about more than that. Government may betray the public's will, but the law—and the criminal law paradigmatically—is the direct expression of popular will. In a democratic republic, where sovereignty resides in the will of the people, "our laws represent the collective moral voice of a free society." For both the victimized and the victimizer, then, punishment represents the reaffirmation of the democratic principles that are undermined when the rule of law is violated. Punishment is at once the declaration of "our" voice, the enactment of our democratic faith, and our recommitment to democratic procedures. Within the cultural logic that Reagan lays out, justice is state violence wielded upon lawbreakers for the benefit of all: for those who violate the law, those whom law-breakers harm, and the body politic as a whole. Only by state violence may the wounds of the criminally afflicted be healed, only by state violence may those who violate the law come to know responsibility, and only by means of state violence may we collectively sustain the civic faith on which the health of the republic depends.

In his vision of and for justice, what Reagan offers is something like a political theodicy. How, in a country of good people, a country providentially safeguarded by a benevolent God, can suffering nonetheless exist? Reagan's answer is twofold. At the top, the government betrays the will of the people. At the bottom, bad people violate the law. The solution to the former is shrinking the government, where "government" means those agencies dedicated to sustaining the welfare state. At the bottom, the solution is hyper-policing and hyper-containment. By surveilling and incapacitating "the guilty," we honor the good. By casting out these polluting agents from our midst, we suture the social fabric.

The criminological anthropology at work here is also illuminating. If, in his talk of "free individuals," Reagan speaks in universalizing terms, in his easy sorting of good people from bad people, Reagan's designations of "innocent" and "guilty" resound in the key of Calvinist theology. In historical and cultural context, these characterizations are also acutely racialized and classed. As characterological essences—identities abstracted from particular instances—innocence and guilt reliably index certain kinds of violations and certain kinds of harms. Nonstate actors who hurt people or damage property with direct acts of violence: these are the guilty who must be *held responsible*. The powerful, who harm systemically or from a distance, are not who Reagan has in mind. The "innocence" of particular sorts of "victims of crime" is manufactured reciprocally along similar lines. As the Supreme Court would find a few years later in its review of the case of Warren McCleskey, a Black man sentenced to death in Georgia for the murder of a white police officer, those convicted of killing a white person were sentenced to death at more than four times the rate of those convicted of killing a Black person. If state violence is that which ritually purifies the contamination of violent crime, then some crime victims' blood would seem to be more sacred than others.[60]

During the final two decades of the twentieth century, the number of people incarcerated in the United States grew six-fold, and the number of prisons grew at an even faster rate.[61] As Naomi Murakawa, Elizabeth Hinton, and Marie Gottschalk have demonstrated, mass incarceration has been a thoroughly bipartisan effort, engineered by Republicans and Democrats acting both nationally and locally.[62] On the national level, and in the public discourse in which these federal policy preferences were expressed and ratified, it was Bill Clinton, a Democrat, who cemented mass incarceration as the law and logic of the land. Between the 1994 Violent Crime Control and Law Enforcement Act and the 1996 Antiterrorism and Effective Death Penalty Act (AEDPA), Clinton expanded the web in which people were criminalized, surveilled, and punished. In combination, the two bills expanded the federal death penalty, toughened sentencing for a slew of different offenses, made life in prison the default sentence for third-time offenders, mandated the establishment of state sex-offender registries, eliminated higher education for incarnated people, and, through restrictions placed on the right to habeas corpus, substantially curtailed the ability of incarcerated people to contest the constitutionality of their convictions and sentences.[63]

In thinking about mass incarceration as not only a slate of policies but also as a prevailing cultural orientation, perhaps no measure is more revealing than the 1994 crime bill's hate-crime provision, which increased penalties for crimes committed "because of the actual or perceived race, color, religion, national origin, ethnicity, gender, disability, or sexual orientation of any person."[64] By mandating tougher punishments for crimes deemed especially heinous, as a warning to other bigots, and as the staunch public affirmation of the value of marginal and otherwise vulnerable people, hate crime legislation remains today relatively popular among progressive groups. By demonizing criminals and prescribing state vengeance as the means for individual and collective healing, hate-crime laws express Ronald Reagan's conceptualization of the relationship between law and justice. For the left as well as the right, justice had become identified with the vigorous enforcement of the criminal code, with punishment as its primary means.

Another "progressive" component of the 1994 crime bill, the Violence Against Women Act (VAWA), ably illustrates the political economy in which American mass incarceration came to make sense. In Great Britain, where the welfare state remained comparatively more robust, what was then called "the battered women's movement" produced a range of ameliorative measures, including housing, healthcare, and other supports to enable women who were being abused to leave their partners and to live independently. In the United States, by contrast, with the welfare state in retrenchment, VAWA's approach was substantially narrower. VAWA did beef up the existing network of shelters for temporary housing and established a domestic violence hotline, but, overwhelmingly, protecting and caring for women meant prosecuting and punishing the men who hurt them. The punishment of offenders was the medium through which the value of harmed women was to be civically conferred.[65]

In his 1994 State of the Union speech, President Clinton took his crime bill to the people. In his remarks, "crime" occurs twenty times, "law" fourteen, "poverty" three, and "justice" not at all. Pivoting out of an optimistic survey of foreign policy, Clinton struck a dark chord: "While Americans are more secure from threats abroad, I think we all know that in many ways we are less secure from threats here at home. Every day the national peace is shattered by crime." As Clinton would have it, the default condition for Americans is "peaceful." Only when the law is violated via violent crime are Americans thrown into precarity or hurt. Clinton listed a diverse series of high-profile violent crimes: a girl murdered during a slumber party, a shooting on the Long Island Rail Road, a Black man in Florida nearly burned alive, a policeman murdered. "Violent crime and the fear it provokes are crippling our society," Clinton asserted, "limiting personal freedom, and fraying the ties that bind us."[66]

For a secularist wonk like Clinton, changes in law are made not to bring the law in closer proximity to an ideal of justice, but simply to make the law more effective. But effective how? Effective in stomping out the agents of evil as informed by a law-and-order notion of what this evil is. The "tough and smart" crime bill achieved its aims principally by structuring the law around a small group of very bad men. Specifically, it targets the "small percentage of criminals . . . who commit repeated, violent crimes." In a climate of fear, vengeance was repackaged as public safety, and prisons were proffered as the antidote.

Using heinous high-profile crimes as its template, the crime bill provided measures to eradicate or incapacitate bad men. Borrowing nomenclature from an altogether different sphere of the American sacred—baseball—the bill's three-strikes-and-you're-out provision radically expanded the use of the sentence of life without parole. In the years to come, in states around the country, men and women judged to be incorrigible would be sentenced to die in prison for crimes as measly as stealing a set of golf clubs, a bicycle, or even, in one famous case, a chocolate chip cookie.[67] People convicted of repeated minor crimes are not seen as social products born of poverty and neglect, of hyper-criminalization and policing. For such people there is no help, no rehabilitation, only incapacitation. With respect to prevention, Clinton's solution was to lend more support to the *good guys*, those who enforce the law, "police who work the streets, know the folks, have the respect of the neighborhood kids."

Clinton was not oblivious to the persistent racism in the criminal justice system, but with the containment or elimination of bad men as the primary goal, civil rights and civil liberties necessarily took a back seat. In this regard Clinton's conflation of law and justice is both a symptom and cause. As he said in a fascinating address on the occasion of Louis Farrakhan's Million Man March, "White America must understand and acknowledge the roots of black pain. It began with unequal treatment, first in law and later in fact. African-Americans indeed have lived too long with a justice system that in too many cases has been and continues to be less than just." But such failures, even when systemic, exist only in practice. Things like "trumped up charges . . . false arrests and police brutality" indeed happen, but when they do they are a function of people "play[ing] by the rules of the bad old days." In this narrative of progress, existing law is framed as unimpeachably just. Fair enforcement may flag, but when it does, this too is a function of the malfea-sance of bad men who betray the law.[68]

In the name of justice, Clinton whittled away at protections for defendants and for incarcerated people. Picking up from where his predecessors left off, meanwhile, he continued to campaign on behalf of crime victims. In a 1996 state-ment in favor of a constitutional amendment codifying victims' rights, Clinton criticized the unfair balance of power that favors criminal defendants at the expense of their victims: "Today, the system bends over backwards to protect those who may be *innocent*, and that is as it should be. But it too often ignores the millions and millions of people who are completely innocent because they're victims, and that is wrong." Like Reagan before him, Clinton appeals to the the-ologically laden figure of the innocent man to initiate a tectonic shift in public policy. Who deserves the protections of due process? Not the poor, not the dis-advantaged, and certainly not, as per classical liberalism, *everyone* who lives sub-ject to the state's sovereignty and who is therefore entitled to certain inalienable rights. For Clinton, rather, legal protections are essential for defendants *who may be innocent*. Crime victims are owed special protections, too, because they *are* innocent. As for the guilty, all they are entitled to is effective punishment. If and where due process unfairly obstructs the rights of innocent crime victims to the justice they deserve, then due process becomes an active obstacle to the adminis-tration of justice. Praise the lamb but lion be damned.[69]

As is true of neoliberalism more generally, in the logic of mass incar-ceration, we witness a substantive retreat from universal principles of the entitlements of citizenship. In the sphere of criminal justice, rights and protections are entitlements rightly owed to the innocent. Regardless of the personal and social circumstances that led to their conviction, people convicted of doing their crime deserve whatever punishment they have coming to them. The innocent are altogether different. Innocence, which renders the incarcerated person a type of victim themselves, makes the incar-cerated person a subject worthy of concern and worthy of rights. It is a very curious thing. In the moral imagination of mass incarceration, Americans are easily able to place themselves in the shoes of someone "wrongly convicted," but Americans have been rendered utterly incapable of imagining them-selves as someone born into poverty in a society in which poverty is crimi-nalized. At what point does a child—a Black or brown child especially—lose the privileges of innocence? As many have observed, the police murder of twelve-year-old Tamir Rice in 2014 offers a harrowing and harrowingly clear answer to this question.[70]

In a variety of ways, the American criminological cult of innocence reflects American culture's Christian heritage. Nothing drives contemporary Americans to conviction like the spilling of innocent blood, and nothing avenges the blood of the innocent like the blood of the guilty. But this is only part of it. The sacred body of the innocent is manufactured precisely via the purported guilt of the guilty. A car wreck, a plane crash, even a mass shooting—should it seem without motivation—is insufficient grounds for collective movement. Rather, what enables catharsis (always) and mobilization (occasionally) is the holy suffering of the innocent painted as a function of the manifest *evil* of the perpetrator. The cultural logic of mass incarceration pairs innocent victim and evil perpetrator, furnishing Americans with the visceral reflex to seek redemption in purifying violence. Systematized and normalized through our systems of punishment, this logic of celebrating the purification of bad violence through good violence informs our entertainment and shapes in a variety of pernicious ways how we relate to one another.

These complementary American cults—the positive cult to crime victims and the negative cult to criminals—have had a productively elastic relationship to American foreign policy, one that germinated during the Cold War, blossomed in the post-1989 interregnum, and has borne massive fruit during the War on Terror.[71] With the consolidation of the Department of Homeland Security, the militarization of local police forces, and the erosions of civil liberties in the surveillance state, militarism and domestic policing are harder and harder to differentiate.[72] As had been the case at the height of the Cold War, the righteous deployment of state violence against problem people represents a unified field of practice and ideology. Justice means little more than *making the bad guys pay*.[73] By the mid-nineties, as James Forman Jr. describes it, a Black D.C. Superior Court judge would routinely evoke the legacy of Martin Luther King to Black children he was sending to jail.[74]

Five years prior to the attacks of September 11, 2001, President Clinton anticipated the next frontier for redemptive American violence. A cocktail of policies nominally advanced in response to the Oklahoma City bombing, AEDPA offered, according to Clinton's signing statement, "a comprehensive approach to fighting terrorism both at home and abroad. . . . As a result, our law enforcement officials will have tough new tools to stop terrorists before they strike and to bring them to justice if they do."[75] "Bring to justice" is quintessentially a lawman's phrase. What it means is to capture and detain law violators and subject them to whatever state violence may be afforded by the law.

When bringing violators to justice, efficiency becomes the watchword. Civil liberties become obstacles to the proper execution of justice, grit in the gears that keep the machine from processing justice smoothly. To maximize efficiency, those who enforce the law were given "new tools" to enable surveillance, arrest, prosecution, and conviction, which correlate inversely to the protections afforded to suspects, defendants, and prisoners. As had been true during his presidential campaign, the death penalty was for Clinton a potent symbol of his seriousness and fealty to this mechanistic conception of justice: "I have long sought to streamline Federal appeals for convicted criminals sentenced to the death penalty. For too long, and in too many cases, endless death row appeals have stood in the way of justice being served." The robust notion of habeas corpus, which placed no time bar on the right of an incarcerated person to appeal their sentence, was a vestige of the era when justice exceeded the proper functioning of the law. Prior to AEDPA, so long as a person's body was in state custody, they had standing to challenge the constitutionality of their conviction and sentence, henceforth, upon conviction, incarcerated people would have only one year to file this appeal. With justice now fully collapsed into the smooth functioning of the criminal justice system, foundational rights became inefficiencies to be eliminated.

By the post-9/11 period, criminal justice and American militarism had been seamlessly combined into a unified Manichean struggle between the innocent and the evil, a struggle to achieve justice by enforcing American rule on terrorists abroad and on criminals at home. Understood in this way, justice is cool and calculating, and as sure as divine wrath. As President George W. Bush put it:

> Justice is one of the defining commitments of America. In our war against terror, I constantly remind our fellow citizens: We seek justice, not revenge. We seek justice for victims. We seek justice for their families. And for justice to prevail in our struggle for freedom, we must rout out terrorist threats wherever they exist. And that's exactly what this country is going to do. And while the war goes on and while our fight for freedom continues, we will continue to work for justice at home, including justice for the victims of violent crime.[76]

In the War on Terror era, American justice is proudly declared as the remedi-ation of evil violence with good violence—good violence, which, as the inno-cents who were attacked, it is our right and duty to inflict. As Bush stipulates, the administration of good state violence might look like revenge, but it is not. Rather, it is justice. Perhaps on account of his evangelicalism, which made his heart a barometer of God's will, and buoyed by the public's love of an au-thoritarian form of masculinity, President Bush pushed the pursuit of justice *beyond* the law. Protecting the innocent against an evil deemed to be exis-tentially necessitated decisive actions by a sovereign executive. Domestically, globally, cosmically, the pursuit of justice demanded that the executive throw off the law's shackles. In a series of memos, Bush administration lawyers wrote this anarchic principle into law.[77] In so doing, the Bush administration accentuated an essential feature of law-and-order politics, which a decade hence the Trump administration would call into even sharper relief: some must follow the law and pay steep consequences for breaking the law; those with vast property and power, however, are more or less free to do whatever they please.

In the realm of rhetoric at least, Barack Obama restored the rule of law to its sovereign position. In August 2014, in public remarks to the press about the simultaneously unfolding "[s]ituations in Iraq and Ferguson, Missouri"—American airstrikes against the Islamic State in Iraq, and the gathering protests against the killing of Michael Brown—Obama demon-strated his fealty to the political theology and theodicy of mass incarcera-tion. The "images of protestors and law enforcement in the streets" showed, Obama said, that "the vast majority of people are peacefully protesting," but not everyone. Obama expressed understanding for "the passions and the anger that arise over the death of Michael Brown," but he admonished the "small minority of individuals" whose means were not peaceful. As he cau-tioned this troublesome minority, "giving into that anger by looting or car-rying guns and even attacking the police only serves to raise tensions and stir chaos. It undermines rather than advancing justice." In Obama's framing, as in Clinton's, the obligation to remain within the law runs both ways. "There's no excuse for excessive force by police or any action that denies people the right to protest peacefully. Ours is a nation of laws for the citizens who live under them and for the citizens who enforce them."[78] Both sides have their bad apples, the police as well as the urban underclass. The key is for the forces of law to triumph over the forces of disorder. Only then will justice prevail.

Without mentioning incarcerated people specifically, Obama gingerly acknowledged some of the problems that fueled the protest. As he concluded his remarks:

> In too many communities around the country, a gulf of mistrust exists between local residents and law enforcement. In too many communities, too many young men of color are left behind and seen only as objects of fear. Through initiatives like "My Brother's Keeper," I'm personally committed to changing both perception and reality. And already, we're making some significant progress, as people of good will of all races are ready to chip in. But that requires that we build and not tear down. And that requires we listen and not just shout. That's how we're going to move forward together, by trying to unite each other and understand each other and not simply divide ourselves from one another. We're going to have to hold tight to those values in the days ahead. That's how we bring about justice, and that's how we bring about peace.[79]

With the green shoots of abolitionism poking up through the soil in Ferguson, Missouri, President Obama was forced to grapple with what his predecessors were free to ignore: for Americans who live in poverty and under a regime of hyper-criminalization, peace is no default condition. As is true for justice, peace as a condition remains aspirational. But if the times were changing, the president's frame for thinking about these struggles was not. For Obama, justice necessitates that one follow the law and respect property rights; and peace entails submission to the law, even and especially in the face of racist, systemic state violence. As a new epoch dawned, Barack Obama proved to be more the child of Kilpatrick than of King.

Notes

1. Martin Luther King, *The Papers of Martin Luther King, Jr.*, vol. 5, *Threshold of a New Decade, January 1959–December 1960*, ed. Clayborne Carson et al. (Berkeley: University of California Press, 2005), 556–564; William P. Hustwit, *James J. Kilpatrick: Salesman for Segregation* (Chapel Hill: University of North Carolina Press, 2013), 110–113; Aniko Bodroghkozy, *Equal Time: Television and the Civil Rights Movement* (Urbana: University of Illinois Press, 2013), 64–65.
2. David Garrow, *Bearing the Cross: Martin Luther King, Jr., and the Southern Christian Leadership Conference* (New York: William Morrow, 1986), 150; King, *The Papers of Martin Luther King, Jr.*, vol. 5, 556n3.

3. The King Archives at Boston University include King's correspondence regarding the debate and his assessment of it. He received various unsolicited offers of assistance for ideas that would make his presentation more persuasive, for which he expressed his gratitude.

4. See King's diverse sources of moral law in his "Letter from a Birmingham Jail," https://www.africa.upenn.edu/Articles_Gen/Letter_Birmingham.html.

5. Natural law is notoriously used in multiple ways, often with little reference to nature or law. King is specifically building on a natural law tradition of the sort described here, with a focus on human nature that images God as a source of normativity. See Vincent W. Lloyd, *Black Natural Law* (New York: Oxford University Press, 2016), chapter 4; and Richard W. Wills, *Martin Luther King Jr. and the Image of God* (New York: Oxford University Press, 2011).

6. King, *The Papers of Martin Luther King, Jr.*, vol. 5, 557; 558.

7. King, *The Papers of Martin Luther King, Jr.*, vol. 5, 559; Vesla M. Weaver, "Frontlash: Race and the Development of Punitive Crime Policy," *Studies in American Political Development* 21, no. 2 (October 2007), 230–265.

8. King, *The Papers of Martin Luther King, Jr.*, vol. 5, 564.

9. Clive Webb, ed., *Massive Resistance: Southern Opposition to the Second Reconstruction* (New York: Oxford University Press, 2005). It could be objected that higher law language lost persuasiveness because of who was using it: once whites, then Blacks. But both whites and Blacks used higher law language to advance civil rights, as they both did to oppose slavery a century earlier.

10. Even King changed his tune to fit with the changing times. While King continued speaking and writing about moral law—including, famously, in his "Letter from Birmingham City Jail"—he decentered God substantially. In the 1963 "Letter," King quickly moves beyond Augustine and Aquinas to offer a secularized account of moral law: "Any law that uplifts human personality is just. Any law that denigrates human personality is unjust." King in fact describes the moral law in several different ways in his "Letter," including ways that were suggested by frustrated viewers of his debate with Kilpatrick. See Lloyd, *Black Natural Law*, chapter 4.

11. David A. Hollinger, *After Cloven Tongues of Fire: Protestant Liberalism in Modern American History* (Princeton, NJ: Princeton University Press, 2015). A Google N-gram search for "evangelical," "secular humanism," and "episcopal" helpfully tracks these changes. The story of evangelical influence is, of course, longer and more complex, with moments of national fervor (e.g., the Great Awakenings) becoming normalized.

12. David L. Chappell, *A Stone of Hope: Prophetic Religion and the Death of Jim Crow* (Chapel Hill: University of North Carolina Press, 2005).

13. Chappell, *A Stone of Hope*; James F. Findlay, *Church People in the Struggle: The National Council of Churches and the Black Freedom Movement, 1950–1970* (New York: Oxford University Press, 1997).

14. Various churches have even named themselves "Beloved Community." For this language on the religious left, see Charles Marsh, *The Beloved Community: How Faith Shapes Social Justice from the Civil Rights Movement to Today* (New York: Basic Books, 2006).

15. Hustwit, *Salesman for Segregation*, 14. Whether or not Kilpatrick's secularism was anomalous among southern segregationists, that his language caught, and made him a powerful national spokesman for segregation, tells us something important about the tectonic shifts in midcentury American political theology.

16. See George Marsden, *Fundamentalism and American Culture* (New York: Oxford University Press, 2006); and Matthew Avery Sutton, *American Apocalypse: A History of Modern Evangelicalism* (Cambridge, MA: Harvard University Press, 2014).

17. See Joel Carpenter, *Revive Us Again: The Reawakening of American Fundamentalism* (New York: Oxford University Press, 1997).

18. In his debate with King, Kilpatrick is explicit that God's relevance pertains only to the afterlife.

19. The latter was central to liberal Protestant politics in the first half of the twentieth century. See Walter Rauschenbusch, *Christianity and the Social Crisis in the 21st Century: The Classic That Woke Up the Church* (New York: HarperOne, 2008); H. Richard Niebuhr and Martin E. Marty, *The Kingdom of God in America*, New edition (Middletown, CT: Wesleyan, 1988); and Gary Dorrien, *The Making of American Liberal Theology* (Louisville, KY: Westminster John Knox Press, 2001–2006).

20. These are broad strokes. Clearly on concrete questions of ethics and politics, things get more complicated, with multiple ideological and theological currents flowing into and around each other and blurring neat distinctions between the personal and the political (paradigmatically, with respect to abortion politics).

21. These were explicitly mentioned by King in his response to Kilpatrick during their debate.

22. On the broad sweep of the role of evangelical Protestantism in American public life, see David Sehat, *The Myth of American Religious Freedom* (New York: Oxford University Press, 2015). On sexual politics, see R. Marie Griffith, *Moral Combat: How Sex Divided American Christians and Fractured American Politics* (New York: Basic Books, 2017). On the postwar period, see Molly Worthen, *Apostles of Reason: The Crisis of Authority in American Evangelicalism* (New York: Oxford University Press, 2016).

23. Robert Bellah, "Civil Religion in America," *Daedalus* 96, no. 1 (Winter 1967), 1–21; Phillip S. Gorski, *American Covenant: A History of Civil Religion from the Puritans to the Present* (Princeton, NJ: Princeton University Press, 2017).

24. Another alternative approach would focus on the ideas of theologians and intellectuals. But the power of religion is in its circulation among the masses, the way it sets the frame for how we see our worlds and for how we think politically; intellectuals' discourses illuminate these issues only indirectly.

25. Adlai Stevenson, "Address Accepting the Presidential Nomination at the Democratic National Convention in Chicago" (August 17, 1956), https://www.presidency.ucsb.edu/documents/address-accepting-the-presidential-nomination-the-democratic-national-convention-chicago.

26. Dwight D. Eisenhower, "Inaugural Address" (January 20, 1953), https://www.presidency.ucsb.edu/documents/inaugural-address-3.

27. Eisenhower, "Inaugural Address"; John F. Kennedy, "Inaugural Address" (January 20, 1961), https://www.presidency.ucsb.edu/documents/inaugural-address-2.

28. See Hannah Arendt, *The Origins of Totalitarianism* (New York: Harcourt, Brace, Jovanovich, 1973), 437–459; and Alexander Solzhenitsyn, *One Day in the Life of Ivan Denisovich* (New York: Signet Classics, 2008). The year it was translated, NBC ran an hour-long dramatization of the novel.

29. Eisenhower, "Inaugural Address." See, for example, George Marsden, *The Twilight of the American Enlightenment: The 1950s and the Crisis of Liberal Belief* (New York: Basic Books, 2014).

30. On the emergence of "law and order," see Michael W. Flamm, *Law and Order: Street Crime, Civil Unrest, and the Crisis of Liberalism in the 1960s* (New York: Columbia University Press, 2007); and Katherine Beckett, *Making Crime Pay: Law and Order in Contemporary American Politics* (New York: Oxford University Press, 1999). For Goldwater's appearances in recent influential accounts, see Michelle Alexander, *The New Jim Crow: Mass Incarceration in the Age of Colorblindness* (New York: New Press, 2010), 42; Marie Gottschalk, *Caught: The Prison State and the Lockdown of American Politics* (Princeton, NJ: Princeton University Press, 2015), 139–143; and Naomi Murakawa, *The First Civil Right: How Liberals Built Prison America* (Oxford; New York: Oxford University Press, 2014), 75–76.

31. Darren Dochuk, *From Bible Belt to Sunbelt: Plain-Folk Religion, Grassroots Politics, and the Rise of Evangelical Conservatism* (New York: W. W. Norton, 2012), 229.

32. Barry Goldwater, "Address Accepting the Presidential Nomination at the Republican National Convention in San Francisco" (July 16, 1964), https://www.presidency.ucsb.edu/documents/address-accepting-the-presidential-nomination-the-republican-national-convention-san.

33. Ibid. While one might read Goldwater as objecting only to false gods, taken on its own terms, his speech leaves no room for a true God to authorize earthly political projects.

34. Robert Brandom, "Freedom and Constraint by Norms," *American Philosophical Quarterly* 16, no. 3 (1979), 187–196; See also Saba Mahmood, *Politics of Piety: The Islamic Revival and the Feminist Subject* (Princeton, NJ: Princeton University Press, 2011). Think of the rules of a language, offering the freedom to write poetry and to communicate.

35. Bernard Harcourt, *The Illusion of Free Markets* (Cambridge, MA: Harvard University Press, 2011).

36. See Flamm, *Law and Order*.

37. David Garland, *The Culture of Control: Crime and Social Order in Contemporary Society* (Chicago: University Of Chicago Press, 2002); Jonathan Simon, *Governing through Crime: How the War on Crime Transformed American Democracy and Created a Culture of Fear* (Oxford: Oxford University Press, 2009).

38. The reporting mechanism for crime statistics changed during this period and incentives were created for reporting higher crime levels, so it is difficult to know whether there were actual changes in crime frequency. Even if there were, the baby

boom generation was coming of age at the time—and coming of age means a higher likelihood to be involved in crime. See Weaver, "Frontlash."

39. In this speech, Goldwater refers to justice once, but it appears to be purely rhetoric, and does not refer to any of the content of the speech: "I would remind you that extremism in the defense of liberty is no vice. And let me remind you also that moderation in the pursuit of justice is no virtue." Goldwater, "Address Accepting the Presidential Nomination."

40. Lyndon B. Johnson, "Remarks before the National Convention upon Accepting the Nomination" (August 27, 1964), https://www.presidency.ucsb.edu/documents/remarks-before-the-national-convention-upon-accepting-the-nomination.

41. Lyndon B. Johnson, "The President's Inaugural Address" (January 20, 1965), https://www.presidency.ucsb.edu/documents/the-presidents-inaugural-address.

42. *United States Kerner Commission, Report of the National Advisory Commission on Civil Disorders* (New York: Bantam Books, 1968). See also Johnson's "Special Message to the Congress on Crime and Law Enforcement," where many of the Kerner conclusions are foreshadowed. Calling on government to address the "roots" of crime, Johnson carved out a role for justice not dependent on crime—a sense of justice as social rather than political: "Our commitment to insuring social justice and personal dignity for all Americans does not flow from a desire to fight crime. We are committed to those goals because they are right." Lyndon B. Johnson, "Special Message to the Congress on Law Enforcement and the Administration of Justice" (March 8, 1965), https://www.presidency.ucsb.edu/documents/special-message-the-congress-law-enforcement-and-the-administration-justice.

43. *Report of the National Advisory Commission*, 1, 2.

44. Murakawa, *The First Civil Right*, chapter 3; Flamm, *Law and Order*; see also Malcolm Feeley and Austin Sarat, *The Policy Dilemma: Federal Crime Policy and the Law Enforcement Assistance Administration, 1968–1978* (Minneapolis: University Of Minnesota Press, 1981).

45. Lyndon B. Johnson, "Statement by the President upon Signing the Omnibus Crime Control and Safe Streets Act of 1968" (June 19, 1968), https://www.presidency.ucsb.edu/documents/statement-the-president-upon-signing-the-omnibus-crime-control-and-safe-streets-act-1968.

46. Richard Nixon, "Inaugural Address" (January 20, 1969), https://www.presidency.ucsb.edu/documents/inaugural-address-1; Richard Nixon, "Oath of Office and Second Inaugural Address" (January 20, 1973), https://www.presidency.ucsb.edu/documents/oath-office-and-second-inaugural-address. For the longer tradition of religiously imploring Americans to embrace social responsibility, see Sehat, *The Myth of American Religious Freedom*; and Robert H. Abzug, *Cosmos Crumbling: American Reform and the Religious Imagination* (New York: Oxford University Press, 1994).

47. Harcourt, *The Illusion of Free Markets*.

48. Ruth Wilson Gilmore, *Golden Gulag: Prisons, Surplus, Crisis, and Opposition in Globalizing California* (Berkeley: University of California Press, 2007), 5–29.

49. Jimmy Carter, "'Our Nation's Past and Future': Address Accepting the Presidential Nomination at the Democratic National Convention in New York City" (July 15,

1976), https://www.presidency.ucsb.edu/documents/our-nations-past-and-future-address-accepting-the-presidential-nomination-the-democratic.

50. Ibid. Carter exemplifies the liberal embrace of justice as just enforcement of the law, which Murakawa, in *The First Civil Right*, ascribes to Democrats for much of the twentieth century. We see a significant break between Johnson and Carter—a break especially visible when we are attentive to religion.

51. See Samuel Moyn, *The Last Utopia: Human Rights in History* (Cambridge, MA: Belknap Press, 2012).

52. Jimmy Carter, "Inaugural Address" (January 20, 1977), https://www.presidency.ucsb.edu/documents/inaugural-address-0.

53. Ronald Reagan, "Address Accepting the Presidential Nomination at the Republican National Convention in Detroit" (July 17, 1980), https://www.presidency.ucsb.edu/documents/address-accepting-the-presidential-nomination-the-republican-national-convention-detroit. Bill Scher, "When Reagan Dared to Say 'God Bless America,'" *Politico Magazine* (July 17, 2015), http://www.politico.com/magazine/story/2015/07/reagan-god-bless-america-120286.html.

54. See Gilmore, *Golden Gulag*, 5–29.

55. See Loïc Wacquant, *Punishing the Poor: The Neoliberal Government of Social Insecurity* (Durham, NC: Duke University Press, 2009), 41–75; Alexander, *The New Jim Crow*.

56. "Excerpts from President's Speech to National Association of Evangelicals" (March 9, 1983), http://www.nytimes.com/1983/03/09/us/excerpts-from-president-s-speech-to-national-association-of-evangelicals.html?pagewanted=all.

57. Ronald Reagan, "Remarks on Signing the Bill Making the Birthday of Martin Luther King, Jr., a National Holiday" (November 2, 1983), https://www.presidency.ucsb.edu/documents/remarks-signing-the-bill-making-the-birthday-martin-luther-king-jr-national-holiday.

58. Ronald Reagan, "Inaugural Address" (January 20, 1981), https://www.presidency.ucsb.edu/documents/inaugural-address-11.

59. Ronald Reagan, "Proclamation 4929—Crime Victims Week" (April 14, 1982), https://www.presidency.ucsb.edu/documents/proclamation-4929-crime-victims-week-1982.

60. *McCleskey v. Kemp*, 481 U.S. 279 (1987).

61. See data at: Prison Policy Initiative, "U.S. Prison Proliferation, 1900–2000," https://www.prisonersofthecensus.org/prisonproliferation.html.

62. Gottschalk, *Caught*; Elizabeth Hinton, *From the War on Poverty to the War on Crime*; Murakawa, *The First Civil Right*.

63. Violent Crime Control and Law Enforcement Act of 1994, H.R. 3355, Pub. L. 103-322; Antiterrorism and Effective Death Penalty Act of 1996, Pub. L. No. 104-132, 110 Stat. 1214.

64. On critical approaches to the hate-crime framework, see James B. Jacobs and Kimberly Potter, *Hate Crimes: Criminal Law and Identity Politics* (New York: Oxford University Press, 2000); and Yasmin Nair, "Saints and Sinners," *In These Times* (October 16, 2013), http://inthesetimes.com/article/15724/saints_and_sinners_matthew_shepard.

65. See Kristin Bumiller, *In an Abusive State: How Neoliberalism Appropriated the Feminist Movement against Sexual Violence* (Durham, NC: Duke University Press, 2008); Marie Gottschalk, *The Prison and the Gallows: The Politics of Mass Incarceration in America* (Cambridge: Cambridge University Press, 2006), 139–164; and Beth E. Ritchie, *Arrested Justice: Black Women, Violence, and America's Prison Nation* (New York: New York University Press, 2012).

66. William J. Clinton, "Address before a Joint Session of the Congress on the State of the Union" (January 25, 1994), https://www.presidency.ucsb.edu/documents/address-before-joint-session-the-congress-the-state-the-union-12. As a matter of fact, the violent crime rate had already begun to fall. For theories as to why the American crime rate both spiked and fell, see Alfred Blumstein and Joel Wallman, eds., *The Crime Drop in America* (New York: Cambridge University Press, 2005); and Franklin E. Zimring, *The Great American Crime Decline* (New York: Oxford University Press, 2008). For historical and cultural context, see Steve Macek, *Urban Nightmares: The Media, the Right, and the Moral Panic over the City* (Minneapolis: University of Minnesota Press, 2006).

67. On the rise of life sentences under President Clinton and after, see Sentencing Project, *Life Goes On: The Historic Rise in Life Sentences in America* (2013), http://sentencingproject.org/wp-content/uploads/2015/12/Life-Goes-On.pdf. We return to the issue of life without the possibility of parole (LWOP) in chapter 3 when we discuss opposition to the death penalty.

68. For a transcript of Clinton's remarks, see http://www.cnn.com/US/9510/megamarch/10-16/clinton/update/transcript.html (October 17, 1995).

69. For further critiques of "innocence," see Ruth Wilson Gilmore, "Abolition Geography and the Problem of Innocence," in *Futures of Black Radicalism*, ed. Gaye Theresa Johnson and Alex Lubin (New York: Verso, 2017); and Wang, *Carceral Capitalism*, 260–295.

70. See, for example, Jelani Cobb, "Tamir Rice and America's Tragedy," *New Yorker* (December 29, 2015), https://www.newyorker.com/news/daily-comment/tamir-rice-and-americas-tragedy; and Robyn D. G. Kelley, "Why We Won't Wait," *CounterPunch* (November 25, 2014), https://www.counterpunch.org/2014/11/25/why-we-wont-wait/.

71. On negative cults, see Émile Durkheim, *The Elementary Forms of Religious Life* (Oxford: Oxford University Press, 2008); and Mary Douglas, *Purity and Danger: An Analysis of the Concepts of Pollution and Taboo* (New York: Praeger, 1966).

72. See Radley Balko, *Rise of the Warrior Cop: The Militarization of America's Police Forces* (New York: PublicAffairs, 2004).

73. In drawing an analogical connection between mass incarceration and Cold War geopolitics, or, in her language, neoliberalism's workfare-warfare state versus the welfare-warfare state of the era that preceded it, Ruth Wilson Gilmore makes a similar point: "The result was an emerging apparatus that, in an echo of the Cold War Pentagon's stance on communism, presented its social necessity in terms of an impossible goal—containment of crime, understood as an elastic category spanning a dynamic alleged continuum of dependency and depravation. The crisis of state capacity

then became, peculiarly, its own solution, as the welfare-warfare state began the transformation, bit by bit, to the permanent crisis workfare-warfare state, whose domestic militarism is concretely recapitulated in the landscapes of depopulated urban communities and rural prison towns." Gilmore, *Golden Gulag*, 85–86.

74. Forman, *Locking Up Our Own*, Introduction and Chapter 6.

75. William J. Clinton, "Statement on Signing the Antiterrorism and Effective Death Penalty Act of 1996" (April 24, 1996), https://www.presidency.ucsb.edu/documents/statement-signing-the-antiterrorism-and-effective-death-penalty-act-1996.

76. George W. Bush, "Remarks on the Proposed Crime Victims' Rights Amendment to the Constitution" (April 16, 2002), https://georgewbush-whitehouse.archives.gov/news/releases/2002/04/text/20020416-1.html. See also George W. Bush's conversation with evangelical pastor Rick Warren, in which the president asserts, "Government is justice and law. Love is—love comes from a higher government and—or a higher calling or from God." George W. Bush, "Remarks at the Saddleback Civil Forum on Global Health" (December 1, 2008), http://www.presidency.ucsb.edu/ws/index.php?pid=85059.

77. On the Justice Department memos and on the legal and extralegal infrastructure of the War on Terror more generally, see Jane Mayer, *The Dark Side: The Inside Story of How the War on Terror Turned into a War on American Ideals* (New York: Anchor Books, 2009).

78. Barack Obama, "Remarks on the Situations in Iraq and Ferguson, Missouri, and an Exchange with Reporters" (August 18, 2014), https://obamawhitehouse.archives.gov/the-press-office/2014/08/18/statement-president.

79. Ibid.

3

The Limits of Reformist Religion

In 1978 a Vietnam veteran named Harry Palmer was struggling to support his family.[1] Decorated in battle, he was now in Elkhart, Indiana, trying to pay his bills—and coming up short. He decided to steal. As Palmer reported it, he was motivated by the desire to provide his children with the sorts of possessions he saw his neighbors' children enjoying. He was caught. Indiana had a strict, ten-year minimum sentence for burglary, but Judge William D. Bontrager had a different idea. After less than a year, Bontrager allowed Palmer to participate in the Victim Offender Reconciliation Program, one of the first experiments in restorative justice in the United States. Instead of serving time, Palmer met with his victims and agreed to pay restitution. He began performing manual labor for his victims' families each week until they were made whole. By all accounts Palmer had been a model prisoner, and he was an enthusiastic and dedicated participant in this alternative dispute resolution process.

The Indiana Supreme Court was less enthusiastic than Bontrager about creative alternatives to incarceration, and it ruled that Palmer must return to prison for the remainder of his ten-year sentence. Bontrager could not bring himself to send Palmer back to jail. He contemplated resigning, but eventually just withdrew from Palmer's case. Another judge stepped in, and the war veteran was returned to prison. The Indiana Supreme Court was miffed at Bontrager's intransigence. They found him in contempt of court, sentenced him to thirty days in jail, a sentence that was suspended, and fined him $500. Bontrager reached a breaking point. He resigned from the bench and returned to his law practice. A few years later he would move to Minneapolis to become the director of Christian Conciliation Service, a nonprofit restorative justice initiative, and he would later educate others on restorative justice principles across the United States and in the former Soviet Union.

The ethical dilemma confronted by Bontrager is as old as Antigone. When my obligations to my god or conscience seem to supersede my duties to secular authorities, what am I to do? Even and especially in secular modernity, this question remains ethically one of the hardest and most vital. For those compelled to give it serious thought, the consequent actions can bring ostracism, incarceration, and even death. For ordinary citizens, no act of political violence— indeed, no act of civil disobedience—is possible that does not first wrestle with this question. As a man charged with the administration of state violence, Bontrager's dilemma was public and pressing. As in the more recent case of Kentucky county clerk Kim Davis, whose job required her to begin authorizing gay marriages in direct refutation of what she took to be God's authority, Judge Bontrager saw the imperatives of his faith as taking precedence over the letter of the law. There was, in his view, an "irreconcilable difference between the laws of Indiana and the laws of God." Bontrager was forced to make a choice. If the choice was a difficult one, ultimately, as Bontrager experienced it, it was actually no choice at all. "If I have to be true to something, I will be true to God and not the law."[2] A prison system that incarcerates a good man for so long, possibly even turning a good man bad, must be disobeyed, even at the cost of one's professional reputation, financial security, and potentially one's freedom.

Bontrager's story is just one of innumerable instances from the early days of mass incarceration in which what we are calling the *abolition spirit* manifested in acts of religious resistance. Archivally closer to hand are responses of religious institutions and elites. While by and large these responses tend toward the reformist end of the spectrum, in these actions one can also sense the abolition spirit shining through. All this is in contrast to certain secularist caricatures in which America's religious communities are sometimes presumed to have been mass incarceration's unambivalent boosters. There is no denying that certain ideas associated with conservative religious communities, evangelical Christians especially, have meshed well with the expansion of the carceral state, and by and large the same can be said for the country's religious liberals. At the same time, however, a slew of religious institutions and actors, conservative and liberal alike, have, over the duration of mass incarceration, collectively levied highly critical pushback against the institution of the prison, in both its quantitative and qualitative dimensions. These religious critics have consistently preached the need to treat prisoners with greater compassion and care, advocated reducing the number of people in prison, and in other ways contested the era's ruling carceral logics. Sometimes, religious actors have imagined a world radically otherwise, a world without prisons. And yet, by means of its expansiveness and elasticity, the caretakers and profiteers of the dominant carceral order have generally had little difficulty deflecting and absorbing these criticisms.

Calls for more humane prisons became grounds for building new prisons, criticism of sentencing disparities lengthened sentences across the board, opposition to the death penalty led to the expansion of life without parole, and voluntaristic enthusiasm for ministering to incarcerated men and women became yet another stanchion of neoliberal prison administration.

To fashion some sense out of this tangled history, in this chapter we first track the way religious elites and institutions responded to the growing prison population. Religious leaders are ostensibly the caretakers of the abolition spirit, but in fact that spirit tends to dim the closer it travels to power and the more it is encoded in bureaucracy. However, at the margins and in the interstices of religious institutions, and in the forms of grassroots experimentation they can make possible, we find glimmers of the abolition spirit. Just as political history is a story of elites and institutions capturing and codifying grand visions of justice, only for those facing domination to cry out for justice anew, religious history follows the same age-old pattern. The charismatics of the New Testament world were molded into Constantinian Christians, the stultifying papacy was enlivened by the gifts of the Franciscans, and the American Great Awakenings became the shrinking behemoth of mainline Protestantism. To the south, meanwhile, the Catholicism that had underwritten colonial domination boomeranged back with the advent of liberation theology. Such oscillations are inevitable; our task is to discern the abolition spirit wherever it is to be found, whether at moments of revival or at moments of institutional sclerosis. For the religious left, the era of mass incarceration has been an ebb, but the book in your hands stands as a testament to the incipient rebound.[3]

Denominational Dissent

In 1975 Martin Luther King's doctoral advisor, L. Harold DeWolf, published a mass-market volume challenging the criminal justice system—one among many published by public intellectuals in the early 1970s.[4] *Crime and Justice in America: A Paradox of Conscience* is dedicated "To the revered memory of my student and cherished friend Martin Luther King, Jr., who stirred many Americans to seek justice with new urgency."[5] DeWolf had served as chair of the National Interreligious Task Force on Criminal Justice (NITFCJ), and the principles of "Christian Ethics" he affirms in his book seem crafted so as to be palatable to an interfaith context: Love and respect for all persons, Seeking to nurture and maintain community, Community of responsibility for sin and righteousness, and so on.[6] "True justice," DeWolf concludes, "is action well designed to move toward restoration of community on terms best serving the valid interests of all persons concerned."[7] Curiously, but also characteristic of his contemporaries' self-presentation, the theologian DeWolf uses virtually no specifically Christian language in considering the issue of incarceration, instead engaging with progressive public policy and philosophy from the secular world accompanied by the language of "Christian" values like love, justice, and community.

The book was barely noticed. Reviewers found it unimpressive and unconvincing.[8] Fifteen years after King lost the debate to Kilpatrick, DeWolf was unable to seize the ground that King had surrendered. America was no longer a nation where Protestant ideas and mainstream political culture blended seamlessly. Needless to say, King's expansive ideal of justice was never a consensus opinion in America, but whereas during the civil rights era it was powerful enough to marshal an army behind it, by the 1970s that power had evaporated.

In his commitment to a suddenly antiquated notion of justice, DeWolf was hardly alone. To leaf through the 1970s archive of the standard-bearing mainline Protestant bimonthly, the *Christian Century,* is to encounter a religious community firmly allied with those incarcerated—a class consistently painted as disproportionately Black and poor—and attuned to the pressing obligations, for Christians and Americans, to ameliorate both the conditions of incarceration and the social structures that underlay it. Secular foci and religious tropes intermingle easily in the pages of the *Christian Century,* with God, love, and the suffering Jesus, himself a victim of state violence, shuffled in with dispassionately secular articulations of social problems and possible political remedies. The witness offered is committed and steady, and yet it evinces little awareness of the tectonic shifts taking place beneath the authors' feet. If the Rockefeller Drug Laws signaled a new epoch, that fact failed to register in the pages of the *Christian Century,* where those laws never received a single mention. In the criminal justice arena, the touchstone event of the 1970s was a different Governor Rockefeller production—"the Attica uprising." If among American prison administrators, Attica signaled the end to leniency and the need to reassume control, for the staff and readership of the *Christian Century,* Attica demonstrated the inevitable consequences of a downtrodden population being pushed to its limit, with the obvious lesson that the lot of incarcerated people must be improved. "Prison reform" was incumbent, but prison abolition was not on the horizon.

In the pages of the *Christian Century* during the early 1970s, the problem of incarceration is painted primarily as a qualitative problem. As they existed and as they were being administered, prisons were, quite simply, bad for people. They took people that were already hurt and made them worse. Rehabilitation was possible and desirable, provided that it was disaggregated from punishment and that it was pursued in an egalitarian manner that empowered prisoner communities to rehabilitate themselves. Drugs and crime were real and pressing social concerns, but to prey on public fears and lean on incarceration as the remedy was to treat only the symptom.

If *The Christian Century* could be accused of playing the unwitting handmaiden to mass incarceration to any degree, it would be on the issue of indeterminate sentencing. Ending indeterminate sentencing—a practice that was seen as ripe for administrative abuses—was, as of 1971, on the forefront of the magazine's criminal justice reform agenda. But by 1979 it had become clear that the shift of power from judges and prison administrators to state legislators and executives had succeeded in leveling the playing the field only by converting the punitive extreme into the new baseline.[9] By decade's end, with the exponential growth of the US prison population under way, the magazine's brief against imprisonment in America stretched beyond quality—that our prisons were "concentration camps," and that our prisoners were "virtually slaves"—to include, as well, quantity. Only the unseemly company of the Soviet Union and South Africa had incarceration rates higher than the United States, a writer observed. Brutal, vindictive, senseless, and unlikely to improve anyone or keep anyone safe—this was our criminal justice system. From street crime to incarceration to recidivism, the responsibility for this pathetic state of affairs was wholly collective; to the extent that Americans shirked these responsibilities, they did it to their own detriment and at their own peril. "Until there is a place in our social system for the human products of our prisons," one *Christian Century* author predicted in 1979, "ex-convicts will continue to support themselves through violence."[10]

That very year, the National Council of Churches (NCC), the umbrella organization for mainline Protestants in the United States, adopted a statement on "Challenges to the Injustices of the Criminal Justice System." The NCC's governing board has a long track record of addressing hot-button issues in a politically progressive voice, and over the years it has called for a reduction in nuclear weapons, an end to violence in Iraq, an end to human trafficking, immigration reform, and government response to climate change. The NCC's 1979 statement begins by defining justice from a Christian perspective. Justice acquires its meaning "in the Being and activity of God and the relationship established with the human community through creation and redemptive covenant." A central facet of this covenant is the "divine image in human beings." By reflecting on our own godly capacities, we can learn how to live justly together. Justice is not about an action or a law; rather, "it is the substance of a community." Justice inheres when a community organizes itself as God would like. Justice is both individual and social, and both axes must be considered in tandem. Because unjust social structures create systematic injustices, it is essential for us all to be vigilant. Those who write the law and those who enforce the law must aspire to justice; laws and enforcement mechanisms that fail to do so are fundamentally unjust. If and when the norms of a community are violated, the proper response is not to excise the criminal but to repair "the damage done to the fabric of justice."[11] Pursuant to this understanding, the statement calls for, among other things, "drastic reductions in the use and length of penal sanctions," reduction of racial bias in the criminal justice system, and the decriminalization of drugs.[12]

"Challenges to the Injustices of the Criminal Justice System" is a laudably progressive statement, but as with DeWolfe's book, it had vanishingly little impact. No secular newspaper mentioned the statement. Times had changed, and the discourse had changed. Liberal Protestants continued to stress the same themes about justice that they had during their midcentury heyday, but few in the broader public were now able to hear them.

Further to the left, theologically and politically, and deeply concerned with criminal justice, were the Quakers. The American Friends Service Committee, the Quaker's social justice arm, published *Struggle for Justice: A Report on Crime and Punishment in America* in 1971. Written at a moment of widespread prison rebellion, *Struggle for Justice* is an urgent document that foregrounds the perspectives and efforts of those behind prison walls.[13] Written by a group that included incarcerated draft resisters, the report urges a range of necessary reforms intended to empower prisoners and foster self-organization, including the creation of prisoners' unions; it urges communities to hold police accountable; and it offers a model prisoners' bill of rights, which includes essentials such as adequate nutrition, opportunities to work at competitive wages, and the restoration of all civil rights upon release.

Struggle for Justice represents the best of religious institutional organizing against American prisons in the 1970s. And yet, blame the demands of genre perhaps, where the rubber met the road, the Quakers translated their radical religious views into a secular idiom, just as DeWolf translated his liberal religious views into a secular idiom.[14] Far from anything sweeping or theological, what was on offer was framed in simple, pragmatic terms: the justice system has deep problems; here is how it can be made to work better.[15] This is not to claim that radical or liberal religious communities would have prevented mass incarceration had they only spoken in thicker theological accents. Our assertion, rather, is that formal ecclesial structures may not be the best spaces to find the abolition spirit at its fullest. Ecclesial leaders were not in lockstep with the emergent logic of mass incarceration like political leaders were, but neither were they entirely embracing the abolition spirit, grounded as it must be in grassroots practices of organizing against domination. Sometimes with funding from national religious organizations, these grassroots practices did exist among religious communities, even if they proved incapable of stemming the carceral tide.

Subsequent years have brought comparable statements from individual liberal Protestant denominations, including the United Methodist Church, the United Church of Christ, and the Unitarian Universalist Association. These denominational statements distance themselves from retribution and revenge as motives for imprisonment. More often than not, such statements commend restorative justice and other models that emphasize the damage inflicted by crime on individuals and communities, and the need to make right what went wrong. In the spirit of the Kerner Report, they call for deeper analysis of the causes of crime, and they often call for community policing.[16] Nonetheless, as the criminal justice system has swallowed whole American's conceptualization and imagination of justice, these statements have become more cautious, and their critiques more piecemeal.

On occasion, these denominational statements have been drafted in explicit collaboration with government officials. Attorney General Janet Reno's 1994 address on criminal justice to the Interfaith Impact Legislative Briefing was printed in the Presbyterian Church, USA's organ, *Church and Society*, along with discussion questions.[17] Reno argued that police and prosecutors should focus their efforts on violent crime. Public safety, meanwhile, depended on increasing support for community policing and for community care. It was in cultivating these networks of auxiliary support where churches could be of greatest assistance. In 2002 the Presbyterian Church would go on to voice its support for restorative justice, and the following year the denomination called for an end to for-profit prisons.[18] But with mass incarceration cemented as national ethos, the prophetic high ground that had once allowed for a comprehensive critique of imprisonment as such had now been ceded.

In "Rebuilding Human Lives" (1973), "A Community Response to Crime" (1978), and "Responsibility, Rehabilitation, and Restoration" (2000), the United States Conference on Catholic Bishops has consistently been a staunch critic of the American criminal justice system. "Rebuilding Human Lives" foregrounds the prison's role as a place to contain the poor and disadvantaged, and it counsels Catholics not only to "visit individuals confined to prison but 'visit' the correctional system itself."[19] Attention to incarcerated individuals is framed as necessary but insufficient. "A Community Response to Crime" connects crime to social injustice more generally by calling attention to the vulnerable groups—"the poor, the minorities, and the elderly"—who are disproportionately targeted by crime.[20] "Responsibility, Rehabilitation, and Restoration," the most comprehensive statement, calls for recognizing the humanity of offenders as well as victims and questions whether more prisons and executions (and less education and treatment) truly make communities safer. The Catholic tradition and faith, the statement argues, offer better alternatives for accountability and rehabilitation, foster the rejection of vengeance, and restore community while "resist[ing] the violence that has engulfed so much of our culture."[21] Catholic critics worried that the bishops' statements were not sufficiently theologically robust. Ethicist and religious prison critic Andrew Skotnicki dismissed the first two statements as being "relatively uninspired mimicry of themes otherwise unfamiliar to the Catholic mind"—that is to say, as too secular.[22] Similarly, with respect to the third, moral theologian Amy Levad criticized the bishops for their caution. According to Levad, the bishops' recommendations "should be based upon questions of justice, not questions of effectiveness alone." Read in combination, these Catholic critics share our animating impulse: once the terms have been ceded to the dominant discourse, common sense and pragmatic remedies will only get us so far.

Public statements issued by the Union for Reform Judaism—American Judaism's largest denomination—evince a similarly accommodationist trajectory. In a 1968 statement on crime, which explicitly endorsed the Kerner Commission's conclusions, the Union emphasized the need to address "causes of crime and disorder and reject proposals which ignore those causes by emphasis upon vengeful or unconstitutional means." The statement emphasized the need to develop "alternatives to prison," but in the years to follow the means proposed, including "probation, community supervision and work furlough programs within the community," would grow in tandem with the prison population rather than stem the number of people in prison and jail.[23] In 1999 a Union statement on "Race and the U.S. Criminal Justice System" leaned heavily on Deuteronomy 16:20's doubled injunction: "justice, justice you shall pursue." Echoing the rabbinic gloss that "our means must be as just as our ends," the statement called for a moratorium on the death penalty and an end to police brutality, discriminatory policing, and sentencing disparities.[24] Fifteen years later, in the wake of the killings of Michael Brown and Eric Garner, the Union revisited these same themes. A 2014 statement was far more cautious than its already mild and reformist predecessor. In calling for a range of tepid policy fixes, including the use of police body cameras, the statement gives a strong sense of where the denomination's disproportionately white, affluent, and suburban membership stands on these hot-button issues. Its first resolution is to "applaud and support law enforcement individuals and agencies who work arduously and appropriately to keep our communities safe and to protect individuals and property from harm."[25]

Evangelical Reformism and the Pull of the Particular

Just as American capitalism affords so many different ways of opting in— up to and including various modes of nominal refusal—so too has mass incarceration secured its legitimacy through an expansive menu of means. Evangelicals' ambivalent but intimate relationship to mass incarceration is a case in point. On the one hand, evangelicals have been a key voting block for the law-and-order politics that furnished mass incarceration with its mandate.[26] On the other hand, due to the centrality of personal conversion in evangelical discourse and the staunch imperative to bring others to Christ, evangelicals have taken a hands-on approach to the problem of mass incarceration. In a partial echo of the early republic, as the state moved away from the obligations of rehabilitating the men and women incarcerated in its institutions, evangelicals moved in to fill the gap. As we will see in the next chapter with respect to Prison Fellowship's InnerChange Freedom Initiative, the evangelical model for rehabilitation—or as it is more commonly called, "transformation"—may well rhyme with the original penitentiary concept, but it also squares nicely with neoliberalism in its punitive mode. As with the administratively needed labor performed by incarcerated people themselves, religious volunteers help to sustain mass incarceration's scalability.[27] Taxpayers furnish the walls and the turrets, but the state's obligations to the incarcerated increasingly end there. The government has neither the responsibility nor the capacity to change your life, but with God's help, individuals may be capable of transforming themselves.[28] As the prison population expanded, so too did the number of state chaplains and outside religious volunteers. For rank-and-file evangelicals in particular, the rise of mass incarceration has been a wellspring for ethically serious engagement with a desperately needy population. For sure, this direct engagement changes lives and saves lives. As a mode, however, prison ministry does little to challenge the precipitating social and political fundamentals pursuant to which we keep millions locked in cages.[29]

But it would be wrong to presume that evangelicals who minister to prisoners are necessarily willing to stop at individual souls. In this regard, no evangelical went further than did than Richard Nixon aide and convicted Watergate co-conspirator Charles Colson.[30] Having found Jesus Christ while awaiting his own prison sentence, Colson launched Prison Fellowship ministry in 1975. This para-church group has become part of the evangelical establishment and has furnished rank-and-file evangelicals a number of conduits for engaging with incarcerated people, including direct ministry, reentry services, and support for incarcerated peoples' families. While Prison Fellowship works inside prisons, its partner organization, Justice Fellowship, works for institutional and systemic reform.[31] Justice Fellowship's name promises to be as much a reference to a theologically informed concept of justice as it is to the criminal justice system. The tone of Justice Fellowship's policy prescriptions is quite different from that of mainline Protestants, and is generally compatible with law-and-order politics. The group promotes restorative justice under the rubric of "victim's rights," and it urges that the criminal justice system be organized principally around the figure of the victim. On policy issues, Justice Fellowship is moderately reformist and tends to advocate for leniency in specific cases while affirming the underlying punitive principle. For example, it believes that some (but not all) sex offenders should be required to register, and that prison sentences for drug offenses should be reduced except for "high-level and international traffickers." On the issue of capital punishment, Justice Fellowship maintains that Christians can respectfully disagree. If the state's right to kill remains open to debate, a host of other things are not. Prison Fellowship's 2012 Statement of Faith affirms a belief in the Trinity, the Resurrection, and the inerrancy of scripture; the sanctity of human life from conception; the sanctity of heterosexual marriage; and the need to witness to faith in Christ. "Justice" appears in Prison Ministry's Statement of Faith only once, a reference to the obligation of the church's evangelism around the world to be "promoting righteousness and justice." That "justice" here signals an individual virtue, and not a worldly state of affairs, shows just how marginal justice-language is in evangelical discourse—even evangelical discourse about prisons.[32]

Since the 1980s, partially as a testament to Colson's influence, the National Association of Evangelicals (NAE), the umbrella organization for evangelicals in the United States, has issued a series of statements about prisons. The NAE would seem an unlikely leader on prison reform; for one thing, unlike many Protestant denominations, it supports capital punishment. Nonetheless, in 1983, noting prison overcrowding and high recidivism rates, the NAE suggested that "Biblically-based sanctions such as restitution would benefit the victim of the crime and society in general, as well as help to rehabilitate the offender."[33] The Association's statement urges support for legislation that would substitute restitution for incarceration in the case of minor crimes, which "would insure sufficient prison space for dangerous offenders." The end of these reforms is not a yet-to-be-realized vision for justice. Indeed, the term "justice" is invoked only once in the NAE's statement, to explain why "criminal offenders should be punished."[34] That is to say, if American mass incarceration could use a stray tweak or two, its basic operating system does not, for the NAE, merit substantive complaint. Three decades hence, justice is still nowhere on the horizon. In 2014 Justice Fellowship and the NAE successfully lobbied Congress to establish the bipartisan Charles Colson Task Force on Federal Corrections to examine prison overcrowding, violence, and rehabilitation programs. The establishment of this task force was reported in both the Christian and the secular press; in no account was the word "justice" ever mentioned without its mate: "criminal."[35]

Of late, as is true of the culture at large, the terrain of religious response to mass incarceration is shifting, and there are new openings for the abolition spirit to play a public role. In recent years, evangelicals have occasionally joined with mainline Protestants to make statements in favor of prison reform. In the landmark California prison overcrowding case that the Supreme Court eventually decided in 2011, the NAE and NCC shared an attorney and jointly filed an *amicus curiae* brief, along with several denominational organizations. As they argued in one voice, not merely is overcrowding cruel and unusual punishment, but, by overloading chaplains' capacities, overcrowding also placed unconstitutional limits on religious freedom. The NAE and NCC invoked the collective authority of their memberships, whose "belief systems, while diverse, all emphasize the intrinsic value of every human being and the importance of a legal system that upholds constitutional principles."[36] In the self-description that accompanied the *amicus* brief, the NAE describes how the organization "believes that religious freedom is a gift from God that government does not create but is charged to protect for all persons including prisoners." None of this breaks from Goldwater's frame: freedom is inviolable, absolute. The task of government is to protect this primordial freedom. To the degree that it pertains to God, this freedom may appear to be a parochial religious concern, but to the degree that this freedom is cast as an act of self-expression, it also betrays a secularist logic. It is certainly heartening to see religious liberals and conservatives join forces to fight for the rights of incarcerated people, and it may well presage what will eventually become the mass movement that ends mass incarceration. To this point, however, where the problematic remains framed in secular (or evangelical) terms, efforts at hand have been essentially reformist, and the will to comprehensive societal overhaul has remained repressed.

To be sure, other forces, both epistemic and practical, have served to tamp down aspirations for revolutionary change into reformism. Discrete abominations have a way of sparking political commitments (and securing funding) in a way that brutal totalities do not. There is a moral and practical sense to this triage logic. As any politician or organizer will tell you, a winnable goal is a necessary component for a successful campaign. But as far as mass incarceration has been concerned, this secular brand of political reasoning has meant a tendency to focus on a particular set of carceral trees and to ignore (or even worse, to reaffirm) the carceral forest. This focusing in and narrowing down has confined religiously liberal responses to mass incarceration no less so than conservative ones. Particular excesses of the US criminal justice system—political prisoners, solitary confinement, prison rape, slave labor, and privatized prisons—are what garner attention. With concerted care, these narrowly focused pushes can be done in a way that connects the particular problem to the problem of the carceral edifice in its entirety, but in the default reformist vein, attention to the particular is generally accrued at the expense of attention to the whole.

In its early days, the National Interreligious Task Force on Criminal Justice, founded in 1968, approached the problem of prisons from an abolitionist position. While the NITFCJ did not explicitly call for an end to the prison, individual members often held strongly anti-prison views. As task force member Virginia Mackey writes, "The goal of drastically reducing or abolishing the use of imprisonment has been a constant. . . . The general expectation has been that those who participate in Task Force work share the conviction that imprisonment is counterproductive, dehumanizing, ineffective, and so costly that we should not continue its support. Perhaps that is why NITFCJ did not formally adopt a moratorium or abolition stance." Indeed, the NITFCJ was only able to gain wide traction, and coalition partners, when it moved from broad questions about prisons and justice to a primary focus on the death penalty.[37]

As a window onto this broader dynamic, opposition to the death penalty merits special comment. During the era of mass incarceration, no issue has done more to domesticate anti-prison resistance—and to foreclose almost entirely the possibility of prison abolition—than has the issue of capital punishment. From 1976, when the Supreme Court reinstated the death penalty, through the 2016 presidential election, this manifest evil has paradoxically given moral cover to the broader systems of brutality in which it plays only a marginal role. The American preoccupation with the death penalty is understandable. Capital punishment is a gruesome and terrifying spectacle. Coldly and clinically, state actors take a human being, bring them into a sterile room, strap them to a table, inject them with poison, and end their life. With its grotesque bureaucratization and administration of premature death, the horror of state violence is laid bare. As compared to the death penalty, even locking a man or woman in a box for sixty or seventy years seems somehow merciful. And indeed, for those who have opposed the death penalty in state houses and in the courts, including the instructively named National Coalition to Abolish the Death Penalty, life without the possibility of parole (LWOP) has been promoted as the fair and just alternative.[38] As of 1970, only seven states had LWOP on the books, and it was rarely used. Between 1971 and 1990, twenty-six more states added LWOP provisions to their laws, and between 1991 and 2012 another seventeen did.[39] As of now, only Alaska has bucked this trend. With its singular focus on state executions, from the Coalition to Abolish the Death Penalty's official vantage point, the expansion of life without parole was seen as a salutary development.[40] As a putative remedy to capital punishment, however, the expansion of death-by-incarceration was a textbook reformist reform, buttressing the system it was trying to confront. Whereas a generation ago we had only the death penalty to abolish, it is now incumbent upon us to abolish death-by-incarceration as well.

The figure of the death row prisoner occupies a curious place in our civil religion. Two-fifths of Americans identify affirmatively as anti–death penalty, with American Catholics and African American Protestants especially prominent in their opposition.[41] Occasionally, a high-profile death row prisoner can become, for a moment, a household name. The death row prisoner—and the innocent God evoked in the ritual of execution—exerts, even for secular Americans, a powerful pull.[42] In 1995 Sister Helen Prejean's book about her ministerial and personal relationships with two Louisiana prisoners sentenced to death and eventually executed, was adapted for the big screen. In its reception, *Dead Man Walking* became something more than a film. Going to see the film became an act of witness. The film delivers what the audience has come for. In its cathartic execution scene, Sean Penn, as Matthew Poncelet, is strapped, arms unmistakably outstretched, to a padded gurney.[43] Trembling, his final words are a simple moral pronouncement: "I think killing is wrong. Don't matter who does it, whether it's me, or y'all, or your government."[44]

When Susan Sarandon collected the best-actress Oscar for her portrayal of Prejean, she concluded her speech with a modest prayer: "May all of us find in our hearts and in our homes and in our world a way to nonviolently end violence and heal."[45] That Sarandon had the death penalty in mind as something that needed to be ended—and from which the country needed to be healed—would have been, to the overwhelmingly white audience in the theater and watching from home, abundantly clear. But with mass incarceration in full swing, of the millions watching from home, only a vanishing few would have connected Sarandon's lament to mass imprisonment more generally, and fewer still would have connected it to *imprisonment* as such. As far as dreams of abolition were concerned, the death penalty—and more to the point, the sacred body of the executed prisoner—had stolen the spotlight.

Religion and Restorative Justice

As discussed in chapter 1 (and later, in the book's final chapter), the frameworks and practices of restorative and transformative justice furnish pivotal tools in the abolitionist arsenal. Simultaneously, however, restorative justice today is as often appropriated by professionals and reformists. In these, its more secularized and bureaucratized iterations, restorative justice largely represses the abolition spirit we saw with Judge William Bontrager's zealous piety. To nurture restorative justice's abolitionist potential, therefore, it behooves us to consider the novelty of restorative justice in the late 1970s and the specific religious context out of which it arose.

North-central Indiana has large Mennonite and Christian Brothers communities. These two closely related denominations—which descend from the Anabaptists—have a long-standing commitment to radical peacemaking and quietist disengagement from state institutions more generally.[46] Though many Mennonites and Brethren do not go so far as their Amish cousins in their refusal to participate in state institutions, the theological and social attitude remains one of wariness and separation.[47] Above all, the state is seen as a site of violence—a violence that even at its least malevolent is wholly inimical to the peace of a true Christian community.

Bontrager's more confrontational edge was in part a matter of provenance. His father had been raised Amish but left that community to further his education. Bontrager himself belonged to the Brethren, taught Sunday school at his church, and lectured at the Associated Mennonite Biblical Seminary. He was also active in Republican politics, and he had served on a statewide criminal justice advisory body. While making restitution to his victims, Harry Palmer, too, became religious: he joined the Mennonites. The religious enthusiasm of each man belonged to a moment in which, as a group, the Mennonites were thinking creatively about how their theological principles could be applied to questions of criminal justice. In 1981, while Bontrager's saga was still unfolding, Elkhart-based Mennonite professor Millard Lind spoke at a denomination-sponsored conference in British Columbia on "Criminal Justice and Christian Responsibility." He queried, "Can we really believe that, as we are obedient, God may yet work a new work, penetrating the legal system which to this moment has seemed impermeable to God's justice?"[48] Bontrager was eager to see such new work through, even at the expense of his career. In a climate in which legislatures were systemically chipping away at judicial sovereignty, he thought it immoral for a judge to reduce himself to the role of computer, mechanistically submitting to preset sentencing guidelines while ignoring the humanity of the men and women standing before his bench.

The Victim Offender Reconciliation Program in which Palmer participated was directed by Howard Zehr, a man who would go on to become one of the most recognizable figures in the restorative justice movement.[49] Zehr now leads the Zehr Institute for Restorative Justice, an outgrowth of Eastern Mennonite University in Harrisonburg, Virginia, which "advocates for restorative justice as a social movement" and trains people, in person and remotely, in restorative practices.[50] The Elkhart program was Zehr's first attempt at putting his ideas into action, and he would spend the rest of his career promoting what he learned in it. Zehr was born on the cusp of the baby boom, in 1944, the son of a pastor who would serve as the head of the Mennonites. Coming of age in the 1960s radicalized Zehr, as it did many other first-generation advocates of restorative justice. After high school in Indiana, Zehr had enrolled in the local Mennonite college, Goshen. During his first year, he attended a lecture by John Howard Yoder, the twentieth century's towering (and personally flawed) Mennonite theologian. Yoder urged the young people in his audience to take risks, to leave their comfort zone. Zehr took this directive literally. He packed up and moved to Atlanta, enrolling in Morehouse College, and in 1966 he became the historically Black school's first white graduate. After earning a master's degree from the University of Chicago and completing coursework for a doctorate at Rutgers—where he would eventually write a dissertation on the history of criminal justice in Europe—Zehr spent seven years teaching at the historically Black Talladega College in central Alabama. There, Zehr saw firsthand the injustices caused by the criminal justice system, and particularly the racism with which the system was infested. It was this experience that motivated him, in 1978, to set aside his academic career, return home to Elkhart, and try out a new approach for achieving justice.

Zehr's efforts soon received a national platform. In 1979 Zehr was appointed director of the Office of Crime and Justice at the Mennonite Central Committee, a position he would hold for almost two decades. Both in the United States and Canada, Mennonites were developing novel ideas and practices around criminal justice issues, and in 1984 the two national denominations joined forces to publish a series of pamphlets that would become seminal works in the restorative justice movement.[51] Zehr compiled the ideas he was developing into the fourth pamphlet, circulated in 1985.[52] The basic premise of *Retributive Justice, Restorative Justice* was that the existing criminal justice system is a complete failure. To make this claim, Zehr stepped back to offer a sweeping overview of criminal justice throughout the history of the West, identifying two paradigms that had coexisted. One type of justice existed outside of a formal legal system: this is how conflicts are traditionally resolved within families and communities. The other type of justice was legalistic; it just meant following the law properly. This latter type of justice had declined during the Middle Ages, but then it re-emerged, first within the Catholic Church, as Roman law served as a model for canon law, and then more broadly, as the growth of capitalism and the emergence of the secular nation-state incentivized legal standardization. According to Zehr, throughout American history, these two ways of understanding and doing justice have coexisted, albeit in tension.

Within Zehr's Mennonite framework, justice codified in law is retributive by nature and aims to take a toll on the offender rather than to create peace among victim, offender, and the community as a whole. Zehr doesn't simply reject formal law in favor of informal processes. Rather, he advances a third model, "covenant justice," which synthesizes the best elements of both types of justice. This third scaffold for justice has been largely forgotten, he asserts, but it has its origins in the Hebrew Bible. "Old Testament law does not have the sense of rigidity and formalism that our law does. Law points a direction, and it must be discussed."[53] For the Hebrew Bible that direction is justice, and it is justice understood as the restoration of a community.

In ancient Israel the laws of the kings were taken as approximations of divine justice. Kings were subordinate to God, and God's norms could trump any put forward by a king. What mattered most in this ancient world, according to Zehr, was the covenant between God and the people, with the state playing a secondary, provisional role. "Covenant justice was making things right, finding a settlement . . . living in peace and harmony with one another in right relationship"—it was "Shalom."[54] Laws and the rules established by the state are tools for establishing that right relationship. This, for Zehr, is Jesus's central message. Relationships are wounded when a crime occurs in a community, and a community ought to respond by attempting to heal that wound. The current criminal justice system's original error is to focus exclusively on the offender. It judges the offender guilty, and it seeks to mete out the punishment warranted by that guilt. Within Zehr's covenantal justice model, by contrast, when a crime is committed the offender is seen as incurring a liability or debt. Rather than an abstract system that punishes the offender, in covenantal justice the offender is obliged to find a way to make things right with their community. Only by repairing damaged relationships can Shalom be restored.

In developing this position, Zehr drew on Mennonite theology, but his thinking was also informed by the new radical criminology emerging in

European academic contexts. While Michel Foucault is, for many English-speaking academics, the most well-known European figure writing about criminal justice at this time—*Discipline and Punish* was published in French in 1975, with its English translation following in 1977—Foucault was somewhat peripheral to the broader currents of particularly Dutch and Scandinavian criminological revisionism. This European scholarship was not widely read in US academic circles, but it was circulating among the Mennonites. Indeed, the first of the Mennonites' pamphlets on criminal justice was a transcript, edited by Zehr and a group of colleagues, of a dialogue with the Norwegian criminologist Nils Christie that took place on the campus of the Mennonite Conrad Grebel College in Waterloo, Ontario.[55] Like many of his European colleagues, including Foucault, Christie takes aim at both the treatment and the deterrence models of incarceration. In the US context, this lesson had been learned the hard way. In Christie's read, the wave of prison reforms of the late sixties and early seventies targeted policies of indeterminate sentencing, which had been ostensibly for treatment but had often been coercively used to shape prisoners' psyches. When these policies were abolished, they were replaced with increasingly harsh mandatory minimum sentences. This transformation hadn't engendered justice for the American criminal justice system and had brought little relief to America's prisoners. Rather, as Christie observed, it had made the situation worse.

Christie's critique was directed at prison administrators, but also at prison reformers who advocated for more programming inside prisons. Singling out the American Friends Service Committee's *Struggle for Justice* for his critique, Christie urges reformers to shift their focus away from the offender. The offender doesn't exist in isolation. Rather, he exists in a relationship with his victim and his community. In the wake of injury there is anger. Administrators and politicians exploit this anger, harnessing it to buttress the state's authority as the agency inflicting pain on the people's behalf. But what really ought to happen, Christie asserts, is that the victim and the offender should be brought together, so that the anger can be aired, so that both parties, and the community around them, can explore and work through the complex facts and the feelings generated by the crime. Socially, the occasion of crime represents a rupture, but it also represents a provocation, and an opportunity. Rather than singling out an offender for punishment, a community could choose, with work, to restore itself. For early restorative justice advocates, what was needed was a comprehensive reassessment of the relationship between state and community. Among the necessary transformations were the popular reclamation of conflict from the state and the complete disaggregation of state violence from justice. In short, in the making of a just social order, prisons have nothing positive to contribute. As such, they should be abolished.

Restoration and Abolition

Howard Zehr found theological grounding for his account of restorative justice in the work of Dutch criminologist Herman Bianchi, whose work resonated with those elements of Mennonite theology that made Zehr acutely skeptical of the state's claim on violence. In "A Biblical Vision of Justice," which Bianchi presented in Waterloo, Ontario, at the 1982 Biennial Seminar on Victim Offender Ministry, and which the Mennonites subsequently published as a pamphlet, Bianchi offers a surprising political theology. How, he asked, in the name of "justice," did a punitive system of criminal law emerge in the modern West? In his answer, Bianchi lays ample blame at the feet of Christianity, but he also recuperates from the Bible tools for generating real justice—or more precisely, something *better* than worldly "justice." For Bianchi, "retaliation" and "retribution" are the cornerstones of the criminal justice system, but by comparing translations of the Torah, Bianchi concludes that these secular categories are in fact early modern mistranslations of *shelem*, the causative form of the root for *shalom*, that is to say, the enactment of peace. Whereas today we have criminal justice, the children of Israel had conflict resolution processes. Moreover, *tzedek*, which modern translators tend to render as "justice," is in fact a much richer concept, which connotes not a justice issued by decree but rather an ethic of righteousness engendered through a life lived in fidelity to Torah. To encompass this rich and somewhat alien concept, Jewish philosopher Martin Buber made up a word, *Bewahrheitung*, "to bring the truth." It was this comprehensive, practical notion of *tzedek* that Jesus was referring to when he answered Pilate, "I am truth." For Bianchi, this godlike capacity is available to each of us. "Everyone can say 'I am truth' when you commit yourself to a just cause and follow the indications of God."[56] "Criminal justice," by contrast which produces not justice and security but rather only criminality, was for Bianchi "an abomination." The necessary response? "You should abolish it." Rather than pursue justice one should seek *tzedaka* (the nominative abstraction of *tzedek*), "charity"; and, just as importantly, *t'shuvah*, "repentance." Accepting

Buber's gloss, *t'shuvah* is the "shock-stop" you experience when you discover that you've been on the wrong path. Embracing this shock-stop necessarily means willing yourself onto a different path and, in cases where you have committed harm, repairing the damage you have done. In Bianchi's reading of the Torah, this practical ethics is what it means to live under God's law.

Bianchi had been writing about these issues since the mid-1960s, and he was firmly established in the Dutch university system, trained as a secular criminologist, serving as a department chair and dean of the law school at the Free University of Amsterdam. It was perhaps this institutional location that helped secure broad support, including that of the mayor and council of the city of Amsterdam, for hosting, in 1985, the second International Conference on Penal Abolition (ICOPA).[57]

Self-described prison abolitionists had been around for over a decade in European academic circles, at least since the 1973 formation of the European Group for the Study of Deviance and Social Control.[58] At the ICOPA gathering, Bianchi hosted leading figures from that group, based primarily in Scandinavia, including Christie, Louk Hulsman, and Thomas Mathiesen. A cadre of North American abolitionists also attended. While there was support for the gathering from the Canadian Quakers and participation from a former Canadian Mennonite staffer, the tone was largely secular. In his own remarks, Bianchi himself turned toward the history of the abolition of slavery rather than to biblical precedents. While the European criminologists occasionally drew on religious traditions for analytic concepts, they tended to keep religion at arm's length.[59]

Traveling country to country, ICOPA was to become a biennial event, gathering a mix of activists, practitioners, and academics. Religious and spiritual themes had been far more prominent two years earlier, at the inaugural conference, which had taken place in Toronto. Not only were these initial proceedings steeped in religious sentiment and authority, the conference itself had been made possible by the financial resources of religious communities.[60] The conference secretary, Jake Friesen, was trained as a Mennonite minister in Elkhart and had worked for the Mennonite Central Committee. And the conference coordinator, Bob Melcombe, a member of the Quaker Committee on Jails and Justice, had been incarcerated three times for his protests against nuclear armament.

In Melcombe's welcome letter, the Mennonite religious language of restorative justice was foregrounded from the start: "As we build justice, we build a sense of community; as we build community, we build peace."[61]

Financial support for the conference came from a few secular social justice groups and Canadian unions, but also from many, many religious communities: Augustinians, Cistercians, Franciscans, Jesuits, Dominicans, Quakers, Mennonites, and others, from far and near. The conference received official endorsement from the United Church of Canada's Criminal Justice sub-unit, the outreach committee of the Presbyterian Church of Canada, the University of Toronto School of Theology, two Quaker organizations, the Canadian office of Charles Colson's Prison Fellowship, and a wide variety of other groups.

In Toronto, at ICOPA's beginnings, we find religious liberals organized alongside a variety of other religious and secular communities—all under the banner of penal abolition. These groups all shared the view that wholesome community and peace are vital social ideals, and the existing criminal justice system, in North America in particular, is an obstacle to, rather than a means for, achieving them. Before this diverse audience, Melcombe did nothing to restrain his rhetoric:

> There is no way to reform what we have—a society based on punishment. There is only one way to create a society based not on punishment but on values positive, creative and just—to abolish the methods of punishment and the system built around them. In plain language, to abolish imprisonment and to abolish criminal law itself.[62]

Among the conference workshops was one titled "Response of the Religious Community." It was jointly led by a Mennonite staffer and the executive director of the Community Programs Division of the Canadian Ministry of Correctional Services—the latter a former clergy member. As a conference theme, religion was roughly as prominent as race and gender, direct action, and outreach to incarcerated people. The conference program anticipates and pushes back against secularist ambivalence: "Marxist analysts have maintained that religion has always been an instrument of oppression, an opiate of the people to maintain the status quo." Today, the program notes, some religious groups are vocal advocates of the death penalty and long mandatory minimums, but religious groups are *also* prominent in "reconciliation movements."[63] That is to say that while religion can and does act as a tool of domination, as the founders of ICOPA well understood, religion can *and does* also serve as a resource in justice organizing.

Eight years later, in 1991, ICOPA came for the first time to the United States, to Bloomington, Indiana.[64] Harold Pepinsky, a professor of criminal justice and East Asian languages at Indiana University, played host, but as Pepinsky noted, it was the resources of the NITFCJ, a project of the National Council of Churches, that had made the event possible. Indeed, Pepinsky was himself the first member of the task force without a denominational affiliation. The conference opened with a prayer by an Ojibwa elder who was also a board member of the World Council of Churches, and the program was chock full of religiously affiliated participants. Wayne Northey of the Canadian Mennonites chaired a session on "Mediation and Restorative Justice." Quaker prison minister and abolitionist activist Fay Honey Knopp, running a New York Council of Churches group, chaired a session on feminist perspectives on prison abolition. Ruth Morris, working for the Quakers in Toronto, was honored as a cofounder of ICOPA. Note how "radical" Protestants (Quakers and Mennonites) are here cooperating with "liberal" Protestant-supported institutions to move in the direction of prison abolition. When we take a bottom-up perspective, rather than focusing on institutional elites, we find the abolition spirit spreading beyond its expected quarters.

At ICOPA V in Bloomington, yet another place the abolition spirit turned up, albeit haltingly, was in reference to Black Christianity. A special session was dedicated to the book *Black Men in Prison: The Response of the African American Church*, a volume edited by Gayraud Wilmore, a Presbyterian minister and one of the founding fathers of Black theology.[65] Designed to circulate among Black churches, *Black Men in Prison* offers sketches of theological frameworks and study guides to help Black church communities analyze the injustices perpetrated by the criminal justice system. It represents one of the few existing treatments of prisons from an African American religious perspective. Another would not appear until 2011, with the publication of James Cone's *The Cross and the Lynching Tree*.[66] As an indication of just how removed these issues were from mainstream Black religious concerns, in the compilation of key Black theology documents that he edited along with Cone, Wilmore chose not to include any of his edited volume, or any other work on criminal justice. This obviously does not mean that Black Christians ignored prisons. Rather, it marks the generally subterranean nature of the abolition spirit, an enduring cultural strain that surfaces only when the circumstances are just right.

The Indiana ICOPA meeting illustrates the variety of such subterranean possibilities, and it provided a safe space for them to speak out and nurture each other. The meeting featured a plenary panel on racism and the criminal justice system that included Seiichi Michael Yasutake from the National Council of Churches' Interfaith Prisoners of Conscience Project.[67] An Episcopal priest of Japanese-American descent, Yasutake had been interned during the Second World War for a year and a half. He was freed when he was admitted to the University of Cincinnati, but his studies were cut short when he was expelled for refusing to take a loyalty oath due to his opposition to American militarism. Yasutake's career was in some ways unique, but in other ways it represents well the American religious-liberal practices around criminal justice issues at this time—and hints at one shape the abolition spirit takes. Ecumenical, multiethnic coalitions were fostered by parachurch groups maintained by social justice–minded individuals with strong personalities. Yasutake embraced his multicultural background, ministering simultaneously to Japanese and white congregations, and he advanced his advocacy work by making use of a loose affiliation with the liberal Protestant bureaucracy. He had been radicalized both by his experience of internment and by his years as a campus minister during the 1960s, when he supported activists protesting the Vietnam War. What started as liberal Protestant advocacy developed, as the twentieth century drew to a close, into the Interfaith Prisoners of Conscience Project, a group transcending religious boundaries much in the manner that Yasutake managed to stand astride racial divides.

Regardless of the diminished voice of liberal religious elites in the public square, and regardless of whatever difficulty they were having at rallying their own congregations, liberal denominations maintained the resources to operate behind the scenes, by means of which they occasionally supported radical work—nurturing the abolition spirit. In 1974, for example, Beacon Press, the Unitarian Universalist Association's publishing house, put out Marie Buckley's *Breaking into Prison: A Citizen Guide to Volunteer Action*, which encouraged radicalization through engagement in educational and religious programming.[68] While working for the American Friends Service Committee, the Dutch-born former Nazi-detainee and United Church of Christ minister Jan Marinissen approached the Unitarian Universalist Service Committee about working together toward a prison-construction moratorium.[69] With continuing support from the Unitarians as the cornerstone of its ecumenical coalition, the project would come to life as the National Moratorium on Prison Construction, and it would lobby on Capitol Hill from 1975 until the mid-1980s.[70]

Yet another example of grassroots religious organizing that manifested the abolition spirit is found in the life and labors of Fay Honey Knopp.

With resources from the New York Council of Churches, Knopp founded the Prison Research Education/Action Project in 1975. Though based in Syracuse, New York, its mission was national, and the abolitionist pamphlet that it put out with a grant from the Quakers, *Instead of Prisons: A Handbook for Abolitionists*, circulated widely.[71] *Instead of Prisons* is a wonderful mixture of exhortation, critique, and practical tools for decarceration (shrinking the prison system) and *excarceration* (building up the system to replace it)—and the text remains a valuable tool for abolitionists today. Interesting for present purposes, however, is how in its rhetoric, the *Handbook* framed its religious witness at the frontier of the secular.[72] The religion is here: "Abolitionists believe that it is only in a caring community that corporate and individual redemption can take place. We view the dominant culture as more in need of 'correction' than the prisoner. The caring communities have yet to be built."[73] For those with an ear for it, "caring community" and "redemption" are plainly religious notes, as, elsewhere (and more negatively), is the *Handbook*'s condemnation of Americans' "worshipping the Golden Calf of caging."[74] But, even in sum, these religious notes feel deliberately muted.

A few years hence, the window for radical religious critique had seemingly closed. When the National Moratorium on Prison Construction campaign put out a booklet on "Alternatives to Imprisonment," their reasoning was, with the exception of a vague gesture toward justice-beyond-the-law, entirely secular and pragmatic. "In the long term," they wrote, "alternatives to imprisonment involve social, political, and economic changes which would result in a just society. In the short term, they involve a variety of programmatic and procedural changes in the criminal (in)justice system which reduce the numbers of people locked up."[75] With the problems of incarceration now so pressing and obvious, efforts toward broader social transformation took a necessary backseat to essential administrative fixes. Liberal Protestant institutional resources counted to support such work, but thrown into a rearguard crouch, the will to re-envision justice wholesale was no longer articulable. Instead of such prophetic speech, arguments leveraged the reformist spirit and intuitions about justice held in what had become a secular public square.

ICOPA's abolitionism would drift in a similar direction. A gathering once made possible by religious communities with an agenda shaped by religious leaders secularized over time. In 2014 the ICOPA meeting was sponsored by the University of Ottawa and secular community groups.[76] The conference had no religious sponsors, and with the exception of a single feminist critique of the way evangelicals and liberal feminists aligned to criminalize prostitution, the stuff of religion was entirely absent from the discussion.

Indigeneity and Beyond

ICOPA's 2012 meeting in Trinidad and Tobago also lacked religious sponsors and featured only two presentations that touched at all on religion. The two talks were "Hindu and Muslim Perspectives on Justice and Peace" and "Amerindian Spirituality and Blessing."[77] The theme of "Amerindian Spirituality"—and the ambiguity of this designation—is particularly significant in the history of the restorative justice movement.[78] It points to yet another moment when the abolition spirit promises to manifest—and yet another moment when the forces of law-and-order threaten to void that promise. Because they are impersonal, bureaucratized, and professionalized, criminal justice systems express, and in turn engender, alienation. As with the turn away from organized religion, turning away from the state's system of justice and "returning" to a more organic system of justice, supposedly indigenous, promises wholeness and peace. Moreover, in our spiritual-but-not-religious age, indigenous religion seems fitting—even for Christians who want their message to resonate with the broader culture. Indeed, the impulse that animates the turn to "Amerindian spirituality" may, perhaps, be seen in the Mennonites' turn to what they presume as the more ancient way of life found in the Hebrew Bible.

The path that connects indigenous spirituality to restorative justice in the United States is circuitous. The first attempt to implement a restorative justice model is sometimes credited to the Minnesota Restitution Center in 1972, when that state's Department of Corrections funded an initiative developed by two University of Minnesota graduate students drawing on lessons they were learning from secular criminology scholarship.[79] Over the next two decades—the peak of the prison population explosion—such projects remained sporadic.[80] The restorative justice experiments taking place in North America, against the liberal religious background and shaped by it, attracted international attention even before ICOPA convenings began in the mid-1980s. These models crossed the Pacific, with the government of New Zealand, and then Australia, enthusiastically adopting and institutionalizing restorative justice programs.[81] By 1989, New Zealand employed a restorative justice model in lieu of prison for all juvenile offenders, and by 1994 it had extended the model to include some adults. Australia followed a few years behind, though without quite as widespread an embrace. In these contexts, with the support and funding of the state, restorative justice techniques grew rapidly in reach and sophistication. Among the changes that accompanied this Oceanic embrace was the foregrounding of indigenous terminology and practices. Often connected explicitly with the concept of "spirituality," indigeneity became central to the theory and practices of restorative justice.

The first mention of restorative justice in the *New York Times* took place in an article published in 1995, where restorative justice is framed as a possible ameliorative response to the problem of jail overcrowding.[82] The article's protagonist is Father John Bonavitacola, a minister to incarcerated men in Philadelphia's Industrial Correctional Center. Bonavitacola is blunt in declaring that the criminal justice system is a failure, and he holds up restorative justice as the likely solution to the problem. The *Times* reports how secular liberals, law enforcement, and evangelicals were all beginning to turn away from prisons and toward restorative justice, and how, in dialogue with Colson's Justice Fellowship, even Republican Wisconsin governor Tommy Thompson had declared a statewide moratorium on prison construction and was exploring instead the possible implementation of restorative justice models. Restorative justice, the *Times* reports, is "a spiritual notion that a crime affects more than just a criminal in the justice system. The response to crime must include the victim, society and the community as well."[83] What makes restorative justice "spiritual," it seems, is an emphasis on placing the individual in a communal context and positing individual and collective healing as a goal. That the *Times* goes with "spiritual" and not "religious" may have something to do with the fact that restorative justice's demands on justice itself are to be exacted within the existing justice system, as is perennially so with the reformist impulse. Arguably a victim of its international success, by the time of its American rebirth, restorative justice had crossed over from abolitionist polemic *against* criminal justice to a reformist amendment *to* criminal justice.

When newfound advocates for restorative justice in the United States looked abroad for guidance, the most compelling international models prominently incorporated indigenous elements. The Minnesota Restitution Center, which was originally established with funds from the 1968 crime control bill, changed form over the years as the political winds shifted, but its ethos continued to be shaped by its existence within the Minnesota Department of Corrections. In 1994 a new institutional configuration emerged for restorative justice within the department, and it claimed to be the first US government agency to employ a restorative justice–focused staff member. Through the 1990s and early 2000s, restorative justice flourished in Minnesota—and during those last years, under the leadership of Corrections Department restorative justice coordinator Kay Pranis, it embraced indigenous spirituality.[84] What was restorative justice to look like in practice? In search of answers, Pranis turned to Minnesota's indigenous communities for help.[85] After Pranis's position was eliminated, she took to writing and founded Living Justice Press, a publishing house dedicated to publicizing restorative justice. Prominent in the press's catalogue are titles drawing on the wisdom of indigenous communities. For example, former state prosecutor Rupert Ross tapped into the experiences and practices of a range of First Nations concerning how the Canadian justice system fails indigenous victims, offenders, and communities, and he reflected on indigenous metaphysics and ethics. He published his findings in three widely read volumes: *Dancing with the Ghost: Exploring Aboriginal Reality* (1992), *Returning to the Teachings: Exploring Aboriginal Justice* (1996), and *Indigenous Healing: Exploring Traditional Paths* (2014).[86] Some of Pranis's own work partakes in a similar spirit. Her practical guide, *The Little Book of Circle Processes: A New/Old Approach to Peacemaking*, begins with the following rationale: "Our ancestors gathered around a fire in a circle. Families gather around the kitchen table in a circle. Now, we are learning to gather in a circle as a community to solve problems, support one another, and connect to one another."[87]

The authority restorative justice advocates derive from indigeneity again marks the ambivalence of efforts to embrace the abolition spirit. As with Zehr and Bianchi's reclamation of Israelite "Shalom," idealizations of indigeneity by members of the dominant culture have more than a whiff of primitivism about them. The Israelites may have had an organic system of dispute resolution rooted in and conducive to Shalom, but if their practices were anything like what the Bible claims they were, the Israelites also killed and exiled. Families gather around the kitchen table, but these same families are often infused with patriarchal power and domination. As with a Christian primitivism that projects onto the Israelites an idealized order that repudiates the failures of Christian society to be sufficiently just, Anglo-Americans are predisposed to find peace in indigenous culture.[88]

To name this primitivist longing is not necessarily to debunk it. The hegemony of the secular state invariably leaves one grasping at the margins, at what has been repressed, at alternative ways of life (whether they be residual or emergent) to act as mirror and as guide. In indigenous spirituality, as with fugitive versions of Abrahamic religions, those straining toward a more just justice may find resources for imagination and experimentation, as well as indigenous projects in need of support.[89]

Justice from the Right

The restorative justice movement received a firm boost when it was embraced by evangelical Christian elites, including Prison Fellowship. Aware of and attempting to synthesize developments originating in secular social work contexts and internationally, Colson's team translated restorative justice into an idiom that could be heard by their evangelical audience. The historical entanglement of restorative justice and prison abolitionism had by now been fully obscured.

But Prison Fellowship was aware of restorative justice long before it became a centerpiece of its programming, in part because of William Bontrager. Colson wrote glowingly of the one-time Indiana judge, hailing him as a Christian martyr for religious freedom. Writing in Prison Fellowship's magazine in 1982, Colson tells Bontrager's story rather differently than the liberal Protestant *Christian Century* had depicted it (the contours of which we recount above).[90] In Colson's version, Harry Palmer had "accepted Christ in 1977 while in jail," and Bontrager "had himself been converted to Christ a year earlier." Where in the *Christian Century* it is religious community that makes Bontrager who he is, for Colson, it is Bontrager's personal faith in Jesus Christ. Colson touted Bontrager's heightened sense of Christian mission: as the judge "had been reading the Old Testament prophets, the words of Amos seared his conscience. He knew the Supreme Court's order didn't meet God's standard of justice and righteousness." So impressed was Colson that when he later went to preach at the prison where Palmer was serving the remainder of his ten-year sentence, he invited Bontrager to come along. Colson describes the passionate reunion of the two men, and he concludes that anyone who doubts the resurrection of Jesus Christ need only hear Bontrager tell his story. Bontrager had knowingly sacrificed comfort and respectability for his faith, and for such conviction and courage there could be no worldly explanation.

In the wake of *The New Jim Crow*, a broad swath of liberals have been eager to get involved with prison reform, but in this regard, liberals are latecomers. Evangelicals have been grinding away in this struggle for a long time. Colson's Justice Fellowship aims to alleviate the worst problems of prisons, including overcrowding and indignities, but it separates out these ameliorative measures from any broader challenge to the prison system. Following the lead of Justice Fellowship, in pushing for reform the National Association of Evangelicals draws sharp distinctions between "dangerous" and "nondangerous" offenders. Note the flexibility inherent in this language. In contrast to the common distinction between "violent" and "nonviolent" offenders, which, at least nominally, indexes past events objectively, "dangerousness" purports to script a future and may draw on highly subjective criteria—if, for example, an offender sincerely embraces Jesus Christ as his lord and savior—in order to make this determination.[91]

For dangerous offenders, Colson argues, there is only the cage. For the nondangerous, restorative justice is preferable. In making this claim, Colson doesn't back away from the language of law and order. "The criminal justice system," he writes, "which is absolutely crucial if government is to carry out its first duty—the preservation of order—urgently needs reform."[92] Telling a history of criminal justice in the West very similar to the history recounted in early Mennonite pamphlets, Colson argues that for their narrowness of focus, both rehabilitation and deterrence are inadequate goals for the criminal justice system. The real goal should be to create "a system that *restores* the peace of the community shattered by crime." "Restorative justice," which for Zehr signaled a radical break from American criminal justice, for Colson largely signals an affirmation of the existing order. Colson assures his audience that restorative justice is "rooted firmly . . . in the Judeo-Christian tradition," and he provides a religious genealogy of restorative justice structured around the Christian themes of creation, fall, redemption, and restoration. These are the stages of world history and of the life of individual Christians, and, as Colson argues, these stages also map the path from the criminal act to the restored social order. Though in practice this process is essentially one for individuals, in effect it "can produce both personal redemption and a truly just public order."[93] In Colson's work, restorative justice is located in a thoroughly Christian framework, one that is specifically evangelical—aimed at individual transformation and what is effectively social stasis. The social order is to be maintained, or "restored," by converting individuals to faith in

Christ: it is in this transformation, of one soul at a time, that we may best realize justice.

In the 1980s and 1990s, Prison Ministry and Justice Ministry expanded rapidly. In 1985 Colson broke ground on renovations of a 37,000-square-foot mansion in suburban Virginia that would serve as the two groups' headquarters.[94] By the dawn of the new century, however, growth had slowed. In 2000 and again in 2011, the organizations chose to implement major staff layoffs so as to maintain solvency.[95] As new models of institutionalized ministry became bogged down in legal fights, restorative justice offered an alternative opportunity for growth. With Justice Ministry pushing hard, restorative justice was embraced internationally as a best practice in the realm of criminal justice.[96]

While Colson has queried the limitations of state violence for effecting justice, other conservative Christian elites have taken a more regressive tack. In a 2002 speech at the University of Chicago Divinity School, developed and published as "God's Justice and Ours" in the conservative-leaning ecumenical journal *First Things*, the late Catholic Supreme Court justice Antonin Scalia considered whether a commitment to the dignity of each human being, created in God's image, should trump the law of the land with respect to the death penalty.[97] Scalia argues, first, that in his role as judge he must simply apply the law, as it was intended when it was written, bracketing his religious beliefs. Should his religious convictions profoundly differ from the law of the land on a fundamental issue—say, the death penalty—his obligation would be to resign his position. But, Scalia argues, Catholics can reasonably support the death penalty for a number of reasons. For one, in the Christian view, death is not so bad, given that believers will reach a qualitatively better life after death. Further, in contrast to "the post-Freudian secularist" who is always blaming "history and circumstances" at the expense of individual responsibility, Christians acknowledge that individuals are sinners, with weak wills.[98] Individuals are guilty in the eyes of God, and God delegates to the government the role of administering justice on earth. In a modern democracy, where government seems to originate with the people and remain accountable to the people, it is easy to forget, Scalia argues, that the role of the state is divinely ordained. Scalia has little patience for claims that prison might violate the dignity of the prisoner—according to him, prisons feature "nice clean cells with television sets, exercise rooms, meals designed by nutritionists, and conjugal visits"—so there is no need to think of prisoners as particularly "vulnerable."[99] In a sense, Scalia (and the broader current of conservative Catholicism and evangelicalism that he represents) can agree that justice should bring peace to a community. But in contrast to the first wave of restorative justice, these religious conservatives simply maintain that the American state is the divinely ordained agent of such restoration, and the prison system is the proper means by which such restoration takes place.

In the public debate around incarceration, Scalia-style conservative Christians represent an increasingly marginal voice. In part, this is due to the overwhelming evidence showing just how destructive incarceration is to individuals and communities. With a bipartisan consensus emerging around the need for criminal justice reform, the Colson Task Force on Federal Corrections, led by former Republican and Democratic members of the House of Representatives, assembled a team to explore possible reforms.[100] The task force included two members from evangelical organizations (including one from Prison Fellowship), a number of lawyers and judges, and members from the secular nonprofit world. (Liberal religionists were not given a seat at the table.) The task force took testimony from a more expansive set of institutional representatives, including government officials, the private prison manager Corrections Corporation of America, academics, the ACLU, the American Friends Service Committee, the United Methodist Church, and others. Surprisingly, restorative justice was not highlighted in the task force's menu of proposed remedies. They focused on conventional means of making the system function more smoothly and less expensively, including an increase in prison programming, more fine-tuned classification of prisoners, and better reintegration programs after release. In fact, based on the public presentation of its conclusions, the Colson Task Force took its primary job to be explicating the problem, with its rather bland recommendations relegated to bullet points in a sign-off note.[101]

Meanwhile, under the umbrella of the Interfaith Criminal Justice Coalition, a range of denominations and other religious organizations have come together to push for legislative criminal-justice reforms.[102] Groups represented include the Brethren, Jesuits, Quakers, African Methodist Episcopals, Unitarian Universalists, and Scientologists. Thus far, the coalition's statements have been limited to expressing the gravity of the problem. They acknowledge the limitations of existing legislative proposals and affirm the need for faith communities to do more. This approach seems both necessary and necessarily limited. With institutional religion continuing a downward decline, the moral weight of even a broad denominational coalition is insufficient to the task at hand. Rather than formalized religious institutions, the place to look for new possibilities of religious activism would seem to be at the grassroots, where, in lived experience, denominational boundaries are easily crossed and vital improvisations can engender new religious expressions and political configurations. It is through these creases that hints of the abolition spirit may best be spotted.

Spiritual Revolutions

As promising as legislative initiatives may be, we will not find the abolition spirit distilled in the corridors of power, among denominational lobbyists in Washington, DC. Instead, we should turn instead to places like to Klamath, California, with a population of 779. There, twenty-nine miles south of Pelican Bay Prison, the supermax facility built in 1989 where California keeps its "worst of the worst" under 23-hour-a-day lockdown, is the Yurok Tribal Court.[103] Operated by the largest Indian Nation in California, whose reservation lies on the land they inhabited at the moment of European contact, the Yurok put into practice a vision of justice that represents the polar opposite of Pelican Bay. Yurok justice also stands at some distance from caricatures of indigenous folkways. The paramount aim of the court is not to implement the law or protect order in the community. Rather, its mission is "to protect the values of the [Yurok] people, to support the development of those values within each member of the community, and to ensure that our responsibility to protect our traditions and traditional lands are carried out."[104] For the Yurok, protecting traditions and traditional land is a sacred task—this is an argument they made before the US Supreme Court in what would become one of the twentieth century's pivotal Indian rights and religious freedom cases.[105] In *Lyng v. Northwest Indian Cemetery Protective Association*, the Yurok argued that a road ought not to be built through certain National Forest lands because Indian Nations considered those lands sacred. By the time the case was decided, in 1988, such an expansive vision of religious freedom, oriented toward higher ideals of justice, was only a memory; in an opinion authored by Justice Sandra Day O'Connor, the Court ruled against the Indian Nations.

In the face of this loss, one Yurok wrote an impassioned open letter to Justice O'Connor. Abby Abinanti was, in 2004, serving on San Francisco Superior Court, a position she took after years litigating Indian rights claims and as legal director of the National Center for Lesbian Rights. Abinanti declares that US law is "wrong," and that O'Connor personally was "wrong." In part, O'Connor's error in judgment was rooted in her secularist inability to account for the spiritual life of the Yurok, what, Abinanti translated, "I believe you would call 'the soul.'" Law that ignores the soul, or something like it, is the law of domination; that is, the law that is employed by colonizers to suppress Indian Nations. But such law can never secure the assent of Indian Nations: "I lived complying with your decision, but I never accepted it as anything but bending to brute, irresistible, and immoral force."[106] A few years later, Abinanti engineered a response. She left her chambers in San Francisco and took the position of Chief Judge of the Yurok Tribal Court. Her attitude to justice changed as well. Instead of a robe, she now wears jeans and cowboy boots; instead of a bench, she sits at a table. And instead of enforcing the law, Abinanti is committed to implementing a system of restorative justice that supports Yurok values and sovereignty.[107]

In doing justice, Abinanti attempts to reimagine a time before European contact: "How did we resolve things before our cultural interruption, when invasion occurred? We were village people, and we sat around and had discussions. My purpose is to help you think up how to make it right if you made a mistake." This, she understands, is very much the opposite of the settler-colonial prison system, whose principal mode is "banishment.[108] Indian men and women are disproportionately swept up into the criminal justice system, particularly through alcohol- and drug-related offenses, and tribal courts have very limited jurisdiction.[109] She has, therefore, brokered an agreement with state prosecutors to voluntarily defer to the Yurok Tribal Court in some criminal cases, and she tries to relegate people back into criminal court only as "a last resort." Abinanti brings her San Francisco Superior Court experience into the tribal court, running it with some of the trappings of a regular criminal court, including attention to process. Unlike many Native and Native-inspired restorative practices, Abinanti's court features no talking sticks or peace circles. But at Yurok Tribal Court, if fines cannot be paid with cash, debtors can cut an agreement to pay in salmon. Recovering addicts on probation may have to commit to a program that includes both prayer and sweat lodges.

The Yurok Tribal Court includes a Wellness Court—what in other jurisdictions would likely be called a drug court. The drug court movement has a different origin story than restorative justice, with its beginnings in Miami in 1989 with the innovation of a judge who felt more effective outcomes would be had if the adversarial process were set aside for a focus on treatment. With measurable results dramatically superior to the prison system, drug courts rapidly spread nationally and internationally as an adjunct to the regular court system, with best practices disseminated by the US Department of Justice.[110] While drug courts can problematically blend the restorative and retributive functions of the legal system, and are haunted by the double edge of medicalization, their growing acceptance has opened opportunities for local experimentation where justice can potentially be thought otherwise. The Justice Department resources with grant funding the Southern California–based Tribal Law and Policy Institute, which supports Indian courts in general and wellness courts especially; Abinanti serves as the institute's board president.[111] Instead of disseminating model law codes or, at the other extreme, emphasizing some diffuse indigenous spirituality, the institute describes its mission as "to enhance and strengthen tribal sovereignty and justice while honoring community values."[112] The goal of legal systems is justice, and in this case justice is dependent on sovereignty. The values, including religious values, of Native communities are the foundation of justice, in this view, and they are incompatible with the rule of law as administered—imposed—by federal or state governments.

In an analysis of wellness courts, Joseph Thomas Flies-Away, a Hualapai judge, and Carrie E. Garrow, a Mohawk judge, suggest that the introduction of these venues represents a "jurisprudential spiritual revolution" for indigenous communities.[113] The conquest and genocide of American Indians severed relationships between Indians and the natural world, each other, and themselves. Native value systems—which often nowadays are grouped under the secular category of "spirituality"—had cultivated intimacy in these relationships, and those value systems collapsed. All that was left was the rule, the law, of the conqueror. According to Flies-Away and Garrow, wellness courts "help to restore, rejuvenate, or re-create lost connections between misplaced community members and their relatives or other citizens"—and these connections are healed by means of "spirit."[114] More specifically, this means incorporating Native rituals into the wellness courts, and it means orienting those courts toward restoring right relationships, not in order to wallow in some New Age nirvana, but to cultivate an oppositional sovereignty that refuses the conquerors' claim to the same. Half an hour from Pelican Bay, this is what the Yurok attempt to put into practice: a spiritual revolution in which the carceral logics characteristic of America's settler culture will no longer hold sway.[115]

Building a Common Chorus

In her preface to *The New Jim Crow*, Michelle Alexander correctly gauges her audience to be "people who care deeply about racial justice but who, for any number of reasons, do not yet appreciate the magnitude of the crisis faced by communities of color as a result of mass incarceration."[116] Alexander's book, and the tidal wave of popular enthusiasm it helped draw out, brought the category of "mass incarceration" into the mainstream and helped to launch a broad public conversation about race and imprisonment, which continues to gather momentum nearly a decade later.[117]

The New Jim Crow has vanishingly little to say about religion, but in Alexander's many interviews and speeches in the years since the book's publication, she has been explicit about the role religious communities have to play in the struggle ahead.[118] Early returns suggest some cause for optimism. Across the country, in congregations' social justice committees and elsewhere, people of all races and religions are evincing great concern about racial and criminal justice and are hungry for ways to effect positive social change. *The New Jim Crow* phenomenon was both an expression of this hunger and, in turn, it has become a catalyst. From ad hoc study and reading groups to the Unitarian Universalists' denomination-wide engagement with *The New Jim Crow*, religious individuals and communities in the United States are now grappling with incarceration more than at any time in the past half-century.[119]

For Alexander herself, the potential moral force of religious engagement on the issue of mass incarceration has spurred a shift in vocation. In 2016 she resigned her faculty position at The Ohio State University's law school to take up a post at Union Theological Seminary, where she is now investigating the connections between religion and incarceration. "I believe the experience will enable me to clarify my spiritual beliefs," Alexander explained. "A wide range of people of faith and conscience who sing songs from different keys may be able to join in a common chorus that shakes the foundations of our unjust political, legal, and economic systems, and ushers in a new America."[120]

The vision Alexander articulates gestures at both the possibilities and limitations of potential alliances between religious communities and secular criminal justice reform advocates. *The New Jim Crow* is a decidedly secular book. Using data and a compelling organizing frame, it lurched the public conversation about prisons. By and large, however, it remains if not quite value-neutral, then at the very least value-muted. While it rightly detests racism, its gripe is principally levied at the quantitative phenomenon rather than at its qualitative parts. It does not regard incarceration to be an abomination, and it does not offer an alternative vision of the good around which we must collectively organize.[121] Consistent with the dominant secular mode, for Alexander in *The New Jim Crow*, morals and values are secondary. Rather than adopting an explicitly moral viewpoint, the book leans on the preexisting intuitions of its audience—in support of fairness, against the scourge of racism—to nudge the reader in the direction of action. Because Alexander does not present an alternative moral vision, at the end of the day, the book's problem with mass incarceration remains the "mass" part: too many people are incarcerated, and in particular too many Black people. Grounds for a more sweeping critique—not merely of *mass* incarceration, but of encaging human beings as such—remains in her landmark volume largely unthought.

We fully endorse Alexander's subsequent call to arms, and we endorse the centrality of religion to this mobilization, but we would like to offer a friendly, if substantive, amendment. Whereas King once called for a *crusade*, Alexander's language of "clarifying spiritual beliefs" thinks much smaller. The shortfall between King's appeal and Alexander's is indicative of the headwinds faced by those looking to cultivate religious energies and harness them in the struggle for social and economic justice. In terms of institutional and social power, the liberal Protestant establishment that drove the civil rights movement and the Great Society is ever weaker, and up to 20% of Americans (drawn from the secular left disproportionately) now identify as having no religion at all.[122] Once-powerful religious institutions are now weak, membership is down, and a slate of ideas and practices that possess great disruptive potential have been largely left to rust and rot. The power of progressive religious ideas and institutions to help clarify what real justice might look like has never been weaker. Meanwhile—and, as we have been arguing, not unrelatedly—in contemporary politics, television, and social media, and in the half-empty church pews, carceral logics reign supreme. Justice has come to mean the criminal justice system, and punishment appears as the obvious tool for whatever social ill happens to ail us.

Whereas religious appeals were once collectivist and activist, in today's world, where "spirituality" reigns and religion is more often than not a dirty word, religious appeals are personalized and interiorized.[123] Whereas religious folk were once propelled toward a horizon of God's law, today religious folk are to meet where they are on their individual spiritual journeys. Alexander has succeeded at awakening American "people of faith and conscience," but the power of this collective awaking remains as yet uncollectivized. Personal conversions can only get us so far. Religious folk not only need to be awakened, they also need to march. To move beyond awakening into mobilization, old religious institutions need to be revitalized, and new forms of collectivity need to be fostered. Only by gathering institutional power may once-potent theologies be allowed to speak once again, and may new and newly resonant languages of justice be breathed into life. If the foundational transformation Alexander hopes to spur is to be realized, we need not merely aggregate our existing religious resources. We must deepen and expand these resources, weaponize them, and deploy them.

As the book's final two chapters will show, the good news is that in deliberate and spontaneous ways, this project is already well underway. Long tamped down, the abolition spirit is springing back to life.

Notes

1. The basis of this account of the case is John Bender, "Indiana Justice: Retribution or Reconciliation?," *Christian Century* (December 2, 1981), 1259–1262 .
2. Bender, "Indiana Justice," 1259.
3. Our teacher Jeffrey Stout lays this long, vital story out with great precision. Arguing against the purported Enlightenment separation of religion from politics, and the secularist framing of religion as *essentially* a tool of domination, Stout attends to an alternative tradition of religion: what Hume called "true religion" and what King called "ethical religion." Properly understood, this *other* religion is rooted in virtue, celebrates that which is glorious, and condemns that which is horrendous. In modern terms, this other religion (if we want to call it that) is therefore essentially political inasmuch as it committedly orients itself against domination. What we are calling the "abolition spirit" belongs squarely to this tradition. See Jeffrey Stout's 2017 Gifford Lectures, "Religion Unbound: Ideals and Powers from Cicero to King," https://www.giffordlectures.org/lectures/religion-unbound-ideals-and-powers-cicero-king.
4. DeWolf was a Methodist theologian at Boston University and was later dean of Wesley Theological Seminary.
5. L. Harold DeWolf, *Crime and Justice in America: A Paradox of Conscience* (New York: Harper & Row, 1975).
6. See Virginia Mackey, *Reflections on Twenty-Five Years: The History of the National Interreligious Task Force on Criminal Justice, 1968–1993* (Louisville, KY: Presbyterian Criminal Justice Program, 1993).

7. Ibid., 172.

8. For example, see the short, unsigned review in *Stanford Law Review* 28, no. 4 (April 1976), 838.

9. For analyses of how liberal anxieties about sentencing disparities contributed to longer sentences across the board, see Naomi Murakawa, *The First Civil Right: How Liberals Built Prison America* (New York: Oxford University Press, 2014), 69–112; and Marie Gottschalk, *The Prison and the Gallows: The Politics of Mass Incarceration in America* (Cambridge: Cambridge University Press, 2006), 18–40.

10. "Why Rehabilitation Hasn't Worked," *Christian Century* 96, no. 24 (1979), 734–736. In sum, during the 1970s, the *Christian Century* ran twenty substantive pieces that shed light on the scourge of American prisons and pushed for meaningful reforms. For representativeness of stance and style, see "Johnny Cash on Prison Reform," *Christian Century* 87, no. 39 (1970), 1157; and "Worship and Resistance: The Exercise of Freedom," *Christian Century* 91, no. 10 (1974), 290–292.

11. National Council of Churches, "Challenges to the Injustices of the Criminal Justice System" (November 10, 1979), http://nationalcouncilofchurches.us/common-witness/1979/criminal-justice.php.

12. Yet even the NCC statement itself adopts some of the new discursive conventions. Among the prime injustices addressed are the "arbitrary applications of law." This sounds very much like justice defined as the proper operation of the law. The consequence of such problems, the statements suggests, is "gross violations of human rights."

13. As *Struggle for Justice* sets the scene: "[A] low visibility revolution has taken place around us. In penitentiaries in Indiana and Florida, in jails in New York City and the District of Columbia, in California's San Quentin, to name but a few out of hundreds, prisoners have gone on strike, have lashed out at the symbols of their imprisonment, have even maimed themselves to call attention to their plight." *Struggle for Justice*, vi.

14. This secularizing tendency is especially apparent in the document's concluding section, "Justice as a Public Issue." "Justice" here is treated somewhat loosely as a category. The text pivots back and forth from "system of justice" to "struggle for justice." There is no reflection on the concept of justice itself, however, and no attempt to leverage a notion of higher law that our miserable prisons might be said to betray.

15. In 2006 the American Friends Service Committee updated this document with *Beyond Prisons: A New Interfaith Paradigm for our Failed Prison System* (Minneapolis, MN: Fortress Press, 2006).

16. For an overview, see Mackey, *Reflections on Twenty-Five Years*.

17. Janet Reno, "Addressing the Violence Continuum," *Church & Society* 85, no. 3 (1995), 27–35. The speech was also printed in the Methodists' social justice periodical: Janet Reno, "Addressing the Violence Continuum," *Christian Social Action* 7, no. 5 (1994), 4–8.

18. Office of the General Assembly, "Resolution on Restorative Justice" (Louisville, KY: Presbyterian Distribution Services, 2002); Presbyterian Church (USA) General Assembly, "Resolution Calling for the Abolition of For-Profit Private Prisons," *Church & Society* 93, no. 6 (2003), 9–13.

19. Catholic Bishops of the United States, "Rebuilding Human Lives," *Origins* 3 (1973), 344–350. As quoted in Amy Levad, *Redeeming a Prison Society: A Liturgical and Sacramental Response to Mass Incarceration* (Minneapolis, MN: Fortress Press, 2014), 58.

20. United States Catholic Conference, "A Community Response to Crime," *Origins* 7 (1978), 593–604. As quoted in Levad, *Redeeming a Prison Society*, 59.

21. Catholic Bishops of the United States, "Responsibility, Rehabilitation, and Restoration: A Catholic Perspective on Crime and Criminal Justice" (November 15, 2000), http://www.usccb.org/issues-and-action/human-life-and-dignity/criminal-justice-restorative-justice/crime-and-criminal-justice.cfm#intro

22. Andrew Skotnicki, "The U.S. Catholic Church and Criminal Justice," *New Theology Review* 11, no. 1 (1998), 80. See also Andrew Skotnicki, *Criminal Justice and the Catholic Church* (Lanham, MD: Rowman and Littlefield, 2008).

23. Union for Reform Judaism, "Crime" (May 1968), https://urj.org/what-we-believe/resolutions/crime.

24. Union for Reform Judaism, "Race and the U.S. Criminal Justice System" (1999), https://urj.org/what-we-believe/resolutions/race-and-us-criminal-justice-system.

25. Union for Reform Judaism, "Resolution on the Crisis of Racial and Structural Inequality in the United States" (2014), https://urj.org/what-we-believe/resolutions/resolution-crisis-racial-and-structural-inequality-united-states. Resolutions from Conservative Judaism's Rabbinical Assembly have shown a slow but gathering concern about the excesses of policing and punishment in the United States. In the wake of the Abu Ghraib scandal in 2005, the Rabbinical Assembly issued a statement calling for the "humane treatment of prisoners"; in 2012, it called for ending "prolonged solitary confinement"; and in 2016, its resolution against police brutality—its most substantive by far—called for the end of " 'broken windows' policing," the establishment of civilian oversight boards, and the mandating of police body cameras. See https://www.rabbinicalassembly.org/story/resolution-racial-injustice-and-police-brutality. As far as we can tell, the only prisoner-related statement issued since 1981 by the Orthodox Rabbinical Council of America was a 2007 letter calling for loosening restrictions on religious texts in federal prisons. See http://www.rabbis.org/news/article.cfm?id=100938.

26. In saying this, we do not wish to absolve the liberal rank-and-file that supported the state-level prison expansions under Democratic governors in New York and California in the 1980s, or under President Clinton at the national level in the decade to follow.

27. On prison labor in historical context, see Heather Ann Thompson, "Rethinking Working-Class Struggle through the Lens of the Carceral State: Toward a Labor History of Inmates and Guards," *Labor: Studies in Working-Class History of the Americas* 8, no. 3 (2011), 15–45.

28. On the evangelical notion of "transformation," see Winnifred Fallers Sullivan, *Prison Religion: Faith-Based Reform and the Constitution* (Princeton, NJ: Princeton University Press, 2011); and Tanya Erzen, *God in Captivity: The Rise of Faith-Based Prison Ministries in the Age of Mass Incarceration* (Boston: Beacon Press, 2017).

29. Indeed, both in terms of the circulation of labor and the circulation of affect, if anything, prison ministry further incentivizes mass incarceration. These perverse incentives are in no way limited to *religious* voluntarism. As people invested in higher education for incarcerated people, we readily see how our own efforts could well be cast in this same light. For this critique, see Dylan Rodriguez, *Forced Passages: Imprisoned Radical Intellectuals and the U.S. Prison Regime* (Minneapolis: University of Minnesota Press, 2006), 92–104. For our affirmative defense, see Charles Atkins, Joshua Dubler, Vincent Lloyd, and Mel Webb, " 'Using the Language of Christian Love and Charity': What Liberal Religion Offers Higher Education in Prison," *Religions* 10, no. 3 (2019), 169; https://doi.org/10.3390/rel10030169.

30. Charles W. Colson, *Born Again* (Old Tappan, NJ: Chosen Books, 1976); Jonathan Aitken, *Charles W. Colson: A Life Redeemed* (New York: Waterbook Press, 2005). For a comprehensive study of Charles Colson's work specifically, and of evangelicalism's complicated relationship with mass incarceration in general, see Aaron Griffith, *American Law and Gospel: Evangelicals in the Age of Mass Incarceration* (PhD diss., Duke University Department of Divinity, 2018).

31. Justice Fellowship was merged into Prison Fellowship around 2016.

32. Justice Ministry, "Statement of Faith," https://www.prisonfellowship.org/site/wp-content/uploads/2012/10/Prison-Fellowship-Statement-of-Faith.pdf.

33. http://nae.net/sentencing-reform/.

34. "An Evangelical Perspective on Criminal Justice," http://nae.net/an-evangelical-perspective-on-criminal-justice-reform/.

35. Sophia Kerby, "Prison Task Force Included in Omnibus Appropriations Bill," *Brennan Center for Justice* (January 17, 2014), https://www.brennancenter.org/blog/prison-task-force-included-omnibus-appropriations-bill; Napp Nazworth, "Congress Set to Pass 'Charles Colson Task Force on Federal Corrections' to Facilitate Prison Reform," *The Christian Post* (January 16, 2014), https://www.christianpost.com/news/congress-set-to-pass-charles-colson-task-force-on-federal-corrections-to-facilitate-prison-reform-112791/

36. Brief for Prison Fellowship, et al.

37. Mackey, *Reflections on Twenty-Five Years*, 25. NITFCJ did officially recommend the abolitionist writings of some of its leading members, including *Instead of Prisons: A Handbook for Abolitionists*, coproduced by the New York Council of Churches. See Mackey, *Reflections on Twenty-Five Years*, 163.

38. Signatory members of the Coalition to Abolition the Death Penalty include no fewer than twenty national religious organizations. For a complete list, see http://www.ncadp.org/affiliates/all.

39. See http://sentencingproject.org/wp-content/uploads/2015/12/Life-Goes-On.pdf. More broadly on the language of abolitionism used in relation to the death penalty, see Herbert H. Haines, *Against Capital Punishment: The Anti-Death Penalty Movement in America, 1972–1994* (New York: Oxford University Press, 1999); and Jacques Derrida, *The Death Penalty*, 2 vols. (Chicago: University of Chicago Press, 2014–2017).

40. On the expansion of the use of life sentences and LWOP, see Ashley Nellis, "Life Goes On: The Historic Rise of Life Sentences in America" (Sentencing Project, 2013), https://www.sentencingproject.org/publications/life-goes-on-the-historic-rise-in-life-sentences-in-america/

41. http://www.pewresearch.org/fact-tank/2018/06/11/us-support-for-death-penalty-ticks-up-2018/.

42. On the death penalty's theological resonances, see Melynda Price, *At the Cross: Race, Religion, and Citizenship in the Politics of the Death Penalty* (New York: Oxford University Press, 2015); and Mark L. Taylor, *The Executed God: The Way of the Cross in Lockdown America* (Minneapolis, MN: Fortress Press, 2001).

43. Poncelet is an amalgam of Robert Lee Willie and Elmo Patrick Sonnier, two condemned men whom Prejean had known.

44. Tim Robbins, dir., *Dead Man Walking* (1995).

45. To watch Susan Sarandon's acceptance speech, see https://www.youtube.com/watch?v=JeQdwQLwYUU.

46. Like their early Christian forebears, the experiences of persecution and martyrdom were crucial to emergent Anabaptist identity in the early modern period. For a window into this Christian orientation, see Thieleman Van Bragt and Joseph F. Sohm, *Martyrs Mirror: The Story of Seventeen Centuries of Christian Martyrdom from the Time of Christ to A.D. 1660* (Windsor, ON: Herald Press, 1938).

47. One of the twentieth century's most foundational free-exercise cases stemmed from Amish in the Midwest looking for—and winning—the right to home school their children. See *Wisconsin v. Yoder*, 406 U.S. 205 (1972).

48. Bender, "Indiana Justice," 1260.

49. Randi B. Hagi, "Howard Zehr: Pioneer of Restorative Justice," *Crossroads* (July 20, 2015),   http://emu.edu/now/crossroads/2015/07/20/howard-zehr-pioneer-of-restorative-justice/. Zehr's seminal book is *Changing Lenses: A New Focus for Crime and Justice* (Scottdale, PA: Herald Press, 1990). Canadian Mennonites had created an earlier victim-offender reconciliation initiative, in Kitchener, Ontario, in 1974. Harry Mika, "The Practice and Prospect of Victim-Offender Programs," *Southern Methodist University Law Review* 46 (1993), 2195; Howard Zehr, "Restorative Justice: Beyond Victim-Offender Mediation," *Conflict Resolution Quarterly* 22, no. 1–2 (2004), 305–315. The Elkhart program continues as the Center for Community Justice, though it credits a probation officer with its founding and does not mention Zehr in its history. See http://www.centerforcommunityjustice.org/?page_id=111.

50. http://zehr-institute.org/.

51. The New Perspectives on Crime and Justice papers were published from 1984 to 1994. They are available at http://waynenorthey.com/justice/.

52. Howard Zehr, *Retributive Justice, Restorative Justice*, New Perspectives on Crime and Justice 4 (Elkhard, IN: MCC US Office of Criminal Justice, 1985), http://waynenorthey.com/wp-content/uploads/2016/06/Issue-4.pdf

53. Ibid.

54. Ibid.

55. Nils Christie, *Crime, Pain, and Death*, New Perspectives on Crime and Justice 1 (Elkhard, IN: MCC US Office of Criminal Justice, 1983), http://waynenorthey.com/wp-content/uploads/2016/06/Issue-1.pdf. Christie is author of one of the most read conceptualizations of restorative justice, which he frames as the reclamation of an organic conflict-mediation process, as opposed to the criminal justice system, which, from a Weberian standpoint, he paints as a product of bureaucratization and an agent of alienation. See Nils Christie, "Conflicts as Property," *British Journal of Criminology* 17, no. 1 (January 1, 1977), 1–15.

56. Herman Bianchi, *A Biblical Vision of Justice*, 7, New Perspectives on Crime and Justice 2 (Elkhard, IN: MCC US Office of Criminal Justice, 2016, http://waynenorthey.com/wp-content/uploads/2016/06/Issue-2.pdf.

57. Herman Bianchi and René van Swaaningen, eds., *Abolitionism: Towards a Non-repressive Approach to Crime* (Amsterdam: Free University Press, 1986).

58. One significant episode in the early history of prison abolition movements occurred in 1970 with the founding in France of the Prisons Information Group. As it officially conceptualized itself, however, the Prisons Information Group, which included Michel Foucault, Gilles Deleuze, Jean-Paul Sartre, Jean Genet, and others, had a more modest, fact-finding mandate: "We propose to make known what the prison is: who goes there, how and why they go there, what happens there, and what the life of the prisoners is, and that, equally, of the surveillance personnel." "Manifesto of the Groupe d'Information sur les prisons," http://www.critical-theory.com/43-years-ago-today-foucaults-statement-on-french-prisons/. See also Perry Zurn and Andrew Dilts, eds., *Active Intolerance: Michel Foucault, The Prisons Information Group, and the Future of Abolition* (New York: Palgrave MacMillan, 2016).

59. Deviance Group founder Louk Hulsman was perhaps the exception. In Vincenzo Ruggiero's characterization, Hulsman's thought is properly situated in the context of Christianity: "Hulsman's abolitionism is deeply rooted in the Christian tradition that has long fed radical religious movements, revolutionary theologians, great novelists, and unremitting activists." Hulsman's abolitionism is that of the Gospels and Paul, of Augustine and Francis, of Marx and Engels, of Hugo and Tolstoy: mulishly rooted in the insistence that social injustice is endemic, and that the distillation and consolidation of these complex collective responsibilities onto a single, guilty party requiring punishment is always a sacrilege. Vincenzo Ruggiero, *Penal Abolitionism* (New York: Oxford University Press, 2010), 126.

60. "Program of International Conference on Prison Abolition," Toronto, Canada (May 26–28, 1983), http://www.actionicopa.org/items/85-ICOPA%20I_program.pdf.

61. Ibid.

62. Ibid.

63. Ibid.

64. Harold E. Pepinsky, *Report of the Fifth International Conference on Penal Abolition, Bloomington, Indiana, May 21–25, 1991*, http://www.actionicopa.org/items/163-ICOPAV_Report.pdf

65. Gayraud S. Wilmore, ed. *Black Men in Prison: The Response of the African American Church* (Atlanta: ITC Press, 1990). Wilmore was originally from Philadelphia. He had

taught at Boston University and Colgate, but at this point was based at the historically Black Interdenominational Theological Seminary in Atlanta.

66. James Cone, *The Cross and the Lynching Tree* (Maryknoll, NY: Orbis Books, 2011). The Black ethicist James Samuel Logan penned an earlier book about the prison system, but it did not take a specifically Black approach: *Good Punishment? Christian Moral Practice and U.S. Imprisonment* (Grand Rapids, MI: William B. Eerdmans, 2008).

67. "Tribute to Rev. Seiichi Michael Yasutake," http://www.freedomarchives.org/Documents/Finder/DOC3_scans/3.tribute.seiichi.michael.yasutake.11.9.1996.pdf; Funeral Program, https://www.episcopalchicago.org/files/1913/4800/1018/Mike_Yaustake_from_the_Witness.pdf.

68. Marie Buckley, *Breaking into Prison: A Citizen Guide to Volunteer Action* (Boston: Beacon Press, 1974).

69. Marinissen would later lead the push for determinate sentencing guidelines in California.

70. These papers are housed at Harvard Divinity School. See http://div.hds.harvard.edu/library/bms/16000/bms16132.html.

71. Fay Honey Knopp et al., *Instead of Prisons: A Handbook for Abolitionists* (Syracuse, NY: Prison Research Education Action Project, 1976). The handbook was republished by Critical Resistance in 2005. For a digital version see https://www.prisonpolicy.org/scans/instead_of_prisons/. On Knopp in context, see Scott Christianson, "In Memoriam: A Remembrance of Fay Honey Knopp and the Origins of the Abolition Movement in *Instead of Prisons," Justice Professional* 11 (1998), 251–256.

72. On account of having been sent, as per Luke 4, "to proclaim release for prisoners," Jesus is namechecked on the first page. But this invocation appears in a list of incarceration's critics in which Jesus is the only discernably religious voice. Knopp et al., *Instead of Prisons*, 1.

73. <IBT>Knopp et al., *Instead of Prisons*</IBT>, 11.

74. Ibid., 100.

75. *Alternatives to Imprisonment: A Thoughtful Approach to Crime and Punishment* (Boston: Unitarian Universalist Service Committee and National Moratorium on Prison Construction, 1982 [originally 1978]), 5.

76. The conference was hosted by the University of the West Indies' Institute of International Relations. Conference program and materials available at http://www.actionicopa.org/index.php?epm=1_4.

77. Ibid.

78. See generally Michael L. Hadley, ed., *The Spiritual Roots of Restorative Justice* (Albany: State University of New York Press, 2001).

79. Joe Hudson, "Contemporary Origins of Restorative Justice Programming: The Minnesota Restitution Center," *Federal Probation: A Journal of Correctional Philosophy and Practice* 76, no. 2 (September 2012), http://www.uscourts.gov/sites/default/files/76_2_9_0.pdf.

80. Joe Hudson and Burt Galaway, "Undoing the Wrong," *Social Work* 19, no. 3 (May 1974), 313–318. Canada saw more serious, systemic focus on restorative justice during these early days.

81. The origins story in New Zealand involves a Maori offender who was the son of a bishop, a Quaker victim, and a Presbyterian minister who volunteered to reconcile the two. Howard Zehr visited New Zealand in 1994 and his work was influential in promoting restorative justice ideas in that country. Donald W. Shriver Jr., and Peggy L. Shriver, "Law, Religion, and Restorative Justice in New Zealand," *Journal of Law and Religion* 28, no. 1 (2012–2013), 143–177. Clyde H. Farnsworth, "This Penal Colony Learned a Lesson," *New York Times* (August 10, 1997).

82. Karen de Witt, "Crowded Jails Spur New Look at Punishment," *New York Times* (December 25, 1995). There is an earlier chapter in the story of restorative justice: In the 1970s, interest grew in victim restitution. Sometimes this meant simply financial payment, other times it meant something closer to what is now commonly understood as a restorative justice framework. In the mid-1970s, more than fifty municipalities initiated such programs, and more than a dozen states considered them. See Steve Chesney, Joe Hudson, and John McLagen, "A New Look at Restitution: Recent Legislation, Programs, and Research," *Judicature* 61 (1977–1978), 348–357. The authors were employees of the Minnesota Department of Corrections. See also Joe Hudson, ed., *Restitution in Criminal Justice* (Minneapolis: Minnesota Department of Corrections, 1976).

83. de Witt, "Crowded Jails."

84. Kay Pranis, "Reflections from a Descendant of the Minnesota Restitution Center," in *Restorative Justice Today: Practical Applications*, ed. Katherine S. van Wormer and Lorenn Walker (Los Angeles: Sage, 2013), 15–20. Pranis writes that before the Minnesota government effort in the mid-1990s, "restorative justice was the interest of churches and small nonprofits." In her account, the Minnesota initiative brought together the secular social work strand of restorative justice and the Mennonite strand, with particular reference to Zehr's Elkhart project.

85. Kay Pranis, "The Minnesota Restorative Justice Initiative: A Model Experience," *Crime Victims Report* (May/June 1997), https://www.nij.gov/topics/courts/restorative-justice/perspectives/pages/minnesota.aspx. See also Living Justice Press, http://www.livingjusticepress.org/, and Pranis's Chautauqua talk, https://www.youtube.com/watch?v=4oLLAjBOFTg.

86. See http://www.livingjusticepress.org.

87. Kay Pranis, *The Little Book of Circle Processes* (Intercourse, PA: Good Books, 2005), 3.

88. On Native exoticism, see Philip J. Deloria, *Playing Indian* (New Haven, CT: Yale University Press, 1999).

89. See, for example, Kelly Hayes, "On Justice and Survival: A Native Reflection on International Women's Day," Transformative Spaces (March 8, 2016), https://transformativespaces.org/2016/03/08/on-justice-and-survival-a-native-reflection-on-international-womens-day/. We return to Native justice and Native sovereignty later in this chapter.

90. Charles W. Colson, "Is There Evidence of the Resurrection?," *Jubilee Magazine* (June 1982), http://www.breakpoint.org/search-library/search?view=searchdetail&id=1042. Colson elaborates the next year in his book *Loving God* (Grand Rapids, MI: Zondervan, 1983), chapter 16.

91. Calculations about "future dangerousness" may also be found within the criminal justice system—for example, in the adjudication of the death penalty in Texas. See Eric F. Citron, "Sudden Death: The Legislative History of Future Dangerousness and the Texas Death Penalty," *Yale Law & Policy Review* 25, no. 1 (2006), 143–175.

92. Charles W. Colson, *Justice That Restores* (Wheaton, IL: Tyndale House, 2001), vii.

93. Ibid., viii.

94. "Prison Fellowship Moves Ahead on New Headquarters," *Christianity Today* (March 1, 1985), 40–41.

95. Jody Veenker, "Prison Fellowship Downsizing," *Christianity Today* 44, no. 13 (November 13, 2000), 23; Religion News Service, "Prominent Prison Ministry Fires 72, Citing Economy," *Christian Century* 128, no. 18 (September 6, 2011), 14.

96. After Justice Ministry lobbying, the United Nations Economic and Social Council passed a series of resolutions between 1999 and 2002 commending the framework; see http://restorativejustice.org/about-us/our-impact/; see also the "Basic Principles on the Use of Restorative Justice Programmes in Criminal Matters," http://www.refworld.org/docid/46c455820.html.

97. Antonin Scalia, "God's Justice and Ours," *First Things* 123 (May 2002), 17–21. Scalia was responding to issues raised by Pope John Paul II's encyclical *Evangelium Vitae*, which stated the need for the death penalty was "very rare, if not practically nonexistent," given the "steady improvements in the organization of the penal system." The encyclical also embraced a restorative justice framework: "[T]he primary purpose of the punishment which society inflicts is 'to redress the disorder caused by the offense.'"

98. Ibid., 19.

99. Ibid., 20. In the mid-1990s, Colson joined together with conservative Catholic editor and intellectual Richard John Neuhaus to consider ways that evangelicals and Catholics might work together to advance shared goals. In the 1994 joint statement of Evangelicals and Catholics Together, the evangelicals were perhaps pushed to the edge of their comfort zone with respect to natural law. Colson and Neuhaus were joined by Pat Robertson, Mark Noll, Michael Novak, the Campus Crusade for Christ leadership, and others in affirming, "Together we contend for the truth that politics, law, and culture must be secured by moral truth." Essential to that truth was a commitment to the belief that "in their relationship to God, persons have a dignity and responsibility that transcends, and thereby limits, the authority of the state and of every other merely human institution." The lives of the "most vulnerable" must be particularly protected. The elderly, the disabled, and fetuses are explicitly named, and though incarcerated people aren't, we may see here an opening to be exploited. On the other hand, the signers of the statement are explicit about the need, on their view, to teach "law observance," together with honesty, work, chastity, and other virtues. There remains here a commitment to law above justice, and indeed a striking absence of the justice language. See "Evangelicals and Catholics Together: The Christian Mission in the Third Millennium," *First Things* (May 1994), https://www.firstthings.com/article/1994/05/evangelicals-catholics-together-the-christian-mission-in-the-third-millennium.

100. Charles Colson Task Force on Federal Corrections, *Transforming Prisons, Restoring Lives* (2016).

101. Charles Colson Task Force website.

102. See http://jesuits.org/Assets/Publications/File/Criminal%20Justice%20 Reform%20Principles.pdf. The group is coordinated by the United Methodist Church's General Board of Church and Society. Perhaps representing a shift in the landscape around criminal justice issues, the director of advocacy for the Interfaith Criminal Justice Coalition, Kara Gotsch, moved there from the National Coalition to Abolish the Death Penalty.

103. See Keramet Reiter, *23/7: Pelican Bay Prison and the Rise of Long-Term Solitary Confinement* (New Haven, CT: Yale University Press, 2016).

104. http://www.yuroktribe.org/tribalcourt/.

105. *Lyng v. Northwest Indian Cemetery Protective Association*, 485 U.S. 439 (1988).

106. Abby Abinanti, "Letter to Justice O'Connor," *UCLA Indigenous Peoples' Journal of Law, Culture, and Resistance* 1, no. 1 (2004), 1, 21.

107. Rebecca Clarren, "Judge Abby Abinanti Is Fighting for Her Tribe—and for a Better Justice System," *The Nation* (December 18, 2017), https://www.thenation.com/ article/judge-abby-abinanti-is-fighting-for-her-tribe-and-for-a-better-justice-system/; *Tribal Justice* (PBS August 21, 2017), dir. Anne Makepeace. We are also grateful for conversations with Dana Lloyd who has generously discussed her field-work with the Yurok. See Dana Lloyd, "From Religious Freedom to Indigenous Sovereignty: The Case of *Lyng v. Northwest Indian Cemetery Protective Association* (1988)" (PhD diss., Syracuse University, 2018).

108. Clarren, "Judge Abby Abinanti."

109. On hyper-criminalization and hyper-incarceration among Native people, see Robert Nichols, "The Colonialism of Incarceration," *Radical Philosophy Review* 17, no. 2 (2014): 435–455; and Luana Ross, *Inventing the Savage: The Social Construction of Native American Criminality* (Austin, TX: University of Texas Press, 1998). For rates and numbers, see Jake Flanagin, "Native Americans are the Unseen Victims of a Broken US Justice System," *Quartz* (April 27, 2015), https://qz.com/392342/ native-americans-are-the-unseen-victims-of-a-broken-us-justice-system/.

110. Rebecca Tiger, *Judging Addicts: Drug Courts and Coercion in the Justice System* (New York: New York University Press, 2012); Leslie Paik, *Discretionary Justice: Looking Inside a Juvenile Drug Court* (New Brunswick, NJ: Rutgers University Press, 2011).

111. For the history of federal support of wellness courts, see Thomas Flies-Away, Carrie Garrow, and Pat Sekaquaptewa, *Tribal Healing to Wellness Courts: The Key Components* (West Hollywood, CA: Tribal Law and Policy Institute, May 2014), http://www.wellnesscourts.org/files/Tribal%20Healing%20to%20Wellness%20 Courts%20The%20Key%20Components.pdf.

112. http://wellnesscourts.org/about-us/.

113. Joseph Thomas Flies-Away and Carrie E. Garrow, "Healing to Wellness Courts: Therapeutic Jurisprudence +," *Michigan State Law Review* (2013), 403–450.

114. Ibid., 438.

115. On connections between indigeneity and carcerality in North America more generally, see Launa Ross, *Inventing the Savage: The Social Construction of Native American Criminality* (Austin: University of Texas Press, 2000). See also Robert Nichols, "The Colonialism of Incarceration," *Radical Philosophy Review* 17, no. 2 (2014), 435–455.

116. Michelle Alexander, *The New Jim Crow: Mass Incarceration in the Age of Colorblindness* (New York: New Press, 2010), xiii.

117. Books of this cultural magnitude invariably invite criticism, and of Alexander's book there has been much. See, for example, James Forman, "Racial Critiques of Mass Incarceration: Beyond the New Jim Crow," *New York University Law Review* 87 (2012), 101–146.

118. Amy Frykholm, "Criminal Injustice," *Christian Century* (May 16, 2012), 22–25: "I viewed faith leaders as an important audience for this book. I wanted those people to have a broader understanding of the system and to realize that it wasn't all about individual choices." See also "Michelle Alexander Speaks at Riverside Church" (May 21, 2011), https://www.youtube.com/watch?v=681k5W4MSnw.

119. For example, see Alfredo Garcia, "The New Jim Crow: Churches Respond to Mass Incarceration," *Religion & Politics* (August 13, 2013), http://religionandpolitics.org/2013/08/13/the-new-jim-crow-churches-respond-to-mass-incarceration/.

120. "Michelle Alexander Joins Union Theological Seminary," https://utsnyc.edu/michelle-alexander-joins-union-theological-seminary/.

121. Alexander herself has voiced some of these worries. See, for example, her extensive and illuminating 2013 interview with Bill Moyers, in which, with a somewhat equivocal call for the "abolition of the system of mass incarceration as a whole," Alexander moves in the direction of prison abolition. https://billmoyers.com/episode/incarceration-nation/.

122. Pew Research Center, "America's Changing Religious Landscape" (May 12, 2015), http://www.pewforum.org/2015/05/12/americas-changing-religious-landscape/ . Among the general population, 37% of Americans identify as Republicans; of atheists, 23% identify as Republicans. http://www.pewforum.org/religious-landscape-study/party-affiliation/.

123. See, for example, Courtney Bender, *The New Metaphysicals: Spirituality and the American Religious Imagination* (Chicago: University of Chicago Press, 2010).

4

Prison Religion and Prison Justice

Incarceration has long been a prominent motif in the stories we tell about how a certain kind of hero manages to become what he (or, occasionally, she) eventually becomes. The chained shadow-watchers in Plato's cave; Joseph, in Pharaoh's jail, divining the future from his cellmates' dreams; and John, in exile on Patmos, dreaming in riddles of divine judgment-these are ancient and still resonant examples. Pressed in by prison walls, these heroes come to understand the world—and enable *us*, therefore, to understand the world—both for what the world already is and what, in inverted reflection, it has the capacity to as yet become.[1]

Prison cells furnished the pressure for two of twentieth-century America's most iconic political figures to formulate their visions for justice, visions which were, each in its way, fundamentally religious. Martin Luther King Jr. was already a nationally acclaimed civil rights leader when he penned his open letter from a jail cell in Birmingham, Alabama, written in the margins of a newspaper and smuggled out of his cell. Malcolm X's prison conversion to Islam would only become central to his image after his death, but in his epic self-telling, it was in prison that Malcolm first discerned the contours of white supremacy and began to cultivate his opposition. In both cases, the condition of imprisonment served to clarify the acute oppression that King and Malcolm already felt, and steeled them for the long struggle to will its abolition. But prison also offered them the opportunity to preach the limits of the law, for it was the law that authorized their imprisonment, and it was the law (more narrowly in King's case, more broadly in Malcolm's) that must be overturned if justice is to prevail on earth.[2]

"You're still in prison," Malcolm would tell an audience gathered in a Detroit Baptist church. "That's what America means: prison."[3] Back in his cell during his own bid in the Norfolk Prison Colony, Malcolm had chiseled himself into Malcolm X by writing Elijah Muhammad daily and by reading the Messenger's political and esoteric teachings alongside and against the classics of European philosophy and literature. Malcolm learned a new way of seeing the world, and as a result he experienced a new sense of freedom. "I never had been so truly free in my life," he later reflected.[4]

Among the easiest lessons for Malcolm to learn: the white man is the devil. It was obvious. All the whites he had ever encountered, beginning with the men who had murdered his father, had run after evil eagerly. Whites had covered up the true history and achievements of Blacks, which as Malcolm discovered in prison were majestic indeed and ranged from the glories of ancient Ethiopia to the heroic resistance of Africans enslaved in the Americas. Having properly named and discarded lies and distortions of the white world, Malcolm took an expansive view of the Blackness that remained. In and against the existing order, Black men and women found natural solidarity with Indians, Chinese, Africans, and others who suffered under white colonialism.[5] Key to the perpetuation of this global system of white domination was Christianity. Among its many nefarious uses, Christianity had been employed as a tool of whites to degrade nonwhites and to justify white people's "criminal conquests." What they had made legal was, in fact, criminal. Reciprocally, those deemed within white systems of "justice" to be criminals were actually the greatest strivers for justice.

Three years after Malcolm X left prison, King grabbed the national spotlight with his leadership of the Montgomery Bus Boycott. In the years that followed, King would be in and out of jail with relative frequency. A genius at exploiting the emerging media, King understood the dramatic potential of imprisonment and its power to illustrate for white liberals the systemic injustices of the Jim Crow South. The same police power that had maintained the slave economy was used to cripple Black community organizing during Reconstruction, and currently enforced the humiliations of American apartheid was turned with full force against civil rights demonstrators. For white liberals, images of police violence and unjust imprisonment fit uncomfortably with the figures of Black respectability and religiosity. It was obvious that something was desperately wrong with a system of laws that would lock up an eloquent, Northern-educated, suit-clad reverend.

In his now famous letter, King evokes Christianity's august tradition of protesting injustice and rejects the white clergy's call for dialogue in lieu of protest. Society is already caught in the "bondage of myths and half-truths," King says, echoing Malcolm; further dialogue cannot provide the avenue for escape.[6] For freedom—and justice—to come about, conflict must come first, and therein the opportunity for a society to evaluate how far its norms have strayed from its ideals. Too often, King charges, the laws of the land are simply taken for granted. But what of justice? "Law and order" are not an end in themselves; they are at best only a means to achieve justice. The justice here is God's justice, a justice irreducible to worldly terms, but which King, as a Christian, was able to discern, albeit imperfectly, through the tools of that religious tradition.

As Black Power eclipsed the civil rights movement and police surveillance was ratcheted up to sabotage political dissent, the incarcerated Black writer grew into a cultural archetype.[7] Incarceration, for this generation of writers and their readers, was an intensification of American injustice and could not be understood apart from broader systems of racial and economic exploitation that had perverted the souls of Blacks and whites alike. Personal transformation and challenging white supremacy remained central motifs to the prison memoirs of late 1960s, with religion serving as a vessel for each of these projects. However, religion's positive role soon faded from view. Where Malcolm and King had foregrounded religious faith and ideals in the struggle to bring the world into harmony with divine justice, the two most prominent incarcerated Black Power writers, Eldridge Cleaver and George Jackson, had little patience for such matters. Religion, as they positioned it in their stories of self, was the foil to their revolutionary awakenings. Religion is what they had to throw off to arrive at the correct analysis of the world, which for each was a synthesis of black nationalism and Marxism. While King had identified with Jesus as a fellow "extremist for love," the proper object of which was all humankind, Cleaver and Jackson loved much more modestly. Each frames his thoughts as love letters to specific women, and each emphatically subordinates this love to the revolutionary struggle—a struggle defined by each in wholly secular terms.[8]

Cleaver was sent to prison on a drug charge a month after the Supreme Court's 1954 ruling in *Brown v. Board of Education*, which ended the era of de jure segregation. During his time in California prisons, Cleaver underwent a conversion. As Cleaver describes it, he discovered that he was treated poorly, both at an individual and at a systemic level, because he was Black, and that such unfairness was woven into American culture, laws, and institutions. The result: "Inwardly I turned away from America with horror, disgust, and outrage."[9] First, this indignation expressed itself merely as rebellion, as cynicism and nihilism. He vowed to attack all American values—from marriage, to patriotism, to the Constitution, to belief in God. Cleaver had been baptized and confirmed a Catholic while in juvenile prison, not out of any heartfelt belief, but because church attendance was mandatory and whites went to the

Protestant service. A Muslim phase that followed was, in Cleaver's telling, equally motivated by pragmatism. Cleaver was rebelling against whites, whites were identified with Christianity, and Islam provided "language and symbols" that "were nothing but weapons of war."[10] Eventually, for Cleaver, the doctrine of secular revolution provided a more coherent set of words and ideas around which to organize his life. It was, in his view, a vision of justice stripped of all religious mystifications.

Jackson, too, describes his early encounters with religion as fundamentally disingenuous, and fundamentally strategic. When, as a youth, he'd been sent to Catholic schools, "I was really just pretending with the nuns and priests." But he enjoyed the benefits of this feint: "I served mass so that I could be in a position to steal altar wine."[11] As Jackson politicized in prison, he came to realize that the American economic and racial systems, always entwined in his analysis, manifested in his current surroundings, the prison cell, just as they had a century prior in the chains of the enslaved. The "law and order" trumpeted by American politicians was really just a tool for economic efficiency and white supremacy; its effect, among both Blacks and whites, was to take away the capacity for genuine feeling. Social transformation, he concluded, was necessary, and the first step was individual conversion. Conversion entailed turning away from all forms of religion and abstraction, as these dampened the capacity for critical analysis. In effect, the abstractions of religion were really of the same type as the abstractions of law and order, serving to maintain the powers that be. In solitary confinement, Jackson developed regimes of self-discipline to prepare himself for revolutionary struggle. He worked to eliminate his ego, to eliminate his attachments to worldly things and people, to eliminate his softness. With mental and physical exercises, he sought a total alignment between his body, his mind, and the revolutionary cause.

Jackson and Cleaver were both embraced by the nascent Black Panther Party as it developed its radical critique of American society. The Panthers understood themselves to be choosing Malcolm over Martin, repudiating the ineffective and ultimately anesthetic language of peace, love, and nonviolence. But the Panthers did not embrace Malcolm's religious vision for revolutionary transformation. Their vision of justice was discernable through social analysis, expressible in a ten-point program—effectively a program of legal reform. Justice did not stand orthogonal to worldly law. Despite this, or perhaps because of it, because of the clear and direct challenge to worldly law and order, the Panthers were the subject of a brutal and insidious crackdown by the federal government. Prison narratives, and those of political prisoners in particular, became central to Panther organizing. The viral demand to free Huey Newton and, later, Angela Davis were paired with the broader demand to free all political prisoners, and the still broader demand to regard all Black prisoners in the United States as political prisoners.

State repression entailed not only imprisonment, of course. Sometimes, as in 1971 when prison guards shot and killed George Jackson, it meant premature death. Sometimes it meant fanning the flames of internal dissent, as when Eldridge Cleaver, driven to exile in Algeria, split with the Oakland-based Panther leadership. Over the course of the 1970s, Cleaver underwent a slow personal transformation, the drift of which provides the defining theme of this chapter: how, during the era of mass incarceration, American prisoners' aspiration to secular revolution was tamed and domesticated into varieties of individualized religion. In Cleaver's case, that religion was evangelical Christianity. With tropes that would become only more familiar, Cleaver describes a conversion that involved weeping, falling to his knees, and saying the Lord's Prayer. He instantly realized what he must do: acknowledge his disobedience, obey the law, turn himself in, and go to jail.

Cleaver's life in exile ended, and he returned to the United States to serve a prison sentence. Cleaver wrote a new account of conversion, but this time—in *Soul on Ice*'s sequel, *Soul on Fire*—Cleaver narrates his turning away from revolutionary organizing and toward his personal savior, Jesus Christ. It was to Him that Cleaver dedicated *Soul on Fire*, and to a faith which, in a second dedication, Cleaver paired with a vision of justice: "This book is dedicated to the proposition that all human beings are created equal—in sin—with the God-given capacity to rise above themselves."[12] The focus was now on the individual—atomized, sinning, and judged by God. Justice was to be achieved by acknowledging sin and accepting Jesus Christ, not by collective struggle. In telling of his turn to Christ, Cleaver describes how he was exiled in Paris, depressed, when he saw a vision of Castro, then Mao, then Marx. "Finally, at the end of the procession, in dazzling, shimmering light, the image of Jesus Christ appeared."[13]

In chapter 2, we looked at ideas of law and justice circulating among political elites. But when we look from the bottom up, as it were, as in the previous chapter and again here, we find continuously remixed religious beliefs, feelings, images, and texts manifesting the abolition spirit, even as the ideas of elites attempt to manage this insurgent spirit. In King and Malcolm, in Jackson and the early Cleaver, we see this vibrancy—and in the later Cleaver, we see the way elite ideas can filter down and stamp out the justice-seeking intuitions of those incarcerated. The views of incarcerated men and women are sometimes animated by a fierce desire for justice, but sometimes not. At their most potent, in the creative reworking of religious ideas and practices by those incarcerated, we find strivings that refuse worldly limits and the carceral regime, and we find thought and action beyond the limits imposed by worldly concepts.[14] When we attend to the conditions and imaginations of those who have been marginalized, we stumble upon insights, and attendant practices, that challenge the ways that law and politics are conventionally understood. If, as we saw earlier, American politics at the national level gradually foreclosed the possibility of imagining and demanding justice, that possibility is reopened by attending to those most marginalized, to those incarcerated. In this subterranean archive we hope to explore some of the ways incarcerated people practiced religion and what it has to offer to the struggle for justice today. These possibilities, some old and some new, are shaped by national moods, but they are not simple products of those moods, and they signal potential openings for imagining differently in the present day. If it is justice we seek, we ought to attend to these openings. As James Baldwin observed, "If one really wishes to know how justice is administered in a country, one does not question the policemen, the lawyers, the judges, or the protected members of the middle classes. One goes to the unprotected— those, precisely, who need the law's protection most!—and listens to their testimony."[15] In the struggle against prisons, that necessarily entails listening above all to the incarcerated.

Abolition Religion in Three Vignettes

In the early months of 1959, a group of prisoners began to regularly assemble in the prison yard of New York's Clinton State Prison. There, in one of the yard's designated "courts," these men, all African Americans and many of them wearing black caps, would gather for lectures. Animated discourses would come to a halt when a correctional officer approached, and then resume when the CO was again out of earshot. In August, alarmed by the seeming secrecy and militancy they took to spell incipient unrest, prison officials conducted a search of the group's homemade "locker." In the box they found, among other things, the "Constitution" of a group calling itself the "Muslim Brotherhood."[16] Foremost a set of organizational rules and regulations, the Brotherhood's constitution flirts with the tropes of a man-ifesto. It refers to the "despotic anti-brother and anti-Muslim government" and characterizes the condition of its members as living inside "the prison of the enemy." In swearing allegiance to the Brotherhood, members prom-ised five things, the last of these being: "I will, except as a last resort, avoid the use of violence."[17] Construing this admonition for restraint as a declara-tion of aggression, prison officials placed the group's three leaders in solitary confinement. Shortly thereafter, the leaders filed a suit, claiming the viola-tion of their First Amendment rights. The suit would ultimately fail. But in January 1960, the New York Department of Correctional Services (DOCS) issued a memo to its state prison wardens. In it, the DOCS reversed standing policy under which the Koran had been considered contraband, and it gave prisoners the right to acquire any one of four authorized translations. Nowadays, according to one estimate, a fifth of New York's state prisoners practice some form of Islam.[18]

In June 1970, a group of men in the federal prison in Atlanta started a re-ligion that, after a turn of phrase in Revelation 14:3, they called the "Church of the New Song" (CONS). Having already applied for and received by mail his ordination from the Universal Life Church, Harry Theriault, the group's leader and prophet, sued the US Department of Corrections for religious rec-ognition. CONS was at once a tour de force of American religious genius and a self-conscious burlesque of free-exercise litigation.[19] Theriault's scriptures, of which he wrote reams and reams, evince a hodgepodge of Protestant dis-pensationalism and New Age spirituality. But CONS was equally political. In his writing and in his court appearances, Theriault adamantly rejected all state regulation of prisoners' religion—including the Bureau of Prison's em-ployment of prison chaplains—as violations of the Establishment Clause. More pointedly, CONS leadership more than occasionally swore its determi-nation to destroy the prison system. In February 1972, CONS won a lawsuit and garnered protection under the First Amendment.[20] By the time a second federal court found otherwise three years later, a decision that revoked the church's accommodation in the Fifth Circuit, Church of the New Song chapters had sprouted up in prisons across the South and the Midwest.

In July 1981, Frank Africa, a member of the black naturalist sect MOVE, was transferred from Holmesburg Prison, a Philadelphia county facility, to Pennsylvania's State Correctional Institution at Graterford. MOVE was a self-declared "revolutionary organization," whose members rejected the modern world's mores and modes of consumption. Spiritually, MOVE's members were pantheistic vitalists: the world pulsed with life, and all living beings merited respect and care. Members of MOVE were exceedingly self-conscious about the pollutants in the air and water, and they followed a regime of abstemious naturalism. Central to this was a diet committed to simplicity, which consisted primarily of fresh fruits and vegetables. In county jail, Africa had requested and received a special allotment of raw vegetables and fruits, but at Graterford, no such accommodation was guaranteed. Africa sued in federal court. In October, the court ruled that MOVE's beliefs and practices did not rise to the level of "religion" and denied First Amendment protection to the group.[21] To this day MOVE members remain incarcerated in Pennsylvania prisons, and their practices and beliefs garner from the administration no special accommodation.[22]

In these three examples, we find among incarcerated people a creative, confusing synthesis that always takes form in relation to the prison regime but also points emphatically at something beyond. The just world they envision feels achievable in this world, by means of the legal system: law bent hard in the direction of justice. This sequence suggests a particular moment, on the cusp of mass incarceration, when electoral politics moved to embrace the mantra of law and order. With the court system lagging somewhat behind, an opening was created for incarcerated men and women to practice religions in particularly challenging ways. Impolitic and illiberal, members of these groups were not merely seeking to carve out a cozy Sunday morning niche in the chapel for communing with their God. They pushed for much more than that. At the very least they talked about wanting out of the system, in mind and in body. And at most, they talked about bringing the system tumbling down. Let us call the combative religious mood we find in the Muslim Brotherhood, CONS, and MOVE—a religious mood nurtured in collective struggle within and against an oppressive system it vows to destroy—*abolition religion*. This is the abolition spirit captured, organized into religious institutions that fully manifest that spirit.

Custodians of even the most benevolent of social orders tend to look askance at such dissident aspirations, and that was true here, too. In carceral environments where severe repression was the norm, state violence was deployed in varieties both cold and hot. The people in these stories paid high prices with their bodies and spirits—with retaliatory solitary confinement, protracted imprisonment, and, in the case of Frank Africa, who five years later perished in a firebombing, with his life. But for a time, before the returns diminished, these incarcerated religionists got surprising results and made lasting contributions both to the culture of American prisons and to American culture more broadly.

In these stories, a possibility cracks open in the social realm, flickers for a minute, and is then snuffed out. As is perhaps always the case when reflecting on those vanquished social forms that failed to survive to the present in full, the subsequent foreclosure of these one-time possibilities is invariably less surprising than that they ever existed to begin with. Abolition religion flourished in American prisons? How did that happen? What were the anatomical features of this moment? How did it end and what took its place? Or might it never have ended, at least not in full? Might it rather have taken on new forms, its fire not extinguished but smoldering, ready to flame anew when the favorable historical winds once again blow with renewed strength?

The Struggle Within

The abolition religion that once existed as a live option for those incarcerated in America's prisons has been all but forgotten. When it is remembered at all, this tradition is remembered almost exclusively in secular terms. For those allied with the freedom struggle, prisoners' abolition religion was simply *politics*; for those allied against it, it was chicanery. For most, it was nothing at all. This erasure, we contend, says as much about us today as it does about the incarcerated men and women who struggled back when.[23] At the dawn of mass incarceration, abolition religion was a vibrant current in the culture of America's prisons, and its erasure—in fact and in memory—signals a dark triumph of American mass carceral hegemony.

As a tradition, abolition religion was an eddy in a current of Black bodies in motion: bodies stolen in Africa and brought by force to the New World; bodies driven North by terror and opportunity; and in the end, bodies arrested and confined to American prisons. For some, abolition religion was Black Islam, which traced these same lines. For Africans in America, Islam was initially a set of indigenous folkways brought to the New World by kidnapped men and women. These folkways were nurtured, transmitted, and then largely lost before, a century later, Islam was reclaimed and reimagined by a set of religious actors as the spiritual and practical component of a project of collective awakening. With racist immigration laws barring Muslims from Asia, Africa, and the Middle East, space was vacated for this new Islam to blossom in America—and so it did, first tentatively and then spectacularly, among young men in Newark, Detroit, Chicago, Philadelphia, and New York. Diverse and sectarian from the start, the most significant group in the genealogy of radical prison religion was the Nation of Islam, the adherents of which made Islam a tribal totem and a practical program for incarcerated Black men in the protean moment before American mass incarceration began to take shape.[24]

Members of New York's Muslim Brotherhood were, in this process, early adopters. That these men were readers of Elijah Muhammad is clear from the group's constitution. Beyond that, the Brotherhood's brand of religion is murky. Surely, some Brothers had belonged to Muslim groups out on the street and had brought in the Nation's fiery oratorical style with them. But in 1959 the practice of Islam at Clinton Prison remained largely aspirational. Among the duties of the group's officers, the constitution lists Koranic interpretation; the teaching of Muslim law, history, and Arabic; and leading the congregation in prayers. But at this time, the Koran was contraband, and the obligation to lead prayers would commence "when facilities for prayers are obtained." If the Brotherhood's religious observances, narrowly conceived, remain opaque, the same cannot be said of the group's political project. The Muslim Brotherhood's constitution is a performative text. Its goal is to manufacture an alternative order independent of and oppositional to "the despotic anti-brother anti-Muslim" regime. The place of Islam within this monumental struggle is articulated in the constitution's introductory "Aims and Objects:"

1. To maintain ourselves and the Muslim Brotherhood as the vigorous, intellectual vanguard of the struggle for complete unity among our brothers by employing the unifying force of Islam.
2. To secure & maintain the complete intellectual unity & awakening of our brothers by promoting the advantages of unity of action and organization through the study of: Islam; our history which has been concealed from us; the struggle for freedom being made by our brothers at home and abroad; and all other pertinent subjects.
3. To build and train leaders for the future struggle so that each member upon his release shall be so equipped, that he will be able to successfully organize his own group or be an asset to any organization he may join.[25]

An "intellectual vanguard," "to secure intellectual unity . . . through the study of Islam," "to build and train leaders": the instrumental function of

Islam seems unambiguous here. For these men, as Muslim Brothers, God, who by no name or cognate appears in the constitution, would seem to be beside the point. Pivotal instead is each Muslim's evolving relationship with his fellow Muslims. In this social sphere, Islam is cast as a technology for collective awakening and a tool for forging solidarity, but the organizing principle is the struggle for freedom. And in this regard, not any sort of freedom would do. Freedom, as imagined by the Brotherhood, is plainly sociopolitical in kind and internationalist in reach. As a religious orientation, the Brotherhood's is not limited in scope to the individual's "spirituality," and its notion of freedom is not to be satisfied by means of individual peace of mind. This is the freedom that comes only via a mass movement with a revolutionary *telos*. Despots would have to go; the racist, dominating state would have to fall. To rise to this challenge, the need for unity was paramount. To properly serve as the vanguard it felt compelled to become, the Brotherhood's collective affect needed to be zealous but disciplined. In a word, what they needed to be was militant. Thus, unsurprisingly, mixed in the Brotherhood's organizational structure among religious positions like mufti and imam are paramilitary designations like colonel, captain, and lieutenant. The oath of membership entailed full submission to this structure. Members were to promise that they would "irrevocably obey and act upon the orders, commands, instructions" of their leaders and "serve, sacrifice and suffer anything for the cause." Oaths would be accepted, the constitution spells out, only from men who were "sincere" and were willing to go "all the way."[26]

Religion as a tool for individual awakening and uplift mobilized for revolutionary solidarity: abolition religion adheres to what, after its most iconic and influential practitioner, we might call the *Malcolm X paradigm*. And over the course of the decade to come, it became a dominant—indeed, perhaps the *predominant*—religious mode among incarcerated American men.[27] Whether articulated in a secular idiom or in a religious idiom, as a mood, the Malcolm X paradigm is materialist, collectivist, and militant. As we observed in Jackson and in early Cleaver, the Malcolm X paradigm exploits the discipline endemic to carceral monasticism and turns it outside in. Religion, in this mode, is irreducibly a human affair. God matters, as does personal improvement unto salvation, but the driving preoccupation is the building of a more just world. For religionists of this stripe, therapeutic self-transformation is inextricable from the process of world-transformation in the direction of justice.

How precisely did this orientation emerge? The narrow answer pinpoints the Nation of Islam as prototype. Caught between street crime and predatory policing, members of the Black lumpenproletariat brought the styles and tactics of the Nation inside America's prisons. Fanning the flames was the Nation's shrewd tactical decision to sponsor the legal actions of incarcerated Muslims.[28] Neither ideologically nor stylistically was the Nation's brand of abolition religion a discrete phenomenon. Over the course of the 1960s, as driven by the civil rights movement and the emergence of new media, radical thought, oppositional politics, and experimental spirituality all moved from the margin to the cultural center. What was true out on the street was also true in America's prisons. The collectivism and activism that came to characterize prisoners' abolition religion would eventually come to characterize American prison culture as a whole. Read in this way, the Muslim Brotherhood prefigures secular groups like the Black Panthers and activists like George Jackson and Angela Davis. In little more than a decade, as the militants' power grew, tensions mounted, and tactics on both sides of the bars diversified. That which began in the yard in Clinton Prison would eventually flower into the Attica uprising.[29]

Transformative agency from below was eventually matched from above. As enabled by the long postwar economic boom, and as fueled by War-on-Poverty politics, resources were funneled so as to improve the lives of incarcerated people. As informed by a progressive penology that conceptualized crime and violence as collective social failures, controls were loosened and privileges were extended. Prisoners lost their stripes, and prison administrators developed a wide range of educational, artistic, and therapeutic programming. So as to instill the practices of citizenship, incarcerated people were increasingly empowered to organize themselves.[30] In retrospect, one might well see these investments as down payments on the massive prison expansion to come. But at the time, when the future was as yet undecided, what emerged was an animated, creative environment, of which abolition religion was but one articulation. Given the proper room to grow, what started with Black Islam didn't stop at the denominational boundary. Prisoners' Christianity evolved similarly. With its emphasis on social justice, liberation theology—a progressive platform conducive to solidarity-building and ecumenical efforts—came to resonate with many prisoners and chaplains, both Catholic and Protestant, Black and white.

By decade's end, the radical spirit of the Muslim Brotherhood reached its apotheosis in the Church of the New Song. The former's influence on the latter is evident in Harry Theriault's writings, which are peppered with allusions to the Muslims. This was not because of any theological affinity. Like the Muslim Brotherhood, CONS leveraged the First Amendment to carve out sites for oppositional practices. Like the Brotherhood, CONS identified itself as a symptom of state violence, and it flirted with rhetoric that suggested the possibility of turning this violence back against its source. In this regard, both groups appropriated from theologically conservative Protestantism the intimation of a dawning apocalypse when the satanic social order that oppressed them would be beaten back and defeated by the forces of righteousness. But the reach and versatility of prisoner's-rights-era abolition religion is demonstrated less by what the two groups shared than by the many things that set them apart. Surface designators begin to tell the tale: the Muslim Brotherhood was Black, CONS was white; the Brotherhood was in a state prison in the North, CONS began in a federal prison in the South. Whereas the Muslim Brotherhood was bureaucratic, militant, and humorlessly earnest, CONS was charismatic, chaotic, and carnivalesque. That the Muslim Brothers were soldiers whereas the members of CONS were merry pranksters was, at least in part, a reflection of their founders' sensibilities. If Harlem-born Martin Sostre, the Muslim Brotherhood's leader, was a scholar and revolutionary, Theriault, as the self-proclaimed Bishop of Tellus, was nothing less than a religious genius.[31]

With overwhelming religious confidence, Theriault spoke for God, interpreted signs, and forecast the future. More often than not, Theriault found himself in solitary confinement, and it was largely in the confines of such maddening isolation that his scriptural works were revealed. As with the grand tradition of Abrahamic prophecy, the theological content of Theriault's writings is not easily disaggregated from its political content. This is evident from the preface to Theriault's *Gospel of the New Song for the People of the Light*. His revelation, Theriault writes, "does not merely testify; it shows the spirit . . . breaking into history." This revelation's arrival is presented as fundamentally disruptive to the social order. It is "a public dream embracing a symbol that evokes and directs spiritual energy, in such a way as to turn it into a fulfillment of history." "Its aim is the natural organization of a new social order . . . [that will] restore life to splendor." The world Theriault envisions is both religious and political. It "can be a reality spiritually through the Church of the New Song and socially through democratical [*sic*] government."[32]

In his federal court appearance in El Paso, where he fought to retain the Church's religious designation, Theriault fused the Church of the New Song's eschatology into American civic history. With visual aids, he offered up a ty-pological reading whereby the events of Vietnam and Watergate recapitu-lated the events of the Revolutionary War. Calling out the trial judge as an agent of the Devil, he preached the dawning of a coming age when the re-public would be reconstituted, and the American ideals of truth, peace, and freedom would finally be realized. Inasmuch as total social transformation was necessary and inevitable, Theriault's millennialism was intrinsically se-ditious. In court, where the shaman became a showman, the Bishop's defiant charisma spelled his own imminent undoing.

A similar spirit of provocation informed CONS's primary ritual practice, a three-part discussion of life that the Church dubbed a "free-exercise sem-inar." CONS members would, in turn, articulate what was "bugging" them, lay out possible remedies, and counsel one another on potential courses of action. In practice, the express religiousness of the free-exercise seminar was largely limited to its form. That is not to say it didn't meet real spiritual needs—plainly it did. However, as a ritual, CONS's free-exercise seminar was not dissimilar from a meeting of Alcoholics Anonymous; which is to say that whether theological or not, the seminar was a means for fellowship. For CONS, calling this ritual "religious" was both strategic and polemical. It was strategic because it shoehorned what was a secular-seeming practice into the constitutionally requisite rubric. It was polemical because by expressly christening itself in the language of the First Amendment, the "free-exercise seminar" poked fun at the arbitrariness and silliness by which such freedoms are dispensed. Amid its playfulness around the First Amendment, how-ever, CONS pursued a deadly serious directive: creating a space within the carceral system where incarcerated men might gather and organize to chip away at that system from the inside.

How Abolition Religion Was Made to Disappear

As is true of abolition religion more broadly, the Church of the New Song aggressively used state law to advance justice. This was, certainly, a pecu-liar version of justice—but in its time, it was less opaque than it would later come to appear. In CONS's day, American jurists, acting at the intersection of prisoners' rights and the free exercise of religion, took it as their obligation to bring the law ever closer to an as yet unattained justice. Subsequently, as had happened in the domain of electoral politics a decade earlier, this expansive aspiration for the law faded and was replaced by something quite different. The spaces where alternative visions of justice might develop, where moral law might be accessed—in short, spaces that might cultivate abolition religion—these had to be carefully managed. If not explicitly the intention, the result was the foreclosure of alternative legal regimes and the absolute identification of justice with the criminal justice system.[33] Jurisprudentially, this compression of law relative to religious freedom was brought about through careful management, with acceptable religion cleaved from more troublesome religion. And the organized incarcerated men exploiting the law in pursuit of a confrontational politics motivated by a radically alternative vision for justice was troublesome indeed. The repression of abolition religion in America's prisons was therefore secured in part by placing a cap on religious freedom.

Americans tend to regard free religious exercise as an animating impulse from the very beginning of the republic, but it was really only in the twentieth century that religious minorities pushed federal courts to honor their First Amendment rights. The mantle taken up by members of the Salvation Army who wished to bang their drums in the open air, and taken up by Jehovah's Witnesses whose school-age children refused to salute the flag, passed to incarcerated Black Muslims who insisted on the right to practice their religion.[34] The federal jurists of the Warren Court era proved especially receptive to these demands. Some of the receptiveness of these judges was due to the flowering of political liberalism.[35] Softened by the civil rights movement and the Great Society, the federal judiciary of the 1960s proved open to a wide range of minority petitioners. But as a site for accommodation, religion was especially ripe. With the recent incorporation of Catholics and Jews into the ruling cultural order, the 1960s found Protestant hegemony at its most elastic. Suddenly self-conscious of the overwhelming legal and social privileges enjoyed by Protestants as compared to other religious people, federal courts significantly reigned in public Protestantism, and they extended the umbrella of First Amendment protection far and wide, up and down. As pushed by secular humanists, atheists, Buddhists, Black Muslims, and other nontraditional religionists, the Supreme Court came to radically expand the range of what religion entailed—an expansion that both presaged and enabled the radical diversification in American religion that followed the 1965 Immigration and Nationality Act.

In order to authorize an expansion of religious rights, the Court had to first determine what precisely a religion was. Is religion a matter of belief or practice? If the former, then what sorts of beliefs qualify? If the latter, then what place need the practice occupy in order to count? By and large, the federal judiciary had been reluctant to wade into such thorny terrain, but at the limits of the will to accommodate minorities, the Warren Court gave it a shot.[36]

The most determinative answer came in 1965. That year, in *U.S. v. Seeger*, the Court strained to accommodate under the First Amendment minority religionists who wished to conscientiously object to, and therefore refuse to fight in, the Vietnam War. The problem was that under the existing standard, to qualify as a protected believer of a bona fide religion, one had to avow faith in a sovereign Creator, but the earnest Buddhist and secular humanist plaintiffs before the Court claimed no such beliefs. To square this circle, the Court offered an analogical solution. If not a belief in God per se, then religion was something *like* belief in God; that is, "a sincere and meaningful belief occupying in the life of its possessor a place parallel to that filled by the God."[37] To extend the standard in this way, the Court found theological inspiration in the thought of existentialist Protestant theologian Paul Tillich. For Tillich, as quoted by the Court, God is not a projection "out there." He is rather "the ground of our very being." Religion becomes a matter of a person's "ultimate concern, of what you take seriously without any reservation." From the standpoint of Tillich's normative anthropology, every life is built on such epistemic bedrock—or, at the very least, every life *ought to* be.

It was a pluralist standard, and in the jurisprudence to come, it would provide protection to a wide range of religious and secular Americans. But even the warmest embrace has its limits, and in establishing limits on religion, the Court established a two-pronged test: the petitioner must possess a "belief that is sincere and meaningful," and this belief must play a role "in the life of its possessor parallel to that filled by the orthodox belief in God." In the subsequent jurisprudence, perhaps no plaintiffs have run afoul of the sincerity standard more gloriously than the Church of the New Song. Granted their First Amendment imprimatur in 1972 by a federal court in Atlanta, the Church's reversal of fortune came two years later. An article in *Newsweek* lampooned CONS for the damning (if wholly decontextualized) detail that the group had requested Harvey's Bristol Cream and porterhouse steaks for its communion ritual. Much ridicule was to follow. Henceforth, the Church of the New Song ceased to be a "religion" and became, rather, in a quite technical sense, a "so-called religion." That is to say, for the purposes of First Amendment protection, it was not a religion at all. As the federal court in El

Paso artfully put it the following year, "The unmistakeable [sic] stench of the skunk is found emanating from that which petitioner has declared a rose." CONS, as the court saw it, was a sham perpetrated by bad men.[38] Much in the way that a decade hence the acquittal of John Hinckley Jr. in the attempted assassination of Ronald Reagan would herald the collapse of the insanity defense, so too would the Church of the New Song's prior success come to spell the end for First Amendment accommodation of abolition religion in America's prisons. For its latter-day critics, that federal jurists ever even considered recognizing the Church of the New Song as a bona fide faith is patently laughable. If, for liberals, the Muslim Brotherhood's inventiveness and determination echo with resonances of the Liberty Bell, the Church of the New Song represents for liberals and conservatives alike the proverbial thirteenth ring of the cuckoo clock.

As liberal as the *Seeger* test might have hoped to be, the normative Protestantism that locates religion as a fixed condition of interiority jibes horribly with what in our age we have all lazily come to "know" about an incarcerated person. That is, within the cultural logic of mass incarceration, to be a prisoner is to be enduringly defined by the crime for which one has been convicted. The prisoner convicted of murder is *essentially* a murderer; the prisoner convicted of rape is *essentially* a rapist, and so on. Common sense therefore dictates that such a person be approached with great caution, and that seemingly earnest claims—such as claims to foundational personal transformation—are to be met with the requisite suspicion. According to this common sense, the prisoner who would assert his innocence or claim that his captors have tortured him is to be presumed to be a liar, a malingerer, a dissembler seeking advantage. Religion, in the Tillichian framework, is the cornerstone of virtue. Were a prisoner's faith bona fide, it would speak volumes to his character, but inasmuch as he is a prisoner, we may be preemptively confident that his professed faith is a lie, and one likely perpetrated for criminal ends. To be clear: we are not endorsing this judgment. Our claim, rather, is that the *common sense* idea that incarcerated peoples' religion isn't *really* religion speaks volumes about the contempt with which present-day Americans regard those whom we keep in cages.[39]

Seeger authorized another means for excluding prisoners' religion, not in the prisoner's presumed religious insincerity but in the prisoner's presumed religious inauthenticity. Thinkers in the West have long differentiated true religion from false religion, and such distinctions have proliferated since the Protestant Reformation. The grounds for making such distinctions have varied. In the First Amendment jurisprudence that attends prisoners' abolition religion, however, one rule abides: whatever real religion might be found, it necessarily excludes the political.

In *Pierce v. LaVallee*, the 1962 case that denied the Muslim Brotherhood First Amendment protection, this logic remains implicit. As stated in the opinion, "The Muslim Brotherhood, as it existed at Clinton Prison, is not a religion. Rather it is an organization which sets itself up as an adjunct to the Islamic faith."[40] The court could have legitimately queried, but didn't, whether the Nation of Islam ought to be considered Islam proper, but this crucial ground the court ceded. The court presupposed the Muslim Brotherhood to be practitioners of a bona fide faith, but decided on account of its organizational structure that as Muslim Brothers the men were not being religious. They were functioning as an "organization." What sphere of human activity this organization involved the court did not feel compelled to state. What it wasn't, however, was religious.

Theriault v. Silber, the 1975 case that found against the Church of the New Song, is clearer. For the El Paso court, Theriault failed *Seeger*'s sincerity test, but he also flunked Seeger's authenticity test—that is, in the language of Paul Tillich, whether a given belief occupies "a place parallel to that filled by the orthodox belief in God." But, if not religion, then what precisely *was* CONS? Following Tillich, the court provided a short list of ways for conceiving that which *wasn't quite* religion. Its "views" were "essentially political." That is, even if Theriault had been sincere (which, the court decided, he wasn't), CONS would still have fallen short of a religion. Religious sincerity was one problem; religious *authenticity* was another. In CONS, the court made clear, the doctrinal core was politics, with religion providing merely a façade: "The claim of Mr. Theriault to be the second Messiah is merely a front for what is essentially a political 'union' or organization with primary goals of establishing a unit to bargain with prison officials and ultimately to establish a new social order . . . with Harry W. Theriault as its head."[41] The court's reasoning here is exceedingly revealing and underscores the way in which "religion" in this carceral jurisprudence is always and essentially *religion within the scope of the secular state*. Religion's "concern" may be ultimate, but religion's sovereignty is subordinate to that of the state, and as the state would have it, to be political, to posit and actively pursue an alternative social order, is to be essentially *not* religious.

On account of its political aspirations, CONS became *prima facie* not religious. This, to the court, became obvious. But take a critical step back and it speaks volumes about what, during the era of mass incarceration, prisoners' "religion" was allowed to be. Inflict Tillich's exclusions onto religion's prototypical cases and the same political stuff that sank Harry Theriault would surely have sunk Moses, Jesus, and the Prophet Muhammad. To wield justice onto the world via the realization of a new social order is not, sayeth the court, religious.

A comprehensive account of the exclusion of the political from the religious in the scope of the law would necessarily need to attend to economics, politics, and race, but how did the court itself make sense of what it was doing? The answer is a surprisingly religious one. Tasked only with the narrow mandate to make sense of "religion" under a political order necessarily presumed to be just, the court felt no compulsion to spell out what it is precisely about an alternative politics that renders it, as a religious orientation, subpar. What, we might reasonably inquire, is *wrong* with living one's politics as religion—which is to say, with living one's politics *all the way*? If the court didn't say, elsewhere the source text is clear. For Tillich, to mistake a subordinate concern like politics for an ultimate concern is nothing less than "idolatry."[42] Material concerns, thought of as fickle and mutable, belong to a lower realm. Devotional objects are fine *in service to* one's ultimate concern, but as for the ultimate concern itself, it is necessarily more abstract than that. A life lived in ultimate fidelity to a person, to a flag, to a political party, to a piece of land, or to a revolutionary social project is judged implicitly to be a life wanting of adequate concern, a life lived in ignorance.

To qualify as religious before the law, would-be religious practitioners were forced to evince fidelity to something higher and more amorphous than a materially minded politics could accommodate. This, the requirement of religion within the scope of the secular, was a language game that the Black populists in MOVE were ill-equipped to play. For the followers of John Africa, MOVE's founder, "the principle of freedom" was inextricable from "the principle of strength, the principle of fitness, the principle of revolution."[43] Such a mishmash might seem strange to a Sunday school teacher, but not to a member of MOVE. How one ate, how one organized one's family, how one prepared for the future, all these were to be lived in refusal of the existing order. For MOVE, the carceral state was the imperialist state was the polluting state, and such a state merited no accommodation. To combat this state, which was manifested all around them in the decomposing and simultaneously militarized Philadelphia of the 1970s, men and women had to go all the way. Withdrawal, repudiation, and the cultivation of a new way of life: for the catastrophe at hand, only a total solution would suffice. This meant fidelity to a *new* Law, a Law that repudiated entirely the law of the state. As Louise Africa explained it in 1975, "Lest the impression be given that we have no respect for the LAW, we'd like to make clear that we know the LAW, and we have the most profound respect for IT. LAW is the very basis of our Organization, it is our Doctrine, it is our—Religion—and when you know what LAW is—you know what 'law' ain't."[44]

Six years hence, with many MOVE members now in prison, representatives of the state could see that in contrast to Theriault, MOVE people appeared earnestly committed to their radical lifestyle. As it considered Frank Africa's case, the Third Circuit concluded, "We are persuaded from our review of the record that Africa's opinions, especially those having to do with his diet, are 'truly held.' " That is to say, MOVE passed the first prong of the *Seeger* test. "We turn, therefore, to the second issue: whether Africa's beliefs, however sincerely possessed, are religious in nature." Repeating the language of the district court, the Third Circuit characterized MOVE as "merely a quasi-back-to-nature social movement of limited proportion and with an admittedly revolutionary design." That is to say, in its categorical rejection of the modern world and the secular state, MOVE was *merely* a social movement. As an organization concerned primarily with "concepts of health and a return to simplistic living," MOVE was judged to be more a "social philosophy" than a religion. The court concluded, "To the extent MOVE deals with 'ultimate' ideas, a proposition in itself subject to serious doubt, it is concerned with secular matters and not with religious principles."[45]

In what would appear to be a catch-22, then, in the purview of the *Africa* court, for a religion to go all the way was for a religion to not go far enough. MOVE lacked "a comprehensive, multi-faceted theology," and it lacked "the defining structural characteristics of a traditional religion." But given the Supreme Court's record of accommodating Buddhists and secular humanists, these purported deficiencies are most certainly red herrings. What doomed MOVE was less what it lacked than what it had in excess. What it had was honest-to-God *politics*; which to say, a vision for a new and different world, and the collective will to bring this world into existence. It was this dangerous quality that excluded MOVE's religion from the ranks of authentic religions in need of protection.

As ends and as means, state violence has a way of providing for its own justifications. With a rationale equally Protestant and secular, mass incarceration era courts had managed MOVE's abolition religion out of existence.

Three years later in West Philadelphia, a far more horrendous act of state violence would destroy the group in sum.[46]

The Religious Life of Mass Incarceration

The bright if blurry line the *Africa* decision drew between the religious and the political reasserted an abiding secular principle, but it also accompanied the emergence of something radically new. The year *Africa* was handed down, the newly inaugurated president, Ronald Reagan, passed mammoth tax cuts, and California launched its prison-building boom with the passage of Proposition 1. Coming down to earth from the airy realm of religious freedom to the brutally concrete terrain of the carceral state, this story once again carries an odor of American exceptionalism, albeit with the privilege inverted. In this story America's gifts to the world are no longer liberal democracy and individual freedom. They are neoliberal terror and technologies of containment for bodies deemed dangerous.[47]

In the dawning era of carceral expansion, the general mandate of prisons would shift dramatically. Prisons, which in the 1960s were said to be about rehabilitating people, in the 1980s became unapologetically about incapacitating them.[48] The prisoners' rights movement had gone too far, legislators, administrators, and the general public agreed, and riots had been the consequence. With public safety and security as the driving concerns, control became both a means and an end. New architecture and new security protocols were developed. Sentences got longer and more rigidly prescribed, and solitary confinement became an elastic tool to be used for punishing rule violators.[49] Softer tools, like television sets, were deployed as well to depoliticize.[50] By such means, prison populations were atomized and terrorized. Practices of oppositional collectivism were rendered a thing of the past. As one young Pennsylvania prisoner pointedly characterized the impossibility of prisoners' solidarity in the era of carceral control, "If you try to stand together, they treat you with Thorazine."[51]

With the Moral Majority wielding influence in the White House, and with the civil rights movement being slowly emulsified into civil religion, the country's dominant religious forms—in and out of prison—changed with the times. If sixties' era prisoners' religion bore the revolutionary spirit of Malcolm X, beginning in the eighties, the mantle of prisoners' religion was passed to another. In 1976 Charles Colson published *Born Again*.

As Colson describes his rapid personal decline stemming from Watergate and his subsequent rebirth, he attributes to an encounter with C. S. Lewis's *Mere Christianity* opening the avowed secularist to personal faith in Jesus Christ. The *sine qua non* of religion became one's personal relationship with God. The evangelical conversion experience so vividly narrated by Colson involved acknowledging a set of divinely ordained laws that human beings necessarily transgress. Jesus Christ offers redemption, but only for those who acknowledge the laws and their own transgressions. The figure of law is essential to this narrative, and it easily slips between the religious realm and the political realm, between that which is divinely ordained and that which is mandated by the American legal system. Just as the sinner must take responsibility before God, the law-breaker must take responsibility before the legal system. In this view, pointing to social causes of law-breaking distracts from the essential task of taking personal responsibility, beyond which lies forgiveness, personal peace, and the guarantee of salvation. For a Christian theory of salvation that places all of its eggs in the basket of personal faith, law remains overwhelmingly sovereign. As Colson puts it, "A Christian really is committed to finding the certainty of the laws. The whole idea of the rule of law is essential to a just society, and this is a clear Christian contribution, going back to the Decalogue."[52] Accepting God's will means accepting the laws of the world, the laws of the American state, aligned as they are imagined to be with the laws handed down from God on Sinai.

As with Eldridge Cleaver, who in fact befriended Colson, in Colson's prison conversion we may see how a field of practice that had once been militant, collectivist, and polemical lurched in the direction of spirituality, individual piety, and deference to the law. By the nineties, Prison Fellowship, the prison ministry that Colson founded in 1976, was a worldwide organization, and it was competing, via its 501(c)(3), InnerChange Freedom Initiative (IFI), for government contracts. As IFI touted its methodology in an early brochure titled "Invest in a Real Crime Stopper," IFI "is based on the belief that real and lasting change happens from the inside out as a person repents of his sin, receives forgiveness and salvation through Christ and draws on His mighty power day by day."[53]

After a successful bid, IFI's evangelical rehabilitation regimen was implemented at Iowa's Newton Correctional Facility. In *Prison Religion*, scholar of religion Winnifred Sullivan describes IFI's tortured attempt at enabling Christian healing in a manner that conformed to the ruling logic of mass incarceration: "Prisoners participating in InnerChange Freedom

Initiative are asked to reinvent themselves as free moral subjects by using the tools of a populist and punitive theory of justice combined with various forms of vernacular Christianity, all the while disadvantaged by addiction, illiteracy, racism, and childhood abuse."[54] In what participants called the "God Pod," men learned to confess their sins and resolve to submit themselves "to all authority." At the same time, they were inculcated with a highly individualist, rational-choice conception of what it is to be a self. In Sullivan's read, for those men who are actually able to walk this tightrope, the selfhood they assimilate is, more or less, that of a Christian capitalist. If, under the residual Malcolm X paradigm, reforming the self was part and parcel of revolutionizing the social order, under the now-dominant Colson model, personal "transformation"—as it is generally called—is judged successful when the one-time deviant subject has brought himself into snug conformity with the ruling social and economic order.

To her credit, Sullivan does not look down at these aspirations to personal transformation, and neither do we. For men and women who have struggled with crime and with addiction, goals like following the law, holding down a job, and becoming a reliable parent and partner aren't merely understandable, they're commendable. But one unmistakable consequence of the punitive system that places people in an impossible situation and then demands that they improve themselves is that it leaves the penitent man or woman precisely *zero* room for social critique, for talk about justice beyond the procedures of the criminal justice system. All criticism must be directed inward. Within Colson's transformative Christianity, for an incarcerated person to criticize the world around him and not him or herself is evidence of a refusal to embrace personal responsibility.

In spite of prominent billing, "freedom" in IFI's disciplinary regime was a surprisingly marginal concept. In their literature and counseling, IFI programmers occasionally spoke of "freedom in Christ."[55] More frequently, however, they talked of "exhibiting the fruits of the spirit"—a condition of psychic relief characterized by "love, joy, peace, patience, kindness, goodness, faithfulness, gentleness, and self-control."[56] Compare the spirituality of "freedom in Christ" to the materiality of Malcolm X, who flatly declared, "You can't separate peace from freedom because no one can be at peace unless he has his freedom." IFI's brand of freedom abandons not only the project of collective social transformation; it refuses as well the view that individual freedom requires material liberation. For one to experience "freedom in Christ," being in prison is no insurmountable obstacle.

When IFI participants did speak of freedom in material terms, this freedom too is wholly contained within prison walls. One man touted IFI for how it offered a "more spacious," "more comfortable," and "much nicer" environment: "[I]t's a different kind of freedom. Even though you still have the fence around you."[57] Marginally nicer cells and other material improvements to one's prison environment: this is indeed a "different kind of freedom."[58]

In 2007, IFI as it was administered in Iowa was found to be in violation of the Establishment Clause. Nonetheless, as sponsored both by state employees and by outside volunteers, the dematerialized and domesticated "freedoms" IFI propagated remain dominant features of incarcerated religion in the age of mass incarceration. In no way are these newer, smaller freedoms limited to conservative Christianity. Rather, a similar defining down (and in) of freedom may be observed in a range of religious traditions and practices. Two further, very different, examples should give a sense of the cultural predominance of this sort of religious orientation.

In 2002, thirty-seven men incarcerated in Alabama's Donaldson Prison participated in a ten-day Vipassana meditation retreat. As with many housed at Donaldson, a good number of the retreat participants had been convicted of homicide and were serving the sentence of life without the possibility of parole. By their own descriptions, the self-selected men had pressing psychic and spiritual needs. The discipline they found in Vipassana was grueling, and the ten days were spent largely in silence. Those who completed the program reported the retreat as being an overwhelmingly favorable, even life-changing, experience.

The Donaldson Vipassana retreat was documented in a 2007 film, *The Dhamma Brothers*. That the film touts Vipassana meditation as a tool for changing lives is undisguised. Interesting for our purposes, however, is the prominent place in this advocacy of the sort of defined-down "freedom" we found in Iowa. Before the viewer sees a single image or hears a single sound, the black screen births the words, "Freedom Behind Bars Productions." This, purportedly, is what the discipline of Vipassana meditation enables. Prisoners who have made it through the grueling, ten-day program provide testimonials about how learning to meditate "helps you deal with life." Meditation, it is said, helped them to control their anger and allowed them to "choose how to react, and not just act." Said one man, "it set me free."[59]

Especially in a prison environment like Donaldson, in which lack of mind control can lose a man to despair, and lack of bodily control can get him killed, the freedom offered by meditation might indeed save a man's life. But without the attendant will to collectively struggle to reshape the world that one finds in the Malcolm X paradigm, as "freedom," this notion is profoundly circumscribed. Prison-Buddhist freedom provides only modest relief from some of the torments that come from being a body, mind, and spirit living in a cage. These crushing preconditions are presumed as merely a given. And so, a prisoner's inability to control himself is configured as a problem entirely his own—not one for which either the society at large or prison administrators bear any responsibility. In sum, to be "set free" in this framework is to successfully will the discipline necessary to bring one's mind and body into the state of perpetual docility that a life without parole demands.

To call the film's celebration of this diminished freedom cynical is to miss the point. Its enthusiasm is rather an expression of faith, but a religious faith and faith in religion that is only too comfortable within the cultural logic of mass incarceration. *The Dhamma Brothers'* brand of rehabilitation is precisely the rehabilitation of the penitentiary model in the original sense, but with the horizon of eventual social reintegration completely erased. For its prisoner practitioners, this faith surrenders fully not merely to the condition of incarceration, but to the condition of incarceration until death. As one featured practicing Buddhist lifer puts it, "Life without parole . . . means you're to be warehoused until you die. This is my home and I'm gonna do what I can to help make it the best place it can be. I want a nice place to live, too." Another man touts the program by comparing it to solitary confinement. It's like "going into lock up, but in a good way." As with Freud's grandson who, by repeatedly throwing his rattle out of his crib, turned the frustration of being a powerless infant into a game where it was he, himself, that wielded the power, Vipassana meditation is, for the residents of Donaldson Prison, the experience of punitive segregation, but where the determinative agency is no longer that of their captors, but theirs alone.[60]

Because of the residual shadow cast by the Nation of Islam, and because the War on Terror breeds a bad faith paranoia that anticipates a deserved comeuppance, people generally assume that incarcerated Muslims today are a politically radical breed.[61] Inasmuch as American prison religion is almost as diverse as American religion, a good number surely are, but, in our day and age, it is nothing like a general rule. At Pennsylvania's Graterford Prison, for one, the abolition religion of Malcolm X has been largely eclipsed.[62] Over the last twenty years, the economically and politically minded activist brand of Islam practiced by the former adherents of the Nation of Islam has all but died out. Taking its place as the predominant orientation has been

Salafism. Many Americans have become aware of Salafism's political incarnation through media representations of Saudi Arabia, but the species of Salafism that dominates at Graterford, and in African American communities more generally, is avowedly apolitical, even quietist. For Graterford's Salafi, the obligations of the Sunnah are limitless, but particular emphasis is placed on matters of individual comportment. Living righteously means praying, eating, and grooming oneself in strict emulation of the Prophet and his companions. To the degree that it is discussed at all, jihad pertains to the individual drive to puritanical perfection. As a set of practices, Salafism at Graterford is as totalizing as MOVE, but with the will to political mobilization hollowed out. As one elder explained his own lack of interest in politics, "first we have to get our own house in order."[63]

While persecution of politically minded African American Muslims since 9/11 has surely had a chilling effect, for the Salafi, the erasure of politics is about proper religious ethics.[64] For the Muslim Brotherhood at Clinton Prison and for the old guard at Graterford, religion was a tool of individual and group uplift; for the Salafi, to instrumentalize the Sunnah this way is anathema. From their perspective, to exploit the Sunnah for social and political ends necessarily means putting something else on par with God. This, for the Salafi, is the ultimate sin: *shirk*, blasphemy.

Without committing ourselves to a narrow causal explanation, it is impossible not to marvel at how, in the era of mass incarceration, the illiberal Islam practiced by Black men in American prisons has been brought into roundabout alignment with the normative liberal Protestantism promoted by the US Supreme Court. It took a couple of decades, but prisoners' religion in America was driven thoroughly inward.

A quarter-century after Cleaver published his Christian prison narrative, California death-row inmate Stanley Tookie Williams published *Blue Rage, Black Redemption*.[65] The book was widely acclaimed, and Williams was nominated for both the Nobel Peace Prize and the Nobel Prize in Literature. Like Cleaver and Jackson, Williams had grown up poor and Black, and he came to see himself as a victim of systemic injustice once he was incarcerated. A generation younger than Cleaver and Jackson, Williams from the start had fully internalized the belief that law and order were essential, personally and socially. Indeed, it had been this faith in law—a faith forged in a world simultaneously imbued with legal surplus (hyper-policing and hyper-incarceration) and legal scarcity (anomie and lawlessness)—that led him to found the Crips, the notorious American street gang. His neighborhood had been dangerous, with small neighborhood gangs constantly engaged in violent feuds. The young Williams consolidated the gang landscape, imposing order on the chaos by means of a super-gang bound by a strict code of conduct. Williams was committed not only to disciplining others, but also to self-discipline, spending hours each day weightlifting. After he was eventually imprisoned and sentenced to death, Williams acknowledged breaking many laws, though he denied committing the specific crime for which he was sentenced to die. In prison, Williams continued striving to maintain law and order on the street, drafting a twenty-two-page "Perpetual Peace Accord for Opposing Gangs," in the form of a legal contract complete with numerous clauses and subclauses. He also wrote children's books in which he admonished the young to follow the law.

Williams had never had much patience for organized religion. As a boy, his mother had taken him to church, but he spent the service flirting with girls. Later, in prison, Williams continued to use organized religion instrumentally, borrowing a dictionary from the prison chaplain and a thesaurus from the prison imam. While Williams never had a conversion moment in the style of evangelical Christianity, his religiosity would come to take the form of an embrace of a twenty-first-century spiritual-but-not-religious ethos. He structures his autobiography around chapters with titles such as "Voodoo Medicine," "Let There Be Light," and "Human Angel." Central to the book—which is, as its title suggests, a story of redemption—is a chapter titled "Moto Ndani," Swahili for "The Fire Within." In it, Williams describes renouncing his membership in the Crips and accepting a spirituality that takes the best parts of all the religions he encounters, including Christianity, Islam, Buddhism, and Afrocentric wisdom. "My intention is to connect with God based on my own merits, to obtain spiritual enrichment rather than focusing on a particular church or religion."[66] This is a thoroughly secular spirituality, one with no embarrassment about its instrumentalism, one, indeed, that conflates the religious with the pragmatic. As Williams explains, "I construct my faith around facts that can best help me to redeem myself."[67] Drawing on the shared wisdom of his incarcerated militant predecessors, Williams finds most useful those religious practices that enable him to craft a regime of self-discipline. He abstains from beef and pork, meditates, and prays facing Africa seven times a day—"or more, depending upon the spirit that moves me."[68]

On December 13, 2005, the state of California took the life of Stanley Tookie Williams. In his final public statement, Williams condemned the death penalty for its barbarism, but he evoked no sense of higher justice. Instead, he describes his faith in secularized evangelical terms and calls for others to join him in conversion. "I have been a wretched person, but I have redeemed myself. And I say to you and all those who can listen and will listen that redemption is tailor-made for the wretched, and that's what I used to be."[69] While, for Williams, recognizing the beauty of his own Blackness had been an important stage on the path to redemption, the vision of redemption that Williams preaches is for everyone, a redemption "not predicated on color or race or social stratum or one's religious background."[70] The vision Williams proclaims is at once personal and universal, and it takes emphatic account of a person's individuality and of the universe in its entirety. What the vision excludes is any criticism of what lies between, and it offers no systemic analysis or theory of social change. Economic, racial, or religious ideas need not be called into question as we each move toward redemption; the social world is left governed by laws—enforced by police and prisons. As big and powerful as God may be, in practice, there is no outside to this system.

A New Era of Protest

In many ways, Sanyika Shakur's life and writings parallel Tookie Williams's. Shakur was also a Crip; indeed, he had been a protégé of Williams. In 1993 he published *Monster*, a memoir of the exploits of his youth, when he went by the nom de guerre Monster Kody Scott.[71] Like Williams, Shakur realized in prison that his struggles as a poor, Black man were part of the systemic degradation of Black life, and he realized that Black is beautiful. The two men embraced a rich tradition of African thought and practice, including the Swahili language. Unlike Williams, Shakur did not then move on to an embrace of post-racial spirituality. Rather, Shakur finds redemption through the Black radical tradition. He renounces gang life in favor of a new identity, marked by a new name, as a member of the Republic of New Afrika, a political organization working toward creating a sovereign Black nation in the South's Black Belt. (They have had some success, particularly when member Chokwe Lumumba was elected mayor of Jackson, Mississippi, in 2013 after an intensive grassroots organizing effort.[72]) Shakur came to regret the way he framed his life as a story of personal redemption in *Monster*, and in a more politically oriented follow-up book published in 2013, he frames his life story as part of a broader struggle against racial and economic injustice.[73] Shakur describes his involvement in the Pelican Bay hunger strikes, portraying the 2011 strikes as building on a decade of organizing among indigenous, Latinx, and Black prisoners, all demanding, most fundamentally, "to be treated as human beings." Shakur remains suspicious of how institutional religions can capture the political energy of prisoners, and he urges that intellectual and practical struggle is needed inside prison walls to discern the form of a new movement for justice. In a sense, Shakur embraces the post-religious ethos of Williams, but he ties it to a version of justice beyond the laws of the world— and he insists that this justice cannot be known by anyone or any group in the world today. Discerning its shape and operationalizing its demands in struggle, in organizing, in opposition to the laws of the land, is rightly conceived as a task for all of us.[74]

Great pressure can only tamp things down for so long. At some point, what has been forced underground is liable to return—and perhaps explode. With Shakur among the group's leadership, on July 8, 2013, an estimated 30,000 men and women, spread across two-thirds of California's prisons, refused to take breakfast, and then lunch, and then dinner. The next day they did the same thing.

The 2013 California action was not *sui generis*. This was the third time in as many years that California's prisoners had gone on a hunger strike—the first two times were in 2011. The California actions eclipsed in size what had briefly been the largest prison strike in American history—a labor strike organized by prisoners across Georgia's prison system in late 2010 that was violently crushed. Since then, strikes of various forms have cropped up in dozens of state prisons, county jails, and immigrant detention facilities.

The present swell of prisoners' solidary actions represents the reclamation of a repressed American tradition of prisoners' resistance. But to limit our telling of emergent prisoners' solidarity to the lower 48 is to miss a crucial component of the story. Essential to the cultivation of this new moment were men kidnapped in Asia and Africa and placed indefinitely on an island beyond the reach of due process. The hunger strikes at Guantanamo Bay's Camp X-Ray began in the facility's first month in existence, in 2002, when an estimated 150 men refused food to protest the desecration of the Qur'an. Since then, groups of men at Guantanamo Bay have undertaken hunger strikes on at least thirteen occasions, and probably significantly more.[75]

Fittingly, it was at Guantanamo Bay, that apt symbol of out-of-control American militarism, and of cruel and unconstitutional punishment, that the new wave of prisoners' solidarity rightfully began. As it has come inland, revivifying the rich indigenous tradition of American prisoner protest, the movement has retained its internationalist vantage point. In an interview with the *Guardian*, one of the leaders of the California action, Todd Ashker, named among his influences Irish hunger striker Bobby Sands and the Arab Spring. A one-time Nazi gang member who is housed at the notorious Pelican Bay Prison, Ashker has been in prison since he was nineteen and has spent the last twenty-five years in solitary following his conviction for killing a fellow prisoner.[76] As the apotheosis of the culture of control, Pelican Bay's Secure Housing Unit (the system's euphemism for solitary) is where California sends its "worst of the worst." The overwhelming majority have been fingered as members of prison gangs, and those who refuse to "debrief" (inform on fellow prisoners) are kept there indefinitely, locked in their cell for all but ninety minutes a day.

From the prison administrator's standpoint—a perspective that within the cultural logic of mass incarceration presents as merely common sense—total confinement is, both as a remedy and a precaution, precisely what "the worst of the worst" are due. That such bad men would bellyache about their conditions goes without saying. As California's secretary of corrections, Jeffrey Beard, explained in an op-ed in the *Los Angeles Times*: "Some prisoners claim this strike is about living conditions. . . . Don't be fooled." In fact, "The inmates calling the shots are leaders in four of the most violent and influential prison gangs in California. . . . We're talking about convicted murderers who are putting lives at risk to advance their own agenda of violence."[77] As we saw with respect to the "so-called" religious organizations of incarcerated people, so too, now, when prisoners organize, what we see is far from what we're really getting. Where once religion was reduced to politics, now politics is reduced to gang violence.

The role of religion in this mass organizing is sometimes difficult to parse out. Inasmuch as the first hunger strikes protested the desecration of the Qur'an, religious commitments were essential to this emergence. In Georgia, a strike leader was a white convert to Islam who found inspiration in the words of the Qur'an, Martin Luther King, Marcus Garvey, and Malcolm X. In California, prison officials insist that the scheduling of the recent strike to coincide with Ramadan was a ruse to inflate the numbers, but this alignment between religion and politics surely says something about the ongoing potential of Muslim identities and practices for the purposes of oppositional mobilization, in and beyond the pragmatic.[78]

Ambiguous as well is just how "abolitionist" these protests are. As compared to the demands of King and Malcolm, of the Muslim Brotherhood and the Church of the New Song, the California hunger strikers' demands were quite modest. What they demanded was the abolition of indefinite lockdown and of mandatory debriefing about fellow prisoners' gang status; compliance with 2006 federal recommendations insuring that incarcerated people "have regular meaningful contact and freedom from extreme physical deprivations that are known to cause lasting harm," and that they are given "the opportunity to engage in meaningful self-help treatment, work, education, religious, and other productive activities relating to having a sense of being a part of the community"; the furnishing of nutritious food and the end to withholding food as punishment; and the development of programming and privileges for those in indefinite solitary confinement.[79] These demands are merely for modest reforms. As Keremet Reiter worries, the California strikes "raise the question of whether systemic change can be achieved without systemic critique."[80] We share this concern, but with a qualification. Thirty-thousand incarcerated men and women standing together at great personal risk to demand the end to systemic brutalities and to assert their entitlement to some semblance of a social world *is* systemic critique. Even when such actions do not explicitly articulate an alternative vision for justice, the mere fact of their existence stands as a broad-stroke gesture toward a new and more just world straining to be born.

In September 2016, on the forty-fifth anniversary of the Attica uprising, this ethos caught fire among prisoners in at least twelve different states.[81] That strike—the largest in the country's history, according to some—had been spearheaded by a religiously eclectic group of those incarcerated at Alabama's Holman Prison, who organized under the moniker of the Free Alabama Movement. Pushing a growing narrative about the Thirteenth Amendment's poisoned pill, the strike was above all else a performative act of labor power: "If we are to end Mass Incarceration and Prison Slavery, which only those caught up in the slave system can do, then we must Unify nationwide from inside of these prisons and we must stop our labor and LET THE CROPS ROT IN THE FIELD."[82] As with the California strikers, the demands of the Free Alabama Movement are not for the abolition of prisons as such. What is abolitionist, however, is the Free Alabama Movement's resurgent commitment to real, material freedom, and its refusal to countenance anything less.

There is no God-talk in "Let the Crops Rot in the Fields," and there is little ground for claiming the manifesto in the name of an earlier generation's abolition religion. What role religion will play in this generation of prison protest remains to be seen. Due to changes in law and prison administration, and also to changes in American religion, we may be certain that the terms of struggle this time around will be different. For one thing, the complete absence of "religious freedom" as a rallying cry for incarcerated people nowadays gives occasion to reflect, in retrospect, how strangely affirmative the oppositional legal discourses of the prisoners' rights era were. For incarcerated people these days, faith in the promises of the Constitution and in the institutions forged in its name are in meager supply. These days, when the Constitution enters the conversation about prisoners' freedom, it is not to invoke the First Amendment, but rather to critique the Thirteenth. Born of a disillusionment as grave as the conditions that cause it to arise, this nonetheless represents an encouraging turn, one that hints at the possibility of radical social transformation. To be sure, lawsuits over unconstitutional convictions, conditions, and prohibitions remain essential weapons in the struggle against prisons, but only with an abolitionist horizon in our sights can such incremental reforms hope to dislodge the entrenched power of the carceral state and prefigure a world without prisons.

Notes

1. Other first-tier canonical entries would include Paul, Boethius, Joan of Arc, Bunyan, Dostoevsky, and Solzhenitsyn, as well as the fictitious heroes of Dumas, Hugo, Kafka, and Nabokov, among many others. Among the many surveys of prison writing, particularly helpful for the US context is Caleb Smith, *The Prison and the American Imagination* (New Haven, CT: Yale University Press, 2011). Unsurprisingly, the United States has contributed bookshelves to this genre. From this vast array, we have chosen to focus on a particular genealogy of spiritual autobiographies penned by our carceral state's paradigmatic prey: African American men. Among those excluded by these parameters would be Jack Abbott, Leonard Peltier, Jimmy Santiago Baca, Jens Soering, Piper Kerman, and Assata Shakur, whom we engage in this book's final chapter. For an alternative survey of some of this literature, also attuned to justice but less focused on transforming conceptions of justice, see Michael Hames-García, *Fugitive Thought: Prison Movements, Race, and the Meaning of Justice* (Minneapolis: University of Minnesota Press, 2004).

2. As King writes in the letter's penultimate paragraph, without need for hyperbole, "We should never forget that everything Adolf Hitler did in Germany was 'legal' and everything the Hungarian freedom fighters did in Hungary was 'illegal.'" Martin Luther King Jr., "Letter from a Birmingham Jail," https://www.africa.upenn.edu/Articles_Gen/Letter_Birmingham.html.

3. Malcolm X, "Message to the Grassroots," in *Malcolm X Speaks: Selected Speeches and Statements*, ed. George Breitman (New York: Grove Press, 1994), 3–17.

4. Malcolm X with Alex Haley, *The Autobiography of Malcolm X: As Told to Alex Haley* (New York: Ballantine Books, 1992).

5. While this is sometimes presented as a late realization on Malcolm's part, a search for allies after his break with the Nation of Islam, it was in fact in prison that Malcolm was able to study the nonwhite world in all its variety.

6. King, "Letter from a Birmingham Jail."

7. On the complicated intersection between American religion and the surveillance state, see Sylverster A. Johnson and Steven Weitzman, eds., *The FBI and Religion: Faith and National Security Before and After 9/11* (Berkeley: University of California Press, 2017).

8. This point is elaborated on in Vincent Lloyd, "Eldridge Cleaver, George Jackson, and the Ethics of Love," in *Anti-Blackness and Christian Ethics*, ed. Vincent Lloyd and Andrew Prevot (Maryknoll, NY: Orbis Books, 2017), 131–149.

9. Eldridge Cleaver, *Soul on Ice* (New York: Delta, 1999), 17.

10. Ibid., 44.

11. George Jackson, *Soledad Brother: The Prison Letters of George Jackson* (Chicago: Chicago Review Press, 1994), 3.

12. Eldridge Cleaver, *Soul on Fire* (Waco, TX: Word Books, 1978), 7.

13. Ibid., 211.

14. Others have ably made this point: Hames-García, *Fugitive Thought*; Dylan Rodríguez, *Forced Passages: Imprisoned Radical Intellectuals and the U.S. Prison Regime* (Minneapolis: University of Minnesota Press, 2006); Joy James, ed., *The New Abolitionists: (Neo)slave Narratives And Contemporary Prison Writings* (Albany: State University of New York Press, 2005).

15. James Baldwin, *No Name in the Street* (New York: Vintage, 2007), 149.

16. This "Muslim Brotherhood" has no relationship to al-Ikhwān al-Muslimūn, the group founded in Egypt and known in English by the same name.

17. *Pierce v. LaVallee*, 212 F. Supp. 865 (1962).

18. Dr. Michael Waller, Testimony, US Senate, Committee on the Judiciary, Subcommittee on Terrorism, Technology and Homeland Security, October 14, 2003.

19. "Religious genius" is a category introduced by William James in *Varieties of Religious Experience*.

20. *Theriault v. Carlson*, 339 F. Supp. 375 (N.D. Ga. 1972).

21. *Africa v. Pennsylvania*, 662 F. 2d 1025 (1981). For background on MOVE's religiosity and litigation, see Richard Kent Evans, "MOVE: Religion, Secularism, and the Politics of Classification" (PhD diss., Temple University, 2018). Evans is expanding

his dissertation into *MOVE: An American Religion* (New York: Oxford University Press, forthcoming).

22. Beginning in 2018, surviving members of the MOVE 9 began to receive parole. As of this writing, only Chuck Sims Africa, Delbert Orr Africa, and Eddie Goodman Africa remain incarcerated. They have been imprisoned since 1978.

23. This secularist tendency is observable in Dan Berger's useful 2014 book, *The Struggle Within: Prisons, Political Prisoners, and Mass Movements in the United States*. Berger counts among the "most significant" prisoners' movements as follows: "the national liberation struggles of Black/New Afrikan, Puerto Rican, Indigenous, and Chicano people; antiracist solidarity and opposition to U.S. imperialism; revolutionary nonviolence against the state's ability to wage war; and, more recently, activists incarcerated for their actions on behalf of earth and animal liberation." Black and ethnic nationalism, anti-racism, anti-imperialism, and environmentalism: all secularist projects. Religious stuff appears in the creases of Berger's story, in, for example, the nonviolent Catholic Plowshares movement and the hunger strikes undertaken by members of the American Indian Movement in pursuit of protection for Native American spiritual practices, but in sum, religious ideas and practices are not credited with playing a constitutive role in the tradition of U.S. prisoners' radicalism. Dan Berger, *The Struggle Within: Prisons, Political Prisoners, and Mass Movements in the United States* (Oakland, CA: PM Press, 2014), 4. For a substantially thicker account of the same terrain, see Berger's *Captive Nation: Black Prison Organizing in the Civil Rights Era* (Chapel Hill: University of North Carolina Press, 2016). See also James, *The New Abolitionists*.

24. Patrick D. Bowen, *A History of Conversion to Islam in the United States: The African American Islamic Renaissance, 1920–1975* (Leiden: Brill, 2017); Michael A. Gomez, *Black Crescent: The Experience and Legacy of African Muslims in the Americas* (Cambridge: Cambridge University Press, 2005); Richard Brent Turner, *Islam in the African-American Experience* (Bloomington: Indiana University Press, 2003).

25. *Pierce v. LaVallee*.

26. Ibid.

27. While the claim would be difficult to quantify precisely, there is reason to assume that the rise of radical religion in American prisons also signaled the rise of religion in prisons more generally. In the canonical prison ethnographies of the prior era, such as Donald Clemmer, *The Prison Community* (Christopher Publishing House, 1940) and Gresham M. Sykes, *The Society of Captives: A Study of a Maximum Security Prison* (Princeton, NJ: Princeton University Press, 1958), religion gets barely a mention. By John Irwin's *The Felon* (Berkeley: University of California Press, 1970), religion, primarily the Nation of Islam, is treated as a central sociological feature.

28. Sarah Barringer Gordon, *The Spirit of the Law: Religious Voices and the Constitution in Modern America* (Cambridge, MA: Harvard University Press, 2010), 112; Garrett Felber, "'Shades of Mississippi': The Nation of Islam's Prison Organizing, the Carceral State, and the Black Freedom Struggle," *Journal of American History* 105, no. 1 (2018), 71–95.

29. If the connection between Martin Sostre, the Muslim Brotherhood founder, and Davis is figurative, the connection between the Muslim Brotherhood and Attica is literal. A key precipitating factor in the rebellion was the perception that undo restrictions were being placed on Muslims' free religious exercise, and once things escalated, members of the Muslim faction labored concertedly to protect the imprisoned prison guards. There is little to be gained from conceptualizing the Attica rebellion as some sort of "Muslim" action, but without the ingredient of militant Islam, Attica would have gone quite differently, and might not have happened at all. On Attica, see Tom Wicker, *A Time to Die: The Attica Prison Revolt* (Chicago: Haymarket, 2011); and Heather Ann Thompson, *Blood in the Water: The Attica Prison Uprising of 1971 and Its Legacy* (New York: Pantheon, 2016).

30. See James Jacobs, *New Perspectives on Prisons and Imprisonment* (Ithaca, NY: Cornell University Press, 1983), 33–60; and Marie Gottschalk, *The Prison and the Gallows: The Politics of Mass Incarceration in America* (Cambridge: Cambridge University Press, 2006), 165–196. This was especially the case in the federal system and in state systems in the North. For the entire historical sweep, see Dan Berger and Toussaint Losier, *Rethinking the American Prison Movement* (New York: Routledge, 2018).

31. Later reincarcerated on a politically motivated, trumped-up charge, Sostre became a cause célèbre. See Vincent Copeland, *The Crime of Martin Sostre* (New York: McGraw-Hill, 1970).

32. *The Gospel of the New Song for the People of Life*, vii–xii. *Theriault v. Silber,* court records.

33. On "jurispathic courts," see Robert Cover, "Nomos and Narrative," *Harvard Law Review* 97, no. 4 (1983), 4–66, especially 40–54.

34. Legal Historian Sarah Barringer Gordon places Martin Sostre and the Muslim Brotherhood into a genealogy of American popular constitutionalism. Gordon's story is one of "stubborn vitality," of "raucous and inventive religious actors" who fought for and secured what came to be perceived as the fundamental First Amendment rights of all Americans (Gordon, *The Spirit of the Law,* 9). In Sostre, Gordon hears the echoes of Frederick Douglass. "Like other black activists in the mid-twentieth century, [the Muslim Brotherhood] deployed the descendant of constitutional claims that were first developed in the great nineteenth-century struggles over slavery" (119). And in so doing, they radically expanded the religious freedoms of incarcerated Americans. The Brotherhood's "activism increased access and rights to practice for all religious groups in prison. To prison officials in the 1960s, the Nation of Islam represented the outer boundary of danger. And yet, because Muslims had the right to practice, other minority faiths were swept into the same protective constitutional embrace" (123).

Framed in this way, prisoners' abolition religion may be placed in the grand Tocquevillian tradition of American democracy. In the historiography of American religion, this story is not unfamiliar. It's a story of how religious outsiders shake up and reanimate the cultural status quo, perhaps most notably, as in this case, by dragging the Constitution—often kicking and screaming, and never all the way— toward the fulfillment of its originary promises. For more on this, see, for example, R.

Laurence Moore, *Religious Outsiders and the Making of Americans* (New York: Oxford University Press, 1987).

35. A case could be made that the publication of political philosopher John Rawls's *A Theory of Justice* in 1971 represented a turning point. For an American elite that grew up on Rawls's text as the cornerstone of contemporary political thought, the book's analytic treatment of justice tamed and contained the concept's earlier ways of imagining justice that were less secular, less constrained by the world's concepts. Thanks to Eric Gregory for this suggestion.

36. For the canonical postmortem on these efforts, see John Sexton, "Toward a Constitutional Definition of Religion," *Harvard Law Review* 91, no. 5 (1978), 1056–1089.

37. *United States v. Seeger*, 380 U.S. 163 (1965).

38. *Theriault v. Silber*, 391 F. Supp. 578 (W.D. Tex. 1975). Writes the court: "The Church of the New Song appears not to be a religion, but rather as a masquerade designed to obtain First Amendment protection for acts which otherwise would be unlawful and/ or reasonably disallowed by the various prison authorities but for the attempts which have been and are being made to classify them as 'religious' and, therefore, presumably protected by the First Amendment."

   In her 2004 appearance on the *The Daily Show* to promote her book *God vs. the Gavel*, legal scholar Marci Hamilton played the sherry and steak bit for laughs to show just how silly 1970s free-exercise jurisprudence had become. Hamilton wrote that because the "Supreme Court's free-exercise jurisprudence bent over backward for believers to the detriment of the public good," the federal court was unable to see the Church of the New Song for what it plainly was: "a game." For Hamilton, the Church was "a classic case of a group testing the waters with insincere claims of religious devotion. Common sense should have sent their free-exercise claims packing." Marci Hamilton, *God vs. the Gavel: The Perils of Extreme Religious Liberty* (New York: Cambridge University Press, 2005), 162–163.

   After poring through many volumes of Harry Theriault's massive corpus, the Church of the New Song remains for us, to a significant degree, an intriguing mystery. But in her brief against CONS, Hamilton confidently goes straight for the steaks and sherry. This is telling. That she appeals to "common sense" in making her case is even more so. Hamilton's classification of CONS as a "so-called religion" capitalizes on the stereotype of the religious prisoner as the paradigmatic exception to the *Seeger* test's sincerity clause. The would-be religious prisoner, Hamilton trusts that her reader knows, is a villain, a player of "games." But unlike the more comprehensive sense of the "game," as one finds it in practice theory, here the "game" is a much more refined entity. It is that which is done self-consciously as artifice. It is fraud. For more on Harry Theriault and the Church of the New Song, see Joshua Dubler, "The Secular Bad Faith of Harry Theriault, Bishop of Tellus," in *Secular Faith*, ed. Vincent W. Lloyd and Elliot A. Ratzman (Eugene, OR: Cascade, 2011), 44–75.

39. For more on this point, see Joshua Dubler, *Down in the Chapel: Religious Life in an American Prison* (New York: Farrar, Straus and Giroux, 2013).

40. *Pierce v. LaVallee*.

41. *Theriault v. Silber,* 452 F. Supp 254 (1978).

42. Paul Tillich, *Systematic Theology,* vol. 1 (Chicago: University of Chicago Press, 1973), 12.

43. John Africa did not record his lessons by hand, but during a period of isolation he received a revelation of God's law that he dictated to his sister and which circulates in manuscript. See Evans, "MOVE."

44. Louise Africa, "On the MOVE," *Philadelphia Tribune* (August 30, 1975), as quoted in Evans, "MOVE." As Evans glosses MOVE people's abolitionist stance toward law: "According to the Teachings of John Africa, the most egregious—indeed the most *sacrilegious*—aspect of humankind's false worship of progress was the creation of law. To MOVE people, belonging to MOVE meant rejecting human law as a sacrilege of divine law, the Law of Mama."

45. *Africa v. Pennsylvania,* 662 F. 2d 1025 (1981). Evans attributes the court's view to anti-Black racism conjoined to secularism, which makes Black religion in need of policing by secularism, in secular terms. See Evans, "MOVE."

46. See Jason Osder, dir., *Let the Fire Burn* (2013).

47. Naomi Klein, *The Shock Doctrine: The Rise of Disaster Capitalism* (New York: Picador, 2008).

48. See Francis A. Allen, *The Decline of the Rehabilitative Ideal: Penal Policy and Social Purpose* (New Haven, CT: Yale University Press, 1981). In the second essay of Nietzsche's *Genealogy of Morals,* punishment is the paradigmatic case for how practices endure even as the meanings of those practices change. Ruth Wilson Gilmore has noted the irony of how philosophically unambitious the 1980s–1990s expansion of the carceral state was. Whereas in earlier eras, prison builders and administrators painted psychologically complex pictures of incarceration's deterrent and rehabilitative effects, cheerleaders for mass incarceration largely spoke about the need to "keep bad guys off the street."

49. See Lorna A. Rhodes, *Total Confinement: Madness and Reason in the Maximum Security Prison* (Berkeley: University of California Press, 2004); Keramet Reiter, *23/7: Pelican Bay Prison and the Rise of Long-Term Solitary Confinement* (New Haven, CT: Yale University Press, 2016). For greater social context, see David Garland, *The Culture of Control: Crime and Social Order in Contemporary Society* (Chicago: University of Chicago Press, 2002).

50. Eric Cummins, *The Rise and Fall of California's Radical Prison Movement* (Stanford, CA: Stanford University Press, 1994).

51. Joshua Dubler, *Down in the Chapel,* 73.

52. Charles W. Colson, *My Final Word: Holding Tight to the Issues That Matter Most* (Grand Rapids, MI: Zondervan, 2015), 97.

53. Quoted in Winnifred Fallers Sullivan, *Prison Religion: Faith-Based Reform and the Constitution* (Princeton, NJ: Princeton University Press, 2011), 32.

54. Ibid., 9.

55. Ibid., 41–42.

56. Ibid., 54.

57. Ibid., 39.

58. Productive counterarguments to these criticisms may be drawn from Svetlana Boym's discussions about Dostoevsky in *Another Freedom: The Alternative History of an Idea* (Chicago: University of Chicago Press, 2012).

59. All quotations from Jenny Phillips, dir., *The Dhamma Brothers* (2008). For similar claims about Vajrayana Buddhism, see Jarvis Jay Masters, *Finding Freedom: Writings from Death Row* (Junction City, CA: Padma Publishing, 1997).

60. Sigmund Freud, *Beyond the Pleasure Principle*, trans. James Strachey, Standard Edition of the Complete Psychological Works of Sigmund Freud, vol. 18 (New York: W. W. Norton, 1990), 14–15.

61. See Mark S. Hamm, *The Spectacular Few: Prisoner Radicalization and the Evolving Terrorist Threat* (New York: New York University Press, 2013).

62. In 2018, Graterford was closed and those who lived there were moved to a new prison on the same grounds, SCI Phoenix.

63. Dubler, *Down in the Chapel*, 227. Worth noting is that in the wake of Supreme Court decisions in *Miller v. Alabama* and *Montgomery v. Louisiana*, which retroactively barred the statutory imposition of the sentence of life without parole on juvenile offenders, this elder was resentenced and released.

64. On Salafism in Philadelphia, see Joel Blecher and Joshua Dubler, "Overlooking Race and Secularism in Muslim Philadelphia," in *Race and Secularism in America*, ed. Jonathon S. Kahn and Vincent W. Lloyd (New York: Columbia University Press, 2016), 122–152.

65. Stanley Tookie Williams, *Blue Rage, Black Redemption: A Memoir* (New York: Simon & Schuster, 2007).

66. Ibid., 293.

67. Ibid.

68. Ibid.

69. Stanley Tookie Williams and Amy Goodman, "Stanley Tookie Williams: I Want the World to Remember Me for My 'Redemptive Transition,'" *Democracy Now!*, http://www.democracynow.org/2005/12/13/stanley_tookie_williams_i_want_the.

70. Ibid.

71. Kody Scott, *Monster: The Autobiography of an L.A. Crip* (New York: Atlantic Monthly Press, 1993).

72. See Kali Akuno and Ajamu Nangwaya, eds., *Jackson Rising: The Struggle for Economic Democracy and Black Self-Determination in Jackson, Mississippi* (Montreal: Daraja Press, 2017).

73. Sanyika Shakur, *Stand Up, Struggle Forward: New Afrikan Revolutionary Writings on Nation, Class and Patriarchy* (Montreal: Kersplebedeb, 2013).

74. For comparable thought among contemporary incarcerated writers, see Mumia Abu Jamal, *Live from Death Row* (New York: Harper Perennial, 1996); and Fred Ho and Quincy Saul, eds., *Maroon the Implacable: The Collected Writings of Russell Maroon Shoatz* (Oakland, CA: PM Press, 2013).

75. In 2013 the military announced that it would no longer disclose hunger strikes to the public. As a spokesman explained, "The release of this information serves no operational purpose and detracts from the more important issues." Associated Press,

"Guantanamo Detainees' Hunger Strikes Will No Longer Be Disclosed by U.S. Military," *Washington Post* (December 4, 2013), https://www.washingtonpost.com/world/national-security/guantanamo-detainees-hunger-strikes-will-no-longer-be-disclosed-by-us-military/2013/12/04/f6b1aa96-5d24-11e3-bc56-c6ca94801fac_story.html.

76. For further biographical information, and for further information on Pelican Bay, see Reiter, *23/7.*

77. Jeffrey Beard, "Hunger Strike in California Prisons Is a Gang Power Play," *Los Angeles Times* (August 6, 2013), http://articles.latimes.com/2013/aug/06/opinion/la-oe-beard-prison-hunger-strike-20130806.

78. The tactic also suggests a cunning for negotiating the administrative will to punish: "Inmates reached by The Times said [the timing] provided a measure of protection for Muslim inmates participating in the protest, who were less likely to be cited for violating rules." Paige St John, "29,000 California Prison Inmates Refuse Meals in 2nd Day of Protest," *Los Angeles Times* (July 9, 2013), http://articles.latimes.com/2013/jul/09/local/la-me-ff-prison-strike-20130710.

79. "Prisoners' Demands," Prisoner Hunger Strike Solidarity (June 3, 2011), https://prisonerhungerstrikesolidarity.wordpress.com/education/the-prisoners-demands-2/.

80. Keramet Reiter, "The Pelican Bay Hunger Strike: Resistance within the Structural Constraints of a US Supermax Prison," *South Atlantic Quarterly* 113, no. 3 (2014), 579–611, 605.

81. Beth Schwartzapfel, "Why America's Incarcerated Have Launched the Largest Prison Strike in Recent History," *AlterNet* (September 28, 2016), https://www.alternet.org/human-rights/why-americas-incarcerated-have-launched-largest-prison-strike-recent-history. Jeff Spross, "Why No One Knows about the Largest Prison Strike in U.S. History," *The Week* (October 18, 2016), http://theweek.com/articles/655609/why-no-knows-about-largest-prison-strike-history.

82. Free Alabama Movement, "Let the Crops Rot in the Fields," https://freealabamamovement.wordpress.com/2015/02/26/let-the-crops-rot-in-the-fields/.

5

The Spirit of Abolition

Denmark Vesey, a leader at the AME Church in Charleston, interpreted the Bible for classes of free Blacks and the enslaved. For his students, the epic of the Israelites' Exodus from Egypt was already widely resonant, but Vesey paid special attention to Exodus 21, in which God mandates death for "he that stealeth a man and selleth him."[1] In Vesey's typological reading, African Methodists were the new Israelites, but his conceptualization of judgment was, in the case of slavery, flat and literal. Those who violated biblical law by stealing and enslaving men and women were justly owed the penalty of death. When, in 1822, he and his followers planned an insurrection to take place on Bastille Day, local authorities caught wind of the conspiracy. Thirty-five men, including Vesey, were arrested, convicted, and hanged, and the church was burned to the ground. The uprising was a failure, but for decades to come, abolitionists would find inspiration in Vesey's dreams and in Vesey's sacrifice.[2]

David Walker, a Black Bostonian, pursued the "holy cause" of abolition with the 1829 publication of his fiery four-part *Appeal . . . to the Colored Citizens of the World*. His demands: that white Christians repent their barbarism and heathenism, and that his fellow colored people rise up in pursuit of liberty. For Walker, slavery made a mockery of the "God of justice," and radical hypocrisy of this sort required unyielding opposition. As Walker wrote, "The Lord has a suffering people, whose moans and groans at his feet for deliverance from oppression and wretchedness, pierce the very throne of Heaven, and call loudly on the God of Justice, to be revenged."[3] Walker's *Appeal* was a cultural sensation. Printed three times, copies of the pamphlet were circulated among enslaved and free Blacks in Virginia and North Carolina, and they were brought by sailors to Charleston and New Orleans.[4]

As Walker was finalizing his *Appeal*, William Lloyd Garrison delivered to his fellow Christians a blistering polemic in lieu of a July Fourth oration. Extolling Christianity's imperial power that had tamed "red men," abolished caste, overthrown pagan gods, and liberated lands from superstition, he marveled bitterly at Christianity's curious powerlessness in the face of anti-Black racism. Is Christianity "yet so weak, in her own dwelling-place, that she can make no impression upon her civil code? Can she contend successfully with cannibals, and yet be conquered by her own children?"[5] Garrison lectured up and down the eastern seaboard and left a smoldering trail of abolitionists in his wake. For Unitarian pastor Samuel May, hearing Garrison lecture was nothing short of a religious experience. "That night my soul was baptized in his spirit, and ever since I have been a disciple and fellow-laborer of William Lloyd Garrison."[6] May was far from alone in this regard. Filled with the abolition spirit, barnstorming Presbyterian minister Charles Finney brought abolitionism to the Burned-Over District (burned over with religious fervor, it was said) of western New York, and he helped to seed the soil for what a decade later would grow into the Underground Railroad. Religious revival stoked and spread a variety of sentiments, but among them was a frontier fervor that all men ought to be free.

In the gathering cultural upheaval that inspired Garrison and the publication of his newspaper, the *Liberator*, men and women, white and Black, founded local anti-slavery societies.[7] At once sanctuaries and incubators, in these social spaces men and women plotted and prayed, read and wrote, convened public demonstrations, and, when called for, stood in solidarity in the face of mob violence.[8] This gathering mass at the center gave cover to more radical forms of direct action, such as when, in 1836, a crowd of two thousand free Blacks rushed the courthouse in Boston to enable two free Black women who were being jailed as fugitive slaves to escape.[9] A civil authority that justified slavery and kidnapping offended God and needed to be confronted. Abolition, these men and women came to believe, was something that needed to happen not eventually, not someday soon, but now.[10] Slavery was still far from over, but the fire that would eventually consume it would not be extinguished until it was. Abolition religion was aflame.[11]

Whence springs the magical intersection of urgency and opportunity required to collectively annihilate monumental injustice? The idea that slavery could and should be abolished under law had percolated for a good hundred and fifty years on American soil before it became for members of the middle class a viable political orientation. For the abolitionists of the nineteenth century, the drive came from without and from below. It was the revolution in Haiti—"the glory of blacks and the terror of tyrants"—that inspired David Walker to author his 1829 *Appeal*.[12] And it was, among other things, Nat Turner's 1831 uprising—"a dastardly triumph, well becoming a nation of oppressors"—that motivated Garrison to convene another group of activists two years later, once again in Philadelphia, and found the American Anti-Slavery Society (AASS).[13] Within seven years the AASS had a quarter of a million members. Much work was left to be done, but the movement that would eventually end slavery had its spirit and was beginning to acquire its necessary mass.

Almost two hundred years later, Americans once again find themselves on the cusp of a social movement to eradicate an entrenched injustice generally thought to be immutable. Once again, the drive has come from without and from below: from the heroes in Tahrir Square and elsewhere who inspired Occupy Wall Street; to a group of young people in Ferguson, Missouri, who, simply by refusing to go home, transformed a generic tragedy into an iconic one; to incarcerated people around the country who, at great risk to themselves, are demonstrating in support of the heretofore radical principle that slave labor is wrong, even in cases where the slave laborer has been convicted of a felony.

As developed first by innovators, and then disseminated and reproduced through social media and local organizing, a new vocabulary of abolitionist ideas and practices has lurched into availability. The day a grand jury announced Michael Brown's killer would not face indictment, 1,400 activists in Boston shut down I-93. Demonstrators blocking traffic risked their bodily integrity in order to disrupt everyday normalcy, calling attention to the ways in which Black and brown bodies are systematically confined and disfigured, much as poor neighborhoods were systematically disfigured in the 1960s when, in the name of urban renewal, highways like I-93 were cut through them. Shortly before 8:30 that evening, the protesters came to South Bay Prison, where they clotted to a raucous halt. In the barred windows above them, incarcerated people, lit from behind by fluorescent lights, appeared in silhouette. Necks craned upward; the crowd chanted "We see you! We see you! We see you!" On the other side of the glass and metal, the prisoners flashed lights off and on, beat on the bars, and shouted silently in return.[14]

The first-draft histories of our new social movements have rendered these struggles in overwhelmingly secular terms.[15] Occasionally, religious organizers get some attention—such as William Barber and the Moral Mondays folk in North Carolina—but religion has in no way been a dominant theme.[16] Some of religion's absence is an elision born of the secularist lenses of the scholars and journalists doing the reporting. But a good part of the absence is expressive of some of what makes this new moment so fresh. Long authorized by tradition and script, aging preachers are no longer the default bearers of moral and communal authority. Instead, a new class of youth leaders rooted in courage and urgency have seized those mantles. As the St. Louis-raised, Baptist-ordained Reverend Osagyefo Sekou characterized this group:

> This movement in Ferguson is not led by cufflink-wearing preachers. It's led by mostly queer young Black women. I take my orders from 23-year-old queer Black women. They push all kinds of buttons of Black respectability because they don't look the way we think they're supposed to look, it doesn't sound the way it's supposed to sound, these young people say, "Fuck the police." Because they're angry, they're hurt, they're broken, and they're not subjugated to the language of comfort and convenience.[17]

The "nones" are here—but they won't end religion in America, they will only end religion in America as we've known it, supplanting what we've come to expect with remixed and innovative forms of religion and irreligion.[18] The generational shift of moral authority is an expression of this new social configuration, and of the incipient power this shake-up portends.

As was on display in the Boston jail vigil, the new era of protest and organizing has shown an intuitive appreciation for the power of religious and religion-like rituals and symbols. Community organizing meetings are awash in ritual creativity. Imbricated by the abolition spirit and will to radical social transformation, community organizers tell stories and solicit stories back; engineer rites of solidarity and commitment; develop liturgies; and foster practices where affects are stirred up, sacred principles are declared and reinforced, mutual accountability is engendered, and collective power is grown.[19]

A religious spirit may also be observed in the more diffuse rituals of the digital age. Consider, for example, hashtag activism—the practice of people signal-boosting a cause or injustice on social media. Placed in the context of Americans' residually religious sensibility, may not hashtag activism rightly be conceived as an act of witness? This is the case when that which is being testified to is simply the declaration of an important truth, and it is especially the case when the practice entails honoring, by word or video, the death of a martyr. Not merely religious, what we're talking about is specifically Christian, though it resonates well beyond the bounds of Christendom, both between religions and beyond religion. Michael Brown, Eric Garner, Sandra Bland, Philando Castile—these are Christological figures, and for those who share their names and admonish others to witness the evidence of their killings, their deaths carry with them the whispered hope of redemption.[20]

"The best of the Black Church tradition," says Newark-based organizer Nyle Fort, is that "death doesn't get to have the last word."[21] In 2014 Fort preached at Trenton's Shiloh Baptist, employing a liturgy that drew inspiration from the final words of seventeen-year old, Jordan Davis. In response to being told by a middle-aged white man at a gas station to turn down his music, Davis said to his friend, "Fuck that, ni—a! Turn that shit up!" Davis was shot and killed. In and to a Black church tempted by the capitalist individualism of the prosperity gospel, Fort announces that he intended to explicate the sacred text produced by Davis: Davis's last words. In so doing, Fort amplified the dissidence:

> We no longer have the language to tell the truth about the hell we're catching as Black people living under the yoke of this American empire. So the miracle of Jordan Davis, my brothers and my sisters, is that he was able to articulate what the church and the larger faith community simply cannot. Now I understand that this may be difficult for some of us to receive, and that's okay. The sun-baked Palestinian and Jewish political prisoner, Jesus, wasn't well received either. Truth . . . is rarely received easily. But the reality is that Jordan Davis did in a few seconds what the church was unable to do for 500 years. That is: call out the demon of white racial supremacy in the name of justice.[22]

Telling the truth necessitates that we name and decry abominable things. "Some things need to be called out and cursed," Fort preached. "Enough is enough. It's time today to curse the American idols of white supremacy and police brutality, of institutionalized racism and anti-Black state violence." Notably and exceptionally, in cursing these American idols, Fort decidedly did *not* do the conventional thing. He did *not* plaintively demand that state violence merely—and at long last—be properly directed toward its rightfully deserving objects. If not this, then what does cursing these abominable things look like in practice? Fort charted a far more affirmative course:

> Every time we love on one another, we curse white supremacy. Every time we reject individualism and organize our communities we curse police brutality. Every time we don't allow ourselves to become a token in and by the system we curse capitalism and its neoliberal nature. . . . Every time we fight

against mass incarceration we curse the history and legacy of slavery. . . .
Every time we challenge oppressive legislation we curse the criminal injustice system.

The will to life-affirming resistance afforded by Christological suffering has
a decidedly double edge, of course. The martyrdoms of Emmett Till and
Michael Brown have catalyzed civil rights struggles, but their blood has done
little to stop the machines generating premature Black death from churning.
Spectacles of Christological suffering, and of Black Christological suffering
in particular, are reliable stirrers of sentiment and conviction, but we worry
about their tendency to promise a deliverance that somehow never arrives.
The martyrdom of Black bodies buried too soon, we would insist, is but one
piece of a vernacular of religious tropes and rituals available to us. This religious stuff has the power to voice prophetic fury at grave injustices all too
systemic, and to help us stammer into speech sketches of what true justice
might look like. Inspired by abolitionists past, in this chapter we look for new
ways of thinking justice and living justly. As we will show, this demands that
we continue to bear witness and to critique, but it also compels us to dream
and to launch experiments in our communities that may prefigure an abolitionist future. We cannot predict what will result from such openings, or
how we get from here to the just world we must collectively struggle to build.
Whatever this new world will eventually be, we are in the earliest stages of
its beginnings. Bringing this new world into existence will take massive collective imagining and collective organizing. But once each of us accepts that
putting human beings in cages isn't necessary—and that indeed any chance
we have of realizing justice on earth demands that we relegate this accursed
practice to history's dustbin—we nudge that new world one step closer to its
realization.

Love and Struggle, Freedom and Restoration

Since #Black Lives Matter began, the words of Assata Shakur have circulated
far and wide on social media, in organizing meetings, and on the streets: "It is
our duty to fight for our freedom. / It is our duty to win. / We must love each
other and support each other. / We have nothing to lose but our chains."[23]
Before she was a cultural icon, before she was a prison escapee in exile, before she was a political prisoner, Shakur was an astute observer of religion. As

she describes in her autobiography, even when she was a child down South, she had never been "holy-holy," but she watched with interest as her fellow Black church congregants " 'got happy' or 'got the spirit' or jumped around all over the place." Up in Queens, New York, she was taken in by, and baptized in, a Catholic church whose rigid ritualism, perverse doctrines, and baroque "spookiness" quite simply "overwhelmed" her. As Shakur later wrote with her inimitable, frank irony, "It was all so spooky i just knew that this had to be the real god."[24]

Once incarcerated, Shakur rejected Christian nonviolence: "[N]obody in the world, nobody in history, has ever gotten their freedom by appealing to the moral sense of the people who were oppressing them."[25] Nor, despite a mild sense of affinity, could Shakur get with Islam. In a world with "enslavement, torture, and murder of Black people," the idea of an omniscient, omnipotent God was for her simply too far-fetched and off-putting.[26] Eschewing revelation religions, Shakur cultivated instead thoughts of her "ancestors," people who had brought babies into this world only to see them tortured but who had survived through struggle. Where Shakur landed spiritually was in an ardent religious naturalism, a fierce commitment to living life in all of its fullness. In the world as we find it—a world that "can be beautiful and so ugly at the same time,"[27] where "cowboys and bandits" presently hold sway—this necessarily entails a life lived in righteous refusal.[28] "I am about life," a pregnant Shakur reminded herself in her jail cell, steeling herself to refuse her prison doctor's recommendation to abort her unborn child. "I'm gonna live as hard as i can and as full as i can until i die. And i'm not letting these parasites, these oppressors, these greedy racist swine make me kill my children in my mind, before they are even born."[29]

Forgoing divinity or transcendence, Shakur finds the experiences of pregnancy, childbirth, and motherhood to be "miraculous" and "deeply spiritual."[30] Shakur's is a spirituality of vitalism, a spirituality of beautiful struggle and glorious survival, a way of being and being fully that connects her to her sisters and brothers, incarcerated and free, that connects her back to "Ghana and Mali and Timbuktu," and that connects her through her body and being to her children, and onward to their children. Her chosen name captures the various components of an abolition spirituality: Assata, "she who struggles"; Olugbala, "love for the people"; and Shakur, "the thankful." A will to fight injustice, a love of kin, and a gratitude to the sources of her being: a model for revolutionary piety, this is the abolition spirit of Assata Shakur.

Whether explicitly abolitionist or not, whether in conjunction with old-time religion or not, the spirit of abolition continues to animate prison protest movements today, in the streets and in our prisons. Across the state of Georgia in 2010, incarcerated people organized what was then the largest prison labor strike in history. With publicity coordinated from the outside by former Black Panther leader Elaine Brown, the strikers demanded a living wage, educational opportunities, decent healthcare, healthy meals, and other prerequisites to human dignity. "No more slavery. Injustice in one place is injustice to all," the prisoners proclaimed.[31] Like subsequent strikes in California, Alabama, and elsewhere, the Georgia work stoppages involved incarcerated white, Black, and Latinx people coordinating their nonviolent collective action. Because of how prison authorities responded, the strike did not remain peaceful; strikers were brutalized and the leaders isolated.

One of those leaders, Imam Hamim Abdullah Muadh-Dhin Asadallah, describes himself as a "European Muslim who sincerely loves Allah and his messenger and all Black people." [32] Mocked by some prison guards as the "white Martin Luther King" for his strike leadership, Asadallah explains that he was beaten by three white guards "because of the prison strike, my religion—my way of life—and because of my love for Black people." Denied medical attention, Asadallah was transferred and had his personal property confiscated—and when it was returned, the photograph of his Black Muslim wife had a racist slur scrawled across it. After months in solitary confinement in a cell whose walls were stained with blood, and allowed only one weekly shower, Asadallah appealed to secular and religious organizations for support. He wrote to the NAACP, the Nation of Islam, the Southern Center for Human Rights, and Dr. Boyce Watkins. To mobilize support, his wife continued in the ecumenical appeal, writing to potential supporters ranging from the Baptist reverend Al Sharpton to the Georgia Green Party. Asadallah ends his account of his suffering, in a letter to a Black community newspaper, "Allah says in the Qur'an: 'Verily with every struggle there is relief.' Allahu-Akbar!"[33] Following the publication of his letter, Asadallah was moved to a cell without a bed and left naked, without food or his prescription medication, for two days. Why such brutality? His wife, Amina, made sense of her husband's infectious power:

It's not that my husband is doing something wrong or trying to be anybody. It's just that he has the ability to awaken the inner consciousness of a person by using human rationale and when a person's inner consciousness awakens after having been in a state of slumber for so long, this inner consciousness becomes enthused and curious and begins a new journey.[34]

Key among the outside support for the Georgia prison strikers and for the Free Alabama Movement that would grow in their shadow was Pastor Kenneth Glasgow. In 1994, while serving a fourteen-year sentence in Florida, Glasgow had a religious epiphany that led him to a life of religious service and to the founding in 2001 of TOPS, The Ordinary People's Society. Based in Dothan, Alabama, TOPS serves as a one-stop resource center for a community riven by poverty and the criminal justice system. TOPS feeds two hundred people a day, offers job skill trainings and counseling, and hosts Bible studies and recovery groups. Working collaboratively with a range of other organizations, including Project South and the Drug Policy Alliance, TOPS serves community members in need and organizes against the carceral policies that cement precarity. Since 2003 TOPS has registered voters in jail, and since 2008, as made possible by a successful federal lawsuit against the state of Alabama, it has registered voters *in prison*.[35] In 2014, a year during which Glasgow was arrested in Montgomery for protesting the governor's refusal to expand Medicaid, the TOPS leader was among the formerly incarcerated activists brought to Washington by the Obama administration to consult with its re-entry task force.[36]

More recently, with seed money from the Open Philanthropy Project, Glasgow is developing the Prodigal Child Project. Named for the biblical parable of the wayward son who returns to his father expecting chastisement only to find himself embraced with open arms, the goal of the project is, as Glasgow puts it, "to change the school-to-prison pipeline into the reentry pipeline."[37] Working with pastors from hundreds of participating churches in Alabama, Georgia, Tennessee, and Mississippi, the project facilitates the comprehensive re-entry of formerly incarcerated men and women into their communities, and it also "will train pastors to do policy work."

In talking to Glasgow, we were looking for explicitly religious arguments for prison abolition, but Glasgow pushed back somewhat. "Those arguments don't come up too often because they're not here-and-now," he told us. "I follow Jesus. I got my epiphany from God," he explained, adding, "Jesus is the biggest revolutionary we know, but people don't want to hear that." Glasgow's wariness of trading in God-talk when he is wearing his organizer hat is primarily out of consideration for how to successfully build a movement in a post-Christian America. As Glasgow says, acknowledging the pluralistic religious landscape of contemporary America, "It's about making it equal and fair for everybody."

Glasgow also shies away from identifying as an "abolitionist." In an allusion to the widespread efforts to abolish solitary confinement and to remove questions about criminal history from job applications, Glasgow said, "We ban boxes. I don't want to put myself in a box." Another reason for reluctance concerning prison abolition is his desire to sidestep the "if not prisons then what?" question. Glasgow isn't interested in talking about what punishment should look like. "What we need to be talking about is: What does freedom look like?" Rather than as an abolitionist, Glasgow identifies as a "restorationist." His commitment is to help "restore everyone to their full being: as a body, as a soul, and as a citizen."

For Glasgow, the new surge of prison organizing is best thought of as the spearhead of a broader cultural movement: "It's not just a great moment in prisoner organizing. It's a great moment in organizing, period." According to Glasgow, everybody is figuring out that "we gotta do it horizontal. . . . We've got to bring everybody together, across different religions, looking beyond barriers." With respect to the church in particular, its function is, on the one hand, practical. It is "a refuge, a safe haven." In comparing the present moment to the civil rights movement, Glasgow explains, "What they had was a unified front, a shared message. We are divided." Some focus on LGBTQ issues, some focus on prison reform, some focus on poverty, and so on. For Glasgow, the divisions between those organizing for racial justice, economic justice, and gender justice are to be managed by each movement embracing the same core organizing principle: those most affected should lead the way. As Glasgow puts it, LGBTQ folk should lead the struggle for the rights and recognition of queer and transgender people, while those incarcerated, the formerly incarcerated, and families of the incarcerated should lead the struggle against mass incarceration. Churches must surrender their presumption of leadership and support the struggle wherever the struggle is already taking place. Organizing along identitarian lines is essential precisely to the degree that it helps to engender solidarity and broad-based power. The same logic applies to the Black church. It is incumbent on churches to lead, but not at the cost of relegating other stakeholders to a subordinate status. As Glasgow explains, "Getting everybody on one accord, one front: that's the role that the church should play. Along with everybody else."[38]

Abolition Theology

One spring evening in 2017, a heterodox group of prison abolitionists gathered in the Oakland Peace Center for an event called "Abolition for a Moral Economy." Organized by a Christian abolitionist named David Brazil, the room contained people of faith, practitioners of spiritual-but-not-religious traditions, and secularists. After hearing from a panelist who framed her anti-prison work in explicitly Christian terms, a young, formerly incarcerated Critical Resistance organizer named Chance Grable translated his secular commitments into the evening's dominant religious idiom: "My faith," Grable said, "is abolition."

Of spaces where contemporary prison abolitionist organizing happens, the Oakland Peace Center event was something of an outlier. Talk of God and religious faith are minority, even fugitive, idioms in abolitionist circles. Nonetheless, in the trenches of the struggle we found no small number of self-identified people of faith, Christian and otherwise, who, in their efforts to build a world without prisons, explicitly draw on religious ideas. While these people share in the same nonsectarian abolitionist faith professed by Grable, in their arguments and organizing they appeal as well to explicitly religious values, practices, institutions, and histories. Of prominent abolitionist organizers, no one is clearer on this point than Jason Lydon. Known as the founder of Black and Pink, a group organizing on behalf of and with incarcerated LGBTQ and HIV+ prisoners, Lydon is an ordained Unitarian Universalist minister who was himself incarcerated and is a survivor of prison sexual violence. In characterizing the prison industrial complex, Lydon leans on a simple religious concept: "evil."

In accounting for this evil, Lydon credits white supremacy and capitalism, but he also understands it within the history of American Christianity. The evil of the prison system stems in part from a terrible theological mistake that is endemic to American culture. Pursuant to a "violent Calvinist theology" that pervades American common sense, those who are not among the elect—the poor, Black people, queer and trans people disproportionately—are opened to varieties of torture. Some of this is wanton; some of it is motivated. Lydon describes a "dangerous sacrificial theology," with the criminal justice system primarily serving a scapegoat function. Politicians and prison administrators frame the prison as an institution that responds to and addresses violence, brutality, and abuse, but in Lydon's view, prisons merely

reroute these pervasive American problems onto the bodies of specially designated victims. "We have public trials of individuals who have done something terrible, and these people take on the sins of all those who have inflicted
harm. In watching these scapegoats be tried, convicted, incarcerated, and experience the many harms and violence of incarceration, survivors of violence
are supposed to receive some kind of healing. This, we are told, is 'justice.'"
Lydon dissents: the public rituals we tell ourselves are about "justice" and
"healing" are merely "spectacles of scapegoating."[39]

A cogent jeremiad against America's Calvinist viciousness, however, is
only half of what Lydon brings to the table theologically. He also brings an
alternative conceptualization of the sacred to supplant the idolatrous notions
that attend American carcerality. Pursuant to Unitarian doctrine, humans
are sacred and human life is to be valued without exception. Human beings
begin not in original sin but in "original blessing." Honoring the oneness of
God necessitates honoring the sacredness of human life. Neither for those
subjected to state violence nor for the public that looks on is there anything
salvific about incarceration. The principle is simple but revolutionary: in their
goodness, human beings deserve better than to be made to suffer. To give God
and human beings what they are properly due means fighting to eradicate
institutions that damage and replacing them with practices that restore.

In mining recent Christian thought for abolitionist precursors, Lydon
leans on an underread book from the nineties, Lee Griffith's *The Fall of
the Prison: Biblical Perspectives on Prison Abolition*. For the theologically
more conservative Griffith, a principal component of Jesus's good news is
that the prison has already been made obsolete. Even and especially in our
imperfect world, the Christian's task is to refuse this material reality and
bring into being the cage-free world that Jesus mandates:

> Jesus' proclamation of liberty for the captives marks the fall of the prison.
> It is precisely in our own age, when we are bombarded with evidence
> of the empirical reality of prisons, when prisons are proliferating and
> overflowing—it is precisely now that we need to hear Jesus' proclamation
> that prisons are unreal, that they have already been defeated, that they have
> already fallen. . . . In the shell of our old world, a new reality is present, and
> we are called to live the new within the shell of the old.[40]

"To live the new within the shell of the old" entails a slate of religious
activities—repentance, prayer, public witness—but it also gestures in the

direction of a wide range of civic activities. Some of these activities pertain directly to incarcerated people, such as visiting prisoners and making room for the formerly incarcerated in our own communities. But surely this new world cannot be so easily contained. To enact this abolitionist world also means abstaining from state violence as a means for rectifying harm, rejecting punitive measures in favor of transformative ones in our homes and our communities, and caring in general for those who require care. Sometimes this will mean flouting the law, and often this will mean allowing conscience to violate custom. Wherever they are bombarded with dehumanizing labels—"criminal, thief, murderer, monster"—Christians, for Griffith, are called upon to insist, as the Bible insists, that all human life is sacred and that we are all brothers and sisters in this divine sacredness.[41]

Griffith's Christian abolitionism also furnishes inspiration to Los Angeles-based Hannah Bowman. Whereas Lydon primarily seeks to organize the most vulnerable, Bowman seeks to organize her own people: white, middle-class, mainline Protestant progressives. An Episcopalian, Bowman was radicalized in part by reading Maya Schenwar's Locked Down, Locked Out, a brief for prison abolition inspired in part by Schenwar's sister's experiences of incarceration. In reading Schenwar's experiences and arguments, and in learning in particular about restorative justice, Bowman found herself accepting a surprising truth: "Okay," she said to herself, "I'm a prison abolitionist." In founding Christians for the Abolition of Prisons and assembling teaching materials for Protestant churches, Bowman hopes to nudge others like her to similar epiphanies, in the hope of uprooting American culture's punitive and carceral mentality.[42]

At its core, Bowman's theological project is to reclaim substitutionary atonement, but from a restorative justice perspective. Whereas many mainline Christians shy away from claims about the salvific power of Jesus's crucifixion, Bowman reappropriates this theologically conservative notion in service of abolition. "We don't have to have prisons anymore," Bowman argues, "because Jesus has done the atonement for us." With Jesus having taken this weight, we are freed from the obligation to retribute and are invited instead to cultivate nobler faculties. As evinced in Matthew 18's parable of the unmerciful servant, in cases of those who have inflicted harm, our task is to forgive "not seven times, but seventy-seven times." This challenge, of overriding the dominant carceral imperatives with the restorative justice that Jesus himself models, makes prison abolition a paradigmatic vantage point for practical ethics. "Prison abolition is making powerful claims about the Kingdom of God in the present reality." As a mode of engagement, prison abolition shows us not just what to do with those who inflict harm, but it also encourages necessary reflection "about God, the eschaton, and the nature of atonement." For any Christian struggling with how to be good or how to be just, "prison abolition has a lot to say to theology."

Across the country from the Oakland Peace Center, this same hunch, that how Christians respond to the crisis of incarceration in contemporary America encodes in it an ethics writ large, supplies Buffalo's Jesus the Liberator Seminary with its mandate. Founded in the nineties as an effort to bring theological resources to poor and at-risk populations, Jesus the Liberator has been working directly and via correspondence with incarcerated women and men. Whereas prison ministry generally seeks to transform incarcerated people, prison theology emphasizes "the need to redeem both individual and social sins"—with an understanding that "the prison system is a reflection of the larger American society."[43] Informed by a Freireian sensibility, seminarians attempt to practice deep listening so as to center the voices of people inside, aiming to listen without judgment, restore dignity, and try to help meet people's basic needs. Meanwhile, prison theology attempts to heal "a society that's addicted to punishment, where every problem is solved through prisons."[44]

At a fall 2018 gathering of abolitionists in Buffalo, seminary affiliates Chris Barbera and Gabrie'l Atchison presented material from their book-in-progress, which focuses on *relational* prison theology. As is true of Bowman's reappropriation of Christ's salvific death on the cross for the abolitionist cause, Atchison recognizes that in her emphasis on one's "personal relationship" with God, she is borrowing a sphere of theological inquiry that generally belongs to Christian conservatives. The God of relational theology needs us just as we need God. This places the pressure squarely on us to love God. As Jesus says in Matthew, we must love God and we must love our neighbor; and as Jesus says in John, loving one another as God loves us requires that we be willing to lay our lives down for those we call our friends.[45] Those who oppress are also damaged, and also require healing, but just as we must not demonize our oppressors, we must resist the impulse to proceed directly to forgiveness before anyone has had the chance to heal. The goal of relational prison theology is to hold space for people to be angry, and to push for real justice—a justice rooted in love rather than fear or resentment, a justice that heals and restores rather than wounds.

In Jesus's admonition to love without exception, the gathering crowd of Christian abolitionists find leverage to push back against the will to punishment that predominates American culture. But Jesus had his angry side as well, and he was not shy about calling out hypocrites, profiteers, and those who fecklessly aligned themselves with the illegitimately powerful. One catches echoes of this hot-blooded, morally exacting Jesus in the abolitionist exhortations of David Brazil. Brazil cut his teeth in the swirl of East Bay organizing that congealed in the aftermath of the 2009 killing of an unarmed BART passenger, Oscar Grant, and culminated two years later with the Occupy Oakland encampment. After the camp was broken up, Brazil, who had grown up "secularish" and was not at that time religiously identified, turned to his wife and asked, "What should we do? Maybe we should go to church?" The two of them went together, to an African American Methodist church—it was Brazil's first time being in church. After a year "in discernment," David was baptized. He is now the pastor of a house church, the Agape Fellowship.

In his deliberate assembly of Christian ideas and practices on behalf of the abolitionist project, Brazil leans hard on the Book of Acts, where early Christian communities "had all things in common." For Brazil, this form of "primitive communism" both portends an abolitionist future and helps clarify the path between where we are and where we are headed. The scourges of poverty and social brokenness that underlie crime are endemic to both capitalism and empire, as are the systems of punishment and control perversely charged with furnishing solutions to these problems. Brazil's Christian commitments compel him to confront these systems. In theory as well as in practice, "if abolition is to be attainable, we must also dismantle capitalism." The prison industrial complex is bigger than prisons, but as for how to think about prisons and prisoners in particular, Brazil derives from the Book of Acts a strident clarity: "Acts is all about prison and who, in the Bible's perspective, is *in* prison." Paul is in prison for much of the book, as is Silas. "Who's in jail?" Brazil asks. "God's people are in jail." While some Christians might stop at bearing witness to this tragic fact, for Brazil, as informed by theologian Dietrich Bonhoeffer and others, being a disciple of Jesus means shouldering more substantive costs. For Brazil, the Christian's task is to set the incarcerated free.[46]

How necessary is it to appeal to the Bible, to speak in explicitly religious terms? For Brazil, there simply is no substitute. The constellation of potency and resonance afforded to scripture in American culture imbues it with unique revolutionary potential. Tens of millions of people read scripture and, within the generally agreed-upon rules of interpretation, anyone can be an authority. "Christian scripture is a *common* for Christians. If someone has an account, you must listen." Some of the Bible's political force, he would be the first to concede, is a function of his own hermeneutic orientation—he approaches scripture from "an anti-racist, womanist perspective"—but the radical potential is also baked into the text. Jesus was a radical, and Jesus's radicalism makes Christian scripture inherently potent. For Brazil, Christian terms are at the nexus of American religion and American secularity, but whereas religion comes with moral force, secularist individualism dilutes these categories and robs people of the power to bear witness. As moral frameworks drift into secularity, they lose their power. For those looking to fundamentally transform American culture into a society capable of effecting real justice, it becomes essential therefore to speak religious truths as religious truths.

With an eye toward abolitionist organizing, Brazil's Oakland comrade Nicole Deane is somewhat more pluralistic. Like Brazil, Deane practices a counter-hegemonic mode of Christianity. Taking Jesus at his word, she aspires "to witness a Christianity that doesn't have to apologize for itself." This means practicing the justice that one preaches and never turning a blind eye to imperialism, capitalism, patriarchy, or other forms of systemic domination. As powerful as scriptural language can be, for Deane, to box oneself into Jesus-talk can be a tactical mistake. "We are not base-builders, we are weavers," she says. In other words: "I try to use the language of whatever space I'm in." For many, Deane recognizes, talk about religion and God are a real turn-off. Deane refers to her "nongregants" among her abolitionist fellow travelers, people without faith commitments, some hostile to religion, but whom she occasionally finds herself pastoring to nonetheless. Among rank-and-file abolitionists, Brazil agrees, anti-religious attitudes—"the vulgar Marxist critique of Christianity"—are quite common.[47]

As Deane rightly points out, however, the same cannot be said of the communities of color most impacted by the prison industrial complex. In those communities people are actively religious or, at the very least, "they are used to being around religion." Within these communities, Deane tends to lean on the languages of "power," of "having power," and of "self-determination."[48] This need to be sensitive to the religious (or nonreligious) sensibilities of one's audience is something Jason Lydon talks about as well in describing his own efforts as an organizer and minister to help others in their "conscientization"—the term Lydon borrows from Paolo Freire for the process of uncovering new truths. This means sometimes toning his message down, even among his co-religionists: "Unitarian Universalists don't relate to the language of evil," he reflects. With or without explicit appeal to theological concepts, these Christian abolitionists self-consciously speak languages that better walk the tightrope across the religion/secular divide, languages of "witness," of "testimony," of "the exposure of hidden things," and, preeminently, of "injustice" and "justice." If, for Deane, God-talk isn't necessarily suited for all occasions or audiences, at the core of Christianity resides an invaluable element for the struggle against the prison industrial complex. "You might need Jesus to get away from vengeance," she says, before hedging: "Or, if we are to get away from vengeance, Jesus is an extraordinary resource."

In offering their testimonies of how they came by their respective abolitionist callings, Deane and Brazil each point to Lynice Pinkard. Pinkard is a Bay Area organizer and is pastor of Oakland's First Congregational Church.[49] In her prolific writing and preaching, Pinkard combines the polemical and prescriptive strains of Jesus's message with the prophetic exhortations of a range of freedom strugglers in service of an arresting abolitionist vision. In an article titled "Revolutionary Suicide: Risking Everything to Transform Society and Live Fully," Pinkard advocates for the embrace of Bonhoeffer's notion of "costly grace." Citing Fannie Lou Hamer, Oscar Romero, Mamie Bradley, Martin Luther King, and Malcolm X as models, she demands that one go all the way. "Revolutionary suicide," as she characterizes it, is an embodied commitment to justice that declares, like Jesus, "No one takes my life; I lay it down." If there is solace to be found in this disquieting idea, it is that for revolutionary suicide to be more than individual vanity, we must all go in on it together. That is because, with injustice as endemic as it is, "we are not individually salvageable." Importantly, salvation is not defined by affinity groups—that is to say, by "identity politics as it is currently practiced under capitalism." Only by means of a comprehensive and wholly collective "commitment to grappling with our identities in relation to domination" may we assemble a winning coalition and generate a new consciousness that prefigures a just world. As far as salvific solidarity is concerned, for Pinkard, there is no sacrificing the wicked in service of the righteous. For any of us to be saved, all of us must be saved together:

No more *us* and *them*. No more save *us* by abandoning *them*. No more heal *us* by injuring *them*. No more free *us* by binding *them*. No more enliven *us* by killing *them*. No more! .... Human life lived in God's image, lived fully, is found in the crossing over from ourselves to the well-being of others—that is what love is. When we cross over from power to weakness, from strength to vulnerability, from inside to outside, from up to down, we rise above ourselves, we transcend ourselves. In other words, the descent into death of our own self-interest—this revolutionary suicide—is actually a rising, a resurrection."[50]

Only by refusing the easy, vicious fixes that white supremacist capitalism affords may we collectively transcend and transform the institutionalized brutality of the present social order.

This categorical refusal to participate in the doomed politics of scape-goating was on breathtaking display in Pinkard's response to the conviction of Johannes Mehserle, the BART officer who killed Oscar Grant. As Pinkard admonished a community bent on retribution, Mehserle must not be substituted for the system he is "serving." Placed in the context of the system that oppresses us, for Pinkard, Mehserle is also a casualty, albeit a murderous one. As she argues, "the language of 'law and order' within law enforcement is used to mask both the *murderous* effect on the oppressed, and the *dehumanizing* effect on the oppressors." To the extent that those filled with hurt and fury at Grant's murder accept the state's offer of Mehserle as a scapegoat, they allow the oppressors to disown and deflect the system's endemic brutality. For Pinkard, to delight in the symptom is to succumb to the disease.

In diagnosing this collective neurosis, Pinkard appeals to the story of Jonah. When a tragedy like the killing of Oscar Grant takes place, we cry for somebody to isolate the evildoer—in biblical terms, the "Jonah" whose presence is blamed for the storm—and we say, "Here, we've got him, we've got him, and we're going to throw him out here in the ocean [or in the profoundly dysfunctional prison system], and then the race storms will subside."[51] In response to tragedy, to anxiety, and to despair, the wounded and scared cry out for blood. In place of such easy and distracting catharses that perpetuate conditions of domination and effects no real healing, Pinkard counsels her friends and neighbors instead to embrace their grief. Pinkard appeals to Jeremiah's prophetic witness: "My joy is gone, grief is upon me; my heart is sick; I cannot even comfort myself because my heart is barely beating within me."[52]

What she counsels, Pinkard concedes, may feel frustrating, but "despair is a fine place to begin." In despair one can begin doing the arduous labor: to bring "love and tenderness to ungrieved losses, relational estrangement, [and] internalized oppression."[53] Beginning soon thereafter, by means of concerted caring spiritual practices—yoga, massage, support groups—the community can begin to heal. At the same time, the community can begin to cobble together from the wreckage the necessary scaffolding to erect its abolitionist future. "We begin to form coalitions to make structural changes—meaningful work that pays a living wage, community safety patrols to replace police presence, restorative justice processes."[54] If "revolutionary suicide" sounds scary, the stuff of saints, the role Pinkard affords faith in these slow processes of social transformation is much easier to embrace. It is a spirit of abolition that inheres in everyday practices of survival and healing, repair and resistance. For what it is worth, this spirit of abolition is also unmistakably and inexorably *religious*:

> We need to see the Gospel's principle of light in darkness; a little light in darkness here and a little light in darkness there will, that's God's promise, transform darkness to light. That is the way of the Spirit. It's not grandiose. It's not self-aggrandizing. Sometimes it is dramatic; often it is not. It is how the Spirit of Life—the life giving, life engendering power of God—will rupture in, healing and repairing what is broken and damaged by the deathly behavior of created beings, and countering the baffling, cunning, death-dealing forces of empire.[55]

At first blush, this quiet opening of the self to the "energies of love" no doubt appears less satisfying than does watching a bad man be sent to prison to suffer. However, if healing is truly the community's goal, this repudiation of imperial violence represents a much healthier—and indeed, the *only*—path. Whether called by the name of God or by some other name, only by embracing "the Spirit of Life" may we collectively "be raised from the dead," transcend our own ugliness and rancor, and live in peace.[56]

For Kempis "Ghani" Songster, sentenced to life without parole in a Philadelphia court for a crime he committed at the age of fifteen, the pursuit of this spirit led him beyond the bounds of organized religion. Songster's study and practice of a variety of religious traditions, Islam especially, were a crucial "step in becoming a revolutionary," but eventually he grew disillusioned with organized religion because of the way, in prison, it kept people divided. For Songster, all divisions between people buttress the control of the state, which is inherently anti-human, anti-life, and precludes connectedness. For this reason he resists all categories that divide people, up to and including the categories of white people and Black people. Instead of religion, Songster emphatically embraces the designation of spirituality, but contrary to most iterations, Songster's spirituality is radically and irreducibly activist, collectivist, and political. Spirituality, the quality that connects individuals to groups and to nature, is "the seed of abolition work." Put another way, "if empathy is the quintessential quality that makes us human then solidarity is its expression." As Songster explains, "a spiritual system that always has been and must be at the heart of all abolition movements and revolutions is that deep sense of connectedness with everyone and everything around you, and a connection to life such that if an injustice happens and if someone is hurt, you feel that, it animates you, it moves you to do something."

Songster found language to articulate this orientation in Ubuntu, the tradition of African humanism sometimes described as *I am because you are.* For Songster, this connectedness undergirds everything. "There can be no abolitionist work if we are all in our own silos of pain and see *ourselves* as the opposition—and that's what Ubuntu is about."[57] Ubuntu prescribes a set of virtues of how we are to be in relation to one another and points the way forward toward "spirituality on a global scale." Through Ubuntu, we might collectively overcome "what the Buddhists call *dukkha*, the state of separation that is at the root of all suffering."[58] *Dukkha* gives rise to the feelings of ownership and dominion, and it engenders the extractive, industrial way of life that places us on the precipice of ecological collapse. Given where we are, abolitionism, for Songster, must also be ecosocialism.[59] The great expropriation of capitalist wealth that attended the emancipation of enslaved people points the way forward for the gathering movement that must cultivate the power we will need in order to keep trillions of dollars of oil in the ground.

In framing the relationship between the local American struggle against the prison industrial complex and the global ecological struggle against global capitalism, Songster quotes James Baldwin: "*Go the way your blood beats.*" That is to say, the battles that call you are the battles you must fight. "But we've got to be eco-warriors first and foremost. Climate change is the great unifier, the heart of intersectionality. All the radicals intersect: capitalism, industrialization, greed, patriarchy, toxic masculinity, the State." And if we lose that battle, all is lost. As Songster put it: "No struggle for justice matters without an inhabitable planet under our feet."

Abolition Ritual, Abolition Practice

In 2008, Seminary of the Street was founded by Lynice Pinkard, Oakland Congregationalist Nichola Torbett, and "a group of feral folks from a variety of faith traditions (Christian, Buddhist, Jewish, Unitarian Universalist, and agnostic) who shared a sadness and a sense of urgency around the state of both the world and our social justice efforts and a hunch that something loosely named spirituality was part of the remedy."[60] Pinkard describes the organization's founding rationale in terms that seek to bridge the silos of identity described by Kenneth Glasgow: "Let's get white lesbians to work with formerly incarcerated Latin and African American men. Let's work together on both marriage equality and on the negative impact of felony convictions, which prevent formerly incarcerated persons from finding gainful employment. In this way both groups will work for justice and learn to be in solidarity, starting with genuine care and concern for each other's suffering."[61]

As is true for all the religious abolitionists we spoke with, the transformative potential of religious ideas is best activated through religious practices, of which pulpit preaching is only one. As their efforts demonstrate, religious traditions come embedded within catalogues of ritual frameworks and moves that can be put to abolitionist ends. To the growing vocabulary of nominally secular rituals—the occupation, the disruption, the die-in, the jail vigil—we may add the mass, the pilgrimage, and the Passover seder. Some of these rituals will necessarily take place in houses of worship, or in the home, but those with the most inflammatory potential will take place in the streets, in what Seminarians of the Street call "liturgical direct actions."[62] A few examples:

In a 2017 action, members of Second Acts, "a direct-action affinity group for followers of the revolutionary Jesus," gathered on the steps of the Alameda County courthouse. Via a series of short speeches, members confessed their own complicity with the violence of the prison industrial complex.[63] When the speeches were finished, people dipped their hands in red paint and left handprints on the courthouse wall. Then, in an arresting display "to visually symbolize the violence of the prison system and particularly the social death of imprisonment," participants poured buckets of "blood" down the courthouse steps.[64]

A stations of the cross Good Friday liturgy, which the same group performed, is spreading across the county, and not only among urban Black radical communities. The purpose of this direct action is to geographically mark the themes of the crucifixion in one's own community to high-light the spaces of systemic oppression, anguish, and hope. In a version of this liturgical direct action conducted by an Episcopal congregation in Nashville, the liturgy began at their own church with the reading of scripture and the singing of hymns. Participants then walked to pivotal sites—the county courthouse, the public defenders office, sites of desegregation demonstrations, of conflicts with police, and of a Black Lives Matter die-in. At each stop participants recited lines that detail the torments of Jesus that preceded his crucifixion.[65]

Religious symbols and imagery are well suited for ritualizing sacrifice and mourning, but they are also adept at conjuring the specter of apocalyptic destruction. In 2013, frustrated with the relative silence of faith organizations during the California prison hunger strikes, members of the Prisoner Hunger Strike Solidarity Coalition conducted what they called the Jericho Ritual. Once a week for seven weeks, they circumnavigated the central office of the California Department of Corrections. As they circled, they recited the hunger strikers' core demands. To date, these walls have not yet tumbled down, but as Marie Levin, one of the organizers, figures, God isn't done yet, and neither are we. As she testified, "We can speak things into existence."[66]

While Christian liturgical themes—and the popular purchase of these themes—make Christian ritual an apt vehicle for speaking about American violence and American punishment, these sorts of actions have not been limited to Christian communities. Inspired by Black Lives Matter, progressive American Jews have been supplementing the Passover liturgy to make explicit the connection between the saga of Israelite enslavement and liberation and the obligation of American Jews to help emancipate those subjected to mass incarceration.[67] In 2014, during the fever of marches that followed the non-indictment of Eric Garner's killer, a moment at which the people's will to take public space had never been stronger, Jews for Racial and Economic Justice organized what can only be called a liturgical direct action on Manhattan's Upper West Side. After convening on 88th Street at B'nai Jeshurun, the crowd marched to the arterial intersection of 96th and Broadway. Many of the protesters were rabbis and many were wearing prayer shawls. With roughly twenty-five participants sitting in the street blocking traffic, the group recited the mourner's Kaddish. One of those blocking traffic, Rabbi Jill Jacobs, executive director of T'ruah, a rabbinic human rights organization, held a sign that quoted the Mishnah Sanhedrin in English and in Hebrew: "Anyone who destroys one soul—it is like destroying the entire world."[68]

It is impossible to speak about abolitionist organizing by American Muslims without first mentioning Mariame Kaba, the indefatigable organizer behind a slew of abolitionist projects, including Project NIA and Survived and Punished.[69] Via these organizations and on her own, Kaba pursues a range of abolitionist strategies and tactics by conducting workshops and trainings, doing public history, and spearheading solidarity campaigns. In her public-facing work, Kaba is relatively secular. She does not generally foreground explicitly religious concepts, and when her public speech veers into God-talk, it is generally to vent her frustration: "Allah be a fence," she sometimes pleads on Twitter in a Muslim appropriation of a gospel idiom; or just as commonly: "Jesus Christ."

Though largely secular in her abolitionist organizing, Kaba is an ardent critic of secular individualism and secular self-craft. "Self-care doesn't make sense to me as a Black woman living in this county. What we need is *community care.*" Simultaneously, for Kaba, deliberate work one does on one-self is an essential component of transformative practice. Having the right convictions, Kaba cautions, isn't particularly difficult, but, as she tweeted, you "gotta actually live your values. that's the hard part."[70] The challenge for would-be abolitionists is actually living out the commitments we profess to hold. This means habituating ourselves to actually respond to the daily injustice that one encounters, and it means doing so in ways that are themselves just. If one is to be truly ethical, then succumbing to despair is simply not an option. This perpetual refusal is also a practice of concerted labor that one must do on oneself—though, as Kaba's tireless regimen of public witness demonstrates, this work is also an ethical act. If, as Kaba likes to say, "Hope is a discipline," then making this hope available to others is a discipline as well.[71]

Kaba doesn't foreground explicitly religious concepts, but she is adamant that mechanistic secular frameworks are woefully inadequate to the challenges at hand. "Abolitionists must make *moral arguments,*" she says. Stop at quantitative diagnoses and pragmatic remedies and we will never uproot the "criminal punishment system" and the attendant systems of state violence that subject people who are already wounded to an "avalanche of traumas." In making this point, Kaba has pointed to the explicitly moral arguments mobilized against capital punishment by death row prisoners in Illinois. In

2011, after consulting with Bishop Desmond Tutu and Sister Helen Prejean, Governor Pat Quinn abolished the death penalty.[72]

In the spring of 2018, Kaba participated in what might well have been contemporary prison abolitionism's first explicitly Muslim collective action. Inspired by the 2017 National Black Mama's Bail Out that raised money to bail out Black mothers in advance of Mother's Day, a group of organizers launched #believersbailout to bail out Muslims incarcerated in Cook County jail.[73] The action was born at a conference in which Kecia Ali, a scholar of Islamic jurisprudence, said to Su'ad Abdul Khabeer, an anthropologist of American Islam, "Wouldn't it be cool if we got people to pay their *zakat* to get people out of jail?"[74]

According to a standard Sunni conceptualization, the principle of *zakat* obligates a Muslim to annually contribute 2.5% of their wealth to charity. According to Sunni legal traditions, among the eight eligible charitable recipients are the poor and needy, people in bondage, and people in debt. As Khabeer put it, "People in jail because they can't pay bail fall into all of those categories." To implement the bail out, the organizers partnered with a wide range of community organizations, religious and secular, in Chicago and beyond, including Chicago Community Bail Fund; the Innercity Muslim Action Network, which does reentry work; Masjid Al-Rabia, a pluralist Chicago masjid that does prison outreach; Sapelo Square, a national Black Muslim organization; MPower Change, a national Muslim social justice advocacy network; and the Nation of Islam, which has long been engaged in prisoner outreach and efforts at prison reform. Launched in advance of Ramadan with the intention of raising $30,000, by month's end #believersbailout had raised over $100,000.

In a June 6 Twitter town hall, organizers and allies demonstrated some of what the Islamic tradition has to offer the project of prison abolition. Participants quoted the Qur'an: "And you do realize what is the steep road? It is the freeing of a human being from bondage." In applying the tradition to the demands of the present, Muslim fashion blogger Hoda Katebi argued, "Justice in the Qur'an is wholly focused on restorative justice rather than punitive. How many times do we say God is الرحيم Al-Rahim, the most merciful while in prayer? Mercy and humanity are CENTRAL to Islam & antithetical to mass incarceration."[75] As Khabeer would explain in a Radio Islam interview, bailouts are only a tactic. The end game is abolishing money bail. "In the meantime, like Abu Bakr freeing Bilal, like our enslaved African ancestors freeing each other, we're going to free ourselves."[76]

Freedom is to be attained by a variety of channels. In 2016, when the Supreme Court decided *Montgomery v. Louisiana*, which applied retroactively its 2012 *Miller v. Alabama* holding that juveniles could not be sentenced by statute to life without the possibility of parole, Ghani Songster knew that his hour of freedom might soon be at hand.[77] As informed by his Ubuntu outlook, however, Songster saw a problem. Violent crime is largely horizontal, with harmers and the harmed coming from the same communities, but the state's adversarial system pitted community members against each other in a zero-sum game in which some had to win and some had to lose. "We were celebrating but not everybody could share in that victory." The family members of those who had been murdered "saw the USSC decisions as taking justice away. They were retraumatized, and that's legitimate. They lost someone." With so many men around him talking about getting ready to go back to the community, Songster found himself wondering, "[B]ut was the community ready for us?"[78]

"Part of political action," according to Songster, must be "healing action." Too often, he laments, this aspect of abolition has been ignored. For Songster, to refuse to care about the hurt of those victimized by crime is to "to succumb to divide and conquer," which "is to succumb to the state" and its violence. To foster healing, Songster looked to Africa for models of post-conflict justice, to Truth and Reconciliation in South Africa and Gacaca in Rwanda.[79] In 2016, while still incarcerated, Songster co-organized an event that took place at St. Joseph's University, which brought together newly paroled former juvenile lifers and the families of those victimized by violent crime. Drawing on Gacaca, men who had killed were afforded the opportunity to admit what they did, to apologize for what they did, to seek forgiveness, and to explore possibilities of atonement. Songster added one original provision of his own: the returning men were invited to pledge to become agents of change in their community. Two years later, Ubuntu Philadelphia staged its second large convocation, this time with Ghani Songster in attendance.

Whither the Abolition Spirit?

We are, for the moment anyhow, a prison nation. Our carceral politics neurotically fixates on the problem of evil (or a targeted subset of it anyhow) and all but ignores the problem of human suffering. Millions are incapacitated in our name, millions more live under government supervision, and whole sectors of the population are earmarked from birth for more of the same treatment. All this, we are generally told, is what "justice" is, and what "justice" can only be. The social catastrophe that is our criminal punishment system is a political problem, an economic problem, and a problem of racial injustice. But as we have shown, it is also a cultural problem and, more specifically, a religious problem. During the era of mass incarceration, we have been conditioned to forget how to collectively dream—and demand—a vision of justice more robust and beautiful than the hideous substitute currently on offer. The secularized theological language of law and order that has so great a hold on our collective imagination must be refused. Even in its more liberal iterations, where the "bad people" have been somewhat more judiciously designated, punishment politics deifies agents of state violence and excludes the possibility for divine justice. All of this is idolatry, and in our prisons, our courts, and our over-policed streets, we sacrifice the vulnerable to the false, vengeful gods of *criminal justice*.

Where are we to go from here? Writing as scholars of religion with religious entanglements of our own, we see in the religious abolitionists detailed in this chapter a vanguard. In collaboration with their secular fellow travelers, these people are drawing on the stuff of American religion to help cure deep cultural maladies and point us toward an abolitionist future in which all are free and cared for. These people may be "radicals," but so in their time were William Lloyd Garrison, David Walker, and Denmark Vesey—until they weren't. With sufficient power, Jason Lydon, Lynice Pinkard, and Mariame Kaba will cease to be radicals and become instead prophets, movement leaders, and eventually, in retrospect, innovators of what will have become the emergent common sense. For this necessary shift to take place, rank-and-file religious people must push their own communities beyond complicity and into abolitionist potency. Models for effecting this awakening and mobilization are to be found all around us, well beyond those who already self-identify as abolitionist.

Consider Bryan Stevenson's rightly acclaimed *Just Mercy: A Story of Justice and Redemption*.[80] Stevenson is an African American lawyer who built a nonprofit legal practice defending men and women on death row in Alabama, and he is increasingly working to contextualize mass incarceration in the long shadow of white supremacy and racialized violence.[81] *Just Mercy* begins with an epigraph from the most celebrated figure of mid-twentieth-century liberal Protestant public theology, Reinhold Niebuhr: "Love is the motive, but justice is the instrument." The ambiguity of justice as an ideal both within and beyond the legal system is a theme haunting *Just Mercy*. Stevenson recalls his initiation into death penalty litigation: As a summer intern, he met with a prisoner on death row. After a long, humanizing conversation, Stevenson feels helpless as a guard painfully shackles the prisoner. Stevenson's instinct is to apologize, to repeat over and over, "I'm really sorry." The man's response is to sing a hymn that Stevenson recognizes from his childhood. Each stanza ends, "Lord, plant my feet on Higher Ground."[82] Stevenson takes away from the encounter a commitment to justice beyond the world, but this justice still must be achieved through worldly—including but not exclusively legal—means.

Stevenson does not simply propose a return to an earlier era's commitment to divine justice. He also weaves into his story a quite modern, quite evangelical sense of personal transformation. Speaking at a small southern church in support of one of his clients facing death, Stevenson urges the community to become "stonecatchers."[83] Instead of throwing stones at those who have sinned, or witnessing others throwing stones, the religious community must catch these stones so as to block them from harming their intended target. This is how Stevenson understands mercy: an acknowledgment that we all are sinners, motivating a desire to protect those who are vulnerable from vengeance. In other words, Stevenson brings together elements of an earlier era's liberal Protestant belief in divine justice as an ideal with real, worldly implications and our present era's evangelical belief in personal sin and redemption—all in the service of organizing communities to work both through and beyond the legal system to abolish the death penalty and end mass incarceration. Even if not explicitly marshaled under the banner of abolitionism, in Stevenson one may rightfully pinpoint the abolition spirit: politically charged religious ideas put in service of a higher justice, precipitating desperately needed legal services and public education.

Some who are infected by the abolition spirit pursue justice outside the prison, others inside. Many, like Stevenson, move between the two worlds. To move between these worlds generally requires an institutional toehold. Whether as lawyer, state employee, or volunteer, social roles that enable one to bridge the wall and enter carceral spaces endow special insights and can also engender certain kinds of blindness. As we saw in the case of Austin Reed, for as long as we've put people in cages, people who aspire to goodness and justice have ventured into these cages with the hopes of educating, ministering to, and healing those encaged. Especially in the neoliberal order, the system feeds off such virtuous intentions. But to the degree that we wish to disrupt the brutal social isolation that mass incarceration both breeds and relies on, such boundary crossing is essential.[84]

Sam Smolinsky is the Catholic chaplain at Pelican Bay, California's notorious maximum security prison.[85] He started working at the prison during the hunger strike. The previous chaplain had died, and it took the church a few years to find a replacement. Smolinsky's background is in business, and he has no religious or theological degree, but he describes himself as spiritual. He moved from one end of California to the other to take the job at Pelican Bay. Smolinsky's parents are from Latin America, and his father is of Polish-Jewish stock, confusing the ethnic intuitions of the men that he works with. He attends two or three chapel services a day—he conducts the Catholic one and he supervises a Protestant or Muslim service. Each service lasts two hours. He carries himself as a man who is tired but not exhausted, as a man who is used to being tired. He looks rather like a quieter, less expressive version of Peter Falk.

When the hunger strike started—a strike that would come to include 30,000 prisoners across the state of California, but that originated in the solitary confinement cells at Pelican Bay—Smolinsky neither embraced nor rejected the mobilization. Of the prisoners' demands, he found some reasonable and others less so. He talked with prisoners about the demands, and he explained his reasons. Smolinsky described an encounter with one of the strike's leaders who had served more than twenty years in solitary confinement, a man Smolinsky referred to as "Gutierrez." When Smolinsky visited him, this man responded with surprise. In his more than two decades at Pelican Bay, he had never seen or even heard of a prison chaplain. The man told Smolinsky to tell the pope about the hunger strike. Of course, Smolinsky responded that this task was well above his pay grade. But Smolinsky did relay what he was seeing to the prison justice coordinator at the California Catholic Bishops' Conference. And she told her colleagues in Rome. And the message made its way through the corridors of the Vatican. A statement—rather neutral, but a statement nonetheless—was issued. The next time Smolinsky visited Gutierrez, in his supposed isolation, Gutierrez was impressed. He had read the statement, and he thanked Smolinsky.

In Sam Smolinsky we have an example, again, of religion—this time, formally institutionalized, organized religion—crossing boundaries in search of justice. Long-standing authorized channels are used, but something unscripted is involved as well. Just as there is nothing inherently disruptive in ministering to incarcerated people, there is nothing inherently redemptive in the pope seeing and acknowledging the struggles for justice of men and women caged in California. But this surprising moment of mutual recognition carries with it a seedling of possibility that, with work and magic, or grace, could contribute to transformative change.

"Let's Circle Up" (LCU) is a prisoner-led program founded in 2007 at Pennsylvania's Graterford Prison by Felix Rosado and Charles Boyd, two men serving life sentences in a state that statutorily bars lifers from parole (ergo, "Death by Incarceration"). LCU's mission is "to build relationships, community, and leaders through experiential, participatory, and collaborative restorative values and principles." By means of workshops and group dialogues, LCU seeks to empower people "to practice RJ [restorative justice] in everyday life with the aim of restoring damaged relationships caused by past harm, to the extent possible, and ending future harm."[86]

Boyd and Rosado are both religiously observant men—Boyd identifies as a Christian; Rosado identifies as a Catholic. Each participates in chapel activities, and each concertedly seeks to live an ethical life within an explicitly religious framework. Over time, however, each man has backed away from a narrow form of sectarian piety and thrown himself into more ecumenical modes of public engagement. As each has come to realize, testifying to sacred values in public requires less talk and more action, and it can sometimes mean translating faith commitments into secular idioms. "There was a time when I thought that faith in the Creator alone would suffice," Boyd writes, but this changed when a close friend from the block, upon getting out of prison and struggling with drug addiction, ended his life by jumping in front of a train. Boyd reports that he "felt like I had failed him because when he was here and cried out for me to help, instead of listening, I tried to convince him that God had him and all would be fine. So perhaps this is why I do not do so much 'faith-talk' anymore because, as the scripture declares, 'faith without works is dead.'"[87]

Rosado is similarly faithful and similarly circumspect. "My walk is my preaching," Rosado says, which is what pulled him out of the chapel and into other modes of social engagement. In his work with Let's Circle Up and in the Quaker-inspired Alternatives to Violence program, you won't hear Rosado engaging in all that much talk about God or about Christ. "Yet," as Rosado explains, "it's all about Christ, God, and other spiritual and religious matters."[88] Rosado locates the roots of contemporary restorative justice in traditional Native American practices and with Mennonites in the 1970s, but its ethos is also, among others, that of Jesus of Nazareth. "The values and principles of restorative justice are Gospel. But by not using explicitly Christian terms, people of all faiths, or none at all, feel welcome, safe—and often share that the restorative justice philosophy resonates with their particular faith, be it Islam, Judaism, Buddhism, or something else." The ecumenical term Rosado uses for the divine and human force that can change individuals and society is *transformative power*. "In brief, it's the belief that there's a power that can transform violent situations and behaviors into constructive and positive outcomes. This power surrounds us all and lies within us and our 'opponents,' however hidden it might be. Sound familiar? Many Christians have come to me afterwards and said, 'Hey, that's the Holy Spirit!'"

By their own accounts, Boyd and Rosado turn to restorative justice practices in an effort to heal their own brokenness. Boyd appreciates the attention given by those with whom he is incarcerated to how the criminal justice system victimizes incarcerated people, but he is adamant that men like him also attend to the "harm we had caused others." According to each man, the capacity to atone for harms caused is a religious value. "Core to most faiths," Rosado writes, "are the ideas of redemption and dignity. Any consequences for harmful behavior, if we're being true to Jesus's teachings, for instance, should be delivered with reintegration in mind. People should have to face the harm they've caused and do something to restore the harmony that was disrupted."

Taken on their own, these penitent notes, which stress the harms caused by the incarcerated, might well call to mind the inward-facing religion of mass incarceration. When placed in broader, practical context, they gesture beyond mass incarceration, in the direction of an abolitionist future. Both men are adamant that the existing systems of punishment in America make real accountability impossible, and those who long for real accountability and justice need to push to transform these violent systems that atomize us and pit us against one another. "Jesus and Paul preached reconciliation with God when we fall away, and with each other when we do wrong to each other," Rosado writes. "Walls and fences prevent reconciliation." While the dance is necessarily delicate, Let's Circle Up is firmly and publicly allied with forces pushing for radical reform in Pennsylvania. In 2011, members of Let's Circle Up worked with organizers from abolitionist collective Decarcerate PA to connect anti-prison activists from Philadelphia to peace church Christians in Montgomery County to oppose a $400-million project to build a new prison, SCI Phoenix, on the land adjacent to Graterford. Rosado himself sits on the advisory committee of the formerly-incarcerated-led Coalition to Abolish Death By Incarceration (CADBI). A group led by Pennsylvania lifers and former lifers, CADBI belonged to the coalition that elected Larry Krasner as Philadelphia's district attorney and organizes for legislative remedies to meaningfully decarcerate the state of Pennsylvania.[89] In Rosado and Boyd's efforts, we see among incarcerated people the abolition spirit partially sublimated into a secular rubric, but simultaneously harnessed in service of transformative social change.

With a steadily growing movement organizing against Pennsylvania's law mandating that its lifers die in prison, Rosado and Boyd will eventually become parole eligible. Someday soon, we hope, like the overwhelming number of people incarcerated in America, they will leave prison. Once outside, they will join the ranks of formerly incarcerated people who are leading the fight to end mass incarceration and remake an American justice worthy of its name. One such person is Susan Burton.

By her own telling, prior to being a juvenile delinquent, a drug addict, a sex worker, and a survivor of intimate-partner violence, and prior to losing her child, Susan Burton was a Christian. For an achingly long time, she cycled between incarceration and addiction. When she was in prison or jail, she went to church every single Sunday. "I didn't feel no spirit moving. I just wanted to get out of that cage."[90] After many cycles of caging and relapse, Burton's religious path took an expected turn when, as a work detail, she was assigned to clerk for the Muslim chaplain. Like Assata Shakur, in Islam Burton found an unexpected affinity; unlike Assata, Burton went with it. "To my surprise, I found a comfort in the religion's discipline and teachings about the love of mankind, the need for self-determination, and being unaffected by worldly possessions. All this was in the Bible, too, but it never seemed as prominent to me in practice as this was. I began to pray, eventually praying five times a day." And though she rejected the idea that God couldn't hear her when she was menstruating, Burton observed the fast of Ramadan: "[I]ts message of self-repentance and sacrifice resonated with me."[91]

Once back on the street, the practices of Islam no longer felt like they fit, but Burton found a connection to God and to her fellows in recovery. As is true for many others in this country ravaged by illegal drugs and prescription pharmaceuticals, in the rituals of Alcoholics Anonymous, which she attended weekly at an Episcopal church, Burton found structure and community, and a renewed personal relationship with God.[92] She also came to wonder why services of this sort were available to women returning to Santa Monica but not to Los Angeles. Recognizing this gross disparity, Burton

224 BREAK EVERY YOKE

cobbled together a life purpose: to provide housing and other vital supports to some of the four thousand women who return every year from prison and jail to Los Angeles County. In 1998, with pooled resources and a mortgage in her nephew's name, Burton bought a house in Watts, and "A New Way of Life" was founded. One day, the County court called: they wanted to release a returning citizen to her care. For Burton, it was plainly a minor miracle. This "God-shot . . . would be the first of many."[93]

As Burton recognized, helping women survive the perilous transition from prison to the streets—"the process of detoxing from prison"—only so as to leave them thereafter to pull themselves up by their own bootstraps wasn't nearly enough.[94] The system itself had to be radically transformed. This meant organizing against California's tough-on-crime regime, with its predatory policing and pro forma public defense, and against the conveyer-belt "justice" in which criminal convictions are little more than "notches on the DA's belt." Meanwhile, the caste of poor people sent to jail and prison, often for nonviolent offenses, are thrown back out into "the wall of No," which places draconian restrictions on their capacity to find housing and employment, and therefore sends them back into despair and addiction, and oftentimes back to jail or prison. Burton is working in coalition with other formerly incarcerated movement leaders, including Kenneth Glasgow and Dorsey Nunn, founder of All of Us or None, as part of a growing effort to shrink the reach and impact of the prison industrial complex in California and across the nation.[95] Named for a fragment of a verse by Bertolt Brecht, All of Us or None has pushed successfully for incremental but meaningful reforms like Ban the Box provisions, which bar employers from asking about criminal histories, and California's Proposition 47 of 2014, which by changing a variety of offenses from felonies to misdemeanors shrunk California's prison population by 13,000 people.[96]

While many of the women Burton serves have some sort of religious practice, and a New Way of Life sometimes partners with neighborhood churches for Bible studies and life-skills trainings, Burton remains somewhat wary of organized religion, which in her experience has been short on inclusiveness and long on buttressing pastoral authority. She carries traces of these formative encounters, and to this day, when navigating a challenge, she sometimes plays hymns in her head to spur herself on: *We are soldiers in arms / We have to hold up the bloodstained banner.* What do these lyrics mean to her? In weathering her own trials and tribulations, she counts herself as part of "the army of righteousness, the army of change; the army of doing good in the world."[97] Residually animating her, too, are the Christian edicts to do unto others and to love her neighbor, but rather than looking outside herself, the faith that sustains is a "connection to God that's inside of me—a moral and spiritual compass." In her work, she feels this inner divinity in others, and the connections she makes to those who depend on her and those upon whom she depends are in part made of this shared godly stuff.

In aggregate, are the preceding examples religious or are they secular? Are they abolitionist or are they reformist? Though we eagerly tackle such questions in our seminars, we are uninterested in adjudicating them here. We concede that there is danger analytically in allowing the category of religion to grow too capacious. As scholar of religion J. Z. Smith once objected, "if all is religion . . . then we've learned nothing."[98] Analogously, and of substantially higher stakes, inasmuch as abolition's power stems from its categorical *No!* to human caging and human disposability, we understand how the refusal to police the boundary between abolition and not-abolition can lead to abolition's cooptation and enervation. We understand those who might be made uneasy when Michelle Alexander, who dubs Susan Burton an "abolitionist and freedom fighter," speaks of "abolishing *mass* incarceration (and not abolishing the prison as such)."[99] There is danger in such slippage, we recognize, but there is also opportunity. For our purposes, it is on this latter, inclusive side that we have chosen to err. By casting this wider net, we hope to spur on a wider array of prison opponents, whether secular or religious, already abolitionist or not yet there. In sum, in the speech and actions of Bryan Stevenson, Sam Smolinsky, Let's Circle Up, and Susan Burton, we hear invitations to think and do justice differently, and to consider the role religion has to play in helping us get there. The carceral logics of American culture have such a hold on us that these openings are generally hazy and uncertain. These incipient possibilities are too easily abandoned, or misunderstood, or reduced back to the dominant terms of the system—to the language of the prison administrator and the secularist. But these openings represent, perhaps, our best chance to envision true justice.

During the time we researched and wrote this book, Barack Obama finished his second term as president, and it looked likely that his legacy would continue with the presidency of another Clinton. "Ending mass incarceration" was moving from radical slogan to a slate of mainstream policy proposals.[100] With the election of Donald Trump, radical change to the criminal punishment system no longer seems quite so inevitable. New classes are being designated for incarceration, and without concerted, widespread pushback their ranks will only grow. Most of this is decidedly *not* new, but with Trump as its vulgar face, for many on the center left, the status of law and order as a weapon deployed by the powerful against the powerless has come into sharp—and for some, shocking—relief.[101] So long as they are tagged as lawbreakers, whistleblowers may be imprisoned, women seeking abortions may be criminalized, and migrant children may be placed in concentration camps. *Is this who we are?* Sadly, for now, the answer is yes. Trump-era innovations in and exacerbations of America's carceral state are, of course, devastating and deadly, but they offer a staunch reaffirmation of why an abolitionist stance is necessary. And so the abolition spirit continues to become manifest. The 2018 national prison strike was bigger still than the 2016 strike, and it included prisoners in no fewer than seventeen states. The next one will be bigger still.[102] We may well be a nation of jailers, prisoners, victims, and bystanders, but increasingly we are also becoming a nation of freedom fighters.

With respect to prisons and policing, but also, and paradigmatically, with respect to climate change, it is in no way hyperbole to say that our survival depends on our collective capacity to imagine and effect abolition-grade change. Toward these monumental ends, our key contribution here is relatively modest: we must not let party politics and reformist wonkery dictate our concept of justice. Rather, we must reinvigorate that noble concept with its broader, higher meaning. As a clear-sighted ideal, justice must remain immune to the pragmatic pressures of the political present. Whether or not in conjunction with explicitly religious ideas, justice must remain in perpetual tension with worldly categories and frontiers. Yet even in this elusiveness— indeed, especially in this elusiveness—higher justice exercises our imagination, solicits our commitment, and stirs us forward. It urges us to struggle: to discern, organize, oppose, and persist, and to insist that all those who live on this planet deserve better than what the powerful would grudgingly dole out.

Putting these divine convictions into practice can take any of a number of shapes, formal or informal, ritual or organizational, within existing institutional structures or by developing new ones. As we ourselves are trying to do within the bounds of this book and beyond, we encourage readers to begin a push to decarcerate where they are, in the institutions and communities in which they live and work. Keeping the devious adaptability of the carceral state in mind, we must move with caution, and we must draw on the practical know-how of people who are immediately impacted and by those who have been fighting already for years.[103] So long as we are trying to shrink the system and not to grow it, we should also feel licensed to try and fail, and to try again.

Martin Luther King Jr. famously told an audience at the Southern Christian Leadership Conference in 1967, "The arc of history is long, but it bends toward justice." King was paraphrasing the abolitionist preacher Theodore Parker. In the decade before the Civil War, while organizing resistance to the Fugitive Slave Act, Parker spoke of justice to his congregation. He preached to those seated in the pews, including runaway slaves he was protecting: "Private cohesions of self-love, of friendship, or of patriotism, must all be subordinate to this universal gravitation towards the eternal right"—to "a profound love of justice inherent in mankind."[104] Where King's phrasing suggests a liberal optimism, foreseeing gradual improvement, Parker was clear that it was impossible to know the path that history would take. A just world was not steadily emerging, but we can have confidence that tyrannies will, sooner or later, collapse. "The leaders of modern civilization have scorned justice," Parker intoned, pointing particularly to religious leaders, business leaders, military leaders, and politicians.[105] In a world where the rich and powerful dominate the rest, where injustice is rife, patience and prayer are not the solutions: "[I]n human affairs the justice of God must work by human means."[106] In a nation infected by such an evil malady as slavery, "You and I may help deepen the channel of human morality in which God's justice runs."[107] As slavery once did, the evil malady of prisons infects our nation today. We are called to respond— to prepare the world for the unpredictable, exuberant flow of divine justice, a justice not yet of this world, the justice each one of us is rightfully owed and rightfully owes in turn.

Notes

1. Douglas Egerton, *He Shall Go Out Free: The Lives of Denmark Vesey* (Lanham, MD: Rowman & Littlefield, 2004), 114.
2. Manisha Sinha, *The Slave's Cause: A History of Abolition* (New Haven, CT: Yale University Press, 2016), 197.
3. David Walker, *Appeal, in Four Articles; Together with a Preamble, to the Coloured Citizens of the World, but in Particular, and Very Expressly, to Those of the United States of America* (September 28, 1829), http://docsouth.unc.edu/nc/walker/walker.html.
4. Sinha, *The Slave's Cause*, 211.
5. William Lloyd Garrison, "Address to the Colonization Society" (July 4, 1829), http://teachingamericanhistory.org/library/document/address-to-the-colonization-society/.

6. Robert Abzug, *Cosmos Crumbling: American Reform and the Religious Imagination* (New York: Oxford University Press, 1994), 153.

7. Sinha, *The Slave's Cause*, 269.

8. Ibid., 238.

9. Peter P. Hinks, "Free Blacks and Kidnapping in Antebellum Boston," *Historical Journal of Massachusetts* (Winter 1992), 30–31.

10. Sinha, *The Slave's Cause*, 214–227. "Interracial immediatism" is how Sinha characterizes the abolitionist ethos of the early 1830s.

11. See Douglas Strong, *Perfectionist Politics: Abolitionism and the Religious Tensions of American Democracy* (Syracuse, NY: Syracuse University Press, 1999); John R. McKivigan, ed., *Abolitionism and American Religion* (New York: Garland, 1999).

12. Sinha, *The Slave's Cause*, 206.

13. Ibid., 219.

14. John Stephen Dwyer, *Black Lives Matter at South Bay House of Correction in Boston*, https://www.youtube.com/watch?v=kvwX9ZYx56g. The same witnessing practice occurred later in protests in Charlotte, North Carolina; see "Charlotte Inmates Flicker Lights as Protesters Outside Jail Chant 'We See You! We Love You!,'" http://www.mediaite.com/online/charlotte-inmates-flicker-lights-as-protesters-outside-jail-chant-we-see-you-we-love-you/.

15. In characterizing the secularity of history's first draft, we are thinking of early interventions like Joshua Clover's *Riot. Strike. Riot: The New Era of Uprisings* (London: Verso Books, 2016); Mark and Paul Engler's *This Is an Uprising: How Nonviolent Revolt Is Shaping the Twenty-First Century* (New York: Nation Books, 2016); Eddie Glaude's *Democracy in Black: How Race Still Enslaves the Soul of America* (New York: Broadway Books, 2016); Sarah Jaffe's *Necessary Trouble: Americans in Revolt* (New York: Nation Books, 2016); and Keeanga-Yamahtta Taylor's *From #BlackLivesMatter to Black Liberation* (Chicago: Haymarket Books, 2016).

16. For William Barber's account of Moral Mondays, see William J. Barber and Jonathan Wilson-Hartgrove, *The Third Reconstruction: Moral Mondays, Fusion Politics, and the Rise of a New Justice Movement*. See also Vincent Lloyd, "How Religious Is #BlackLivesMatter?," in *Humanism and the Challenge of Difference*, ed. Anthony B. Pinn (New York: Palgrave Macmillan, 2018), 215–237.

17. https://www.youtube.com/watch?v=O4Qs3jS3-3U.

18. "Nones" refer to those without any professed religious affiliation. See Michael Lipka, "Religious 'Nones' Are Not Only Growing, They're Becoming More Secular," Pew Research Center (November 11, 2015), http://www.pewresearch.org/fact-tank/2015/11/11/religious-nones-are-not-only-growing-theyre-becoming-more-secular/. Locating the Ferguson protesters in the tradition of James Baldwin, Xavier Pickett characterizes their stance as "*irreligious* Black rage." Personal conversation, December 12, 2018.

19. For thinking constructively about organizing rituals and practices in a Black radical, spiritual-but-not-religious idiom, see Adrienne Maree Brown, *Emergent Strategy: Shaping Change, Changing Worlds* (Chico, CA: AK Press, 2017).

20. For critical consideration of the politics and affects of racialized spectacles of suffering, see Saidiya Hartman, *Scenes of Subjection: Terror, Slavery, and Self-Making in Nineteenth-Century America* (New York: Oxford University Press, 1997).
21. Personal Interview with Nyle Fort, October 12, 2018. Fort's sermon is reproduced in "Last Words: A Black Theological Response to Ferguson and Anti-Blackness," *QED: A Journal of GLBTQ Worldmaking* 2, no. 2 (Summer 2015), 209–212. For video, see https://www.youtube.com/watch?v=MKQ6c12G4sQ. To read more about Fort and others, see Almeda Wright, *The Spiritual Lives of Young African Americans* (New York: Oxford University Press, 2017).
22. https://www.youtube.com/watch?v=MKQ6c12G4sQ.
23. Assata Shakur, *Assata: An Autobiography* (Chicago: Lawrence Hill Books, 2001), 52.
24. Ibid., 41.
25. Ibid., 139.
26. Ibid., 92.
27. Ibid., 124.
28. Ibid., 274.
29. Ibid., 93.
30. Ibid., 123.
31. Michelle Chen, "Georgia Prison Strike: A Hidden Labor Force Resists," *In These Times* (December 17, 2010), http://inthesetimes.com/working/entry/6784/georgia_prison_strike_a_hidden_labor_force_resists; "Georgia Prisoners on Strike?!," Revolution By the Book: The AK Press Blog (December 13, 2010), http://www.revolutionbythebook.akpress.org/georgia-prisoners-on-strike/.
32. Hamim Abdullah Asadallah, "Georgia Prison Striker Tells His Story," *San Francisco Bay View* (April 8, 2011), http://sfbayview.com/2011/04/georgia-prison-striker-tells-his-story/; Amima Asadallah, "Muslim Minister Labeled a White Dr. King Has a Powerful Voice," *San Francisco Bay View* (July 11, 2012), https://sfbayview.com/2012/07/muslim-minister-labeled-a-white-dr-king-has-a-powerful-voice/; "Immediate Justice and Human Rights for Georgia State Prisoner Shawn Whatley!," Socialist Alternative, https://www.socialistalternative.org/sound-fury-oppressed/human-rights-georgia-state-prisoner-shawn-whatley/.
33. For reflection on "Allahu Akbar" as a political-theological tool for abolitionist struggle, see Houria Bouteldja, *Whites, Jews, and Us: Toward a Politics of Revolutionary Love* (South Pasadena, CA: Semiotext(e), 2017), 127–140.
34. Asadallah, "Muslim Minister." Another prominent Muslim voice organizing today among the incarcerated is Siddique Abdullah Hasan. Sentenced to death for his alleged role in the 1993 Lucasville Prison rebellion, Hasan is a Sunni Muslim community leader who was one of the primary organizers of the Free Ohio Movement, which participated in the September 9, 2016 strike. For an interview with Hasan, see https://freepress.org/article/interview-siddique-abdullah-hasan.
35. Felon disenfranchisement rules vary from state to state; in Alabama, only those convicted of "crimes of moral turpitude" are barred from the ballot box. See http://ballot-access.org/2008/10/21/kenneth-glasgow-wins-alabama-lawsuit-over-registering-voters-in-prison/.

36. http://www.dothaneagle.com/news/crime_court/kenneth-glasgow-arrested-in-protest-at-alabama-capitol/article_a4791788-2f91-11e4-89b6-0017a43b2370.html; https://theintercept.com/2016/09/16/former-prisoners-are-leading-the-fight-against-mass-incarceration/.

37. Personal interview, January 30, 2018.

38. In April 2018, in what by all appearances would seem to be a politically motivated prosecution, Glasgow was charged with capital murder for giving a ride to a man who, upon getting out of his car, shot and killed someone. According to Alabama's expansive statute, to aid and abet someone in committing a crime makes one equally liable. See https://www.nytimes.com/2018/07/07/us/kenneth-glasgow-alabama-sharpton.html.

39. Personal Interview, June 7, 2017.

40. Lee Griffith, *The Fall of the Prison: Biblical Perspectives on Prison Abolition* (Grand Rapids, MI: William B. Eerdmans, 1993), 204.

41. Ibid., 228.

42. Hannah Bowman interview, September 3, 2018. Maya Schenwar, *Locked Down, Locked Out: Why Prison Doesn't Work and How We Can Do Better* (Oakland, CA: Berrett-Koehler, 2014).

43. Chris Barbera, "Toward a Christian Prison Theology," *Dialog: A Journal of Theology* 46, no. 2 (2007), 128. See also Paulo Freire, *Pedagogy of the Oppressed* (New York: Continuum, 2000). For the Freireian impulse in contemporary prison education, see Robert Scott, "Distinguishing Radical Teaching from Merely Having Intense Experiences while Teaching in Prison," *Radical Teacher* 95 (2013), 22–32.

44. Chris Barbera, Conference Presentation at Prison Abolition of Western New York (PAWNY), September 22, 2018.

45. Conference presentation at PAWNY, September 22, 2018, supplemented with personal interview with Gabrie'l Atchison, October 12, 2018. For scriptural support, Atchison specifically cites Matthew 22:35–40 and John 15:13.

46. Personal interviews with David Brazil, January 5 and May 26, 2017. Both in his critiques of capitalism and empire and in his conceptualization of radical discipleship, Brazil credits Ched Myer's *Binding the Strong Man: A Political Reading of Mark's Story of Jesus* (Ossining, NY: Orbis Books, 2008).

47. Personal interview with Nicole Deane, May 26, 2017.

48. Deane counts liberation theologian James Cone as a major influence and appeals to George Lakoff's notion of "political frames" in making sense of her abolitionist organizing.

49. Mark Leviton, "Dangerous Love: Reverend Lynice Pinkard on the Revolutionary Act of Living the Gospels," *The Sun* (October 2014), 4–17.

50. Lynice Pinkard, "Revolutionary Suicide: Risking Everything to Transform Society and Live Fully," *Tikkun* 28, no. 4 (Fall 2013), 31–41.

51. Lynice Pinkard, "The Master's Mehserle Can Never Dismantle the Master's House," *Tikkun* 26, no. 1 (2011), 13–14, 88–91. Pinkard is quoting the words of Will D. Campbell. See Will D. Campbell and Richard C. Goode, *Crashing the Idols: The*

Vocation of Will D. Campbell (and Any Other Christian for That Matter) (Eugene, Oregon: Cascade Books, 2010), 53.

52. Pinkard, "The Master's Mehserle Can Never Dismantle the Master's House."
53. Ibid.
54. Ibid.
55. Ibid.
56. Ibid.
57. Personal interview with Kempis "Ghani" Songster, October 28, 2018. On the use of Ubuntu for abolition, see Mecke Nagel, "Troubling Justice: Towards a Ludic Ubuntu Ethic," Human Dignity and Humiliation Studies (2016), http://www.humiliationstudies.org/documents/NagelUbuntu2016.pdf.
58. For an abolitionist mode of Buddhist practice, see Rev. angel Kyodo Williams, Lama Rod Owens, and Jasmine Syedullah, *Radical Dharma: Talking Race, Love, and Liberation* (Berkeley, CA: North Atlantic Books, 2016).
59. For thinking about organizing against climate change, Songster recommends Aric McBay, Lierre Keith, and Derrick Jensen, *Deep Green Resistance* (New York: Seven Stories Press, 2011).
60. See http://www.seminaryofthestreet.org/id30.html (now defunct).
61. Leviton, "Dangerous Love."
62. For more on "liturgical direct actions," see Bill Wylie Kellerman, *Seasons of Faith and Conscience: Explorations in Liturgical Direct Action* (Eugene, OR: Wipf & Stock, 2008). For an influential account of the politics of liturgy developed from anti-Pinochet protests in Chile, see William T. Cavanaugh, *Torture and Eucharist: Theology, Politics, and the Body of Christ* (Oxford: Blackwell, 1998).
63. https://www.facebook.com/savethe12stparcelforthepeople/posts/458349841037251.
64. Nicole Deane, personal email, June 22, 2017.
65. Nicole Deane, personal email.
66. Oakland Peace Center, May 26, 2017.
67. See, for example, Jews for Racial and Economic Justice, "Mixed Multitudes: Nobody's Free 'til Everybody's Free: A Racial Justice Haggadah for Pesach," https://jfrej.org/wp-content/uploads/2016/04/Mixed-Multitudes-Haggadah-for-Download.pdf; and The Jewish Working Group to End the New Jim Crow, "Crying Out against Mass Incarceration: Passover Haggadah Supplement," http://www.truah.org/wp-content/uploads/2017/03/Haggadah_Supplement_Mass_Incarceration.pdf.   For an antecedent, see Arthur Waskow's "Freedom Seder" liturgy from 1969, at https://theshalomcenter.org/content/original-1969-freedom-seder.
68. See https://www.facebook.com/judy.hollander/videos/10205417448100248/. Immanent to the ritual's explicitly Jewish significations, Molly Farneth reads into this action the assertion of a foundational democratic principle: "[T]hese citizens . . . put their bodies in the streets and . . . symbolized and actualized, in word and deed, that notion at the heart of democratic authority: we are responsible." Molly Farneth, *Hegel's Social Ethics: Religion, Conflict, and Rituals of Reconciliation* (Princeton, NJ: Princeton University Press, 2017), 131.

69. See http://www.project-nia.org/ and https://survivedandpunished.org/.

70. https://twitter.com/prisonculture/status/931292682529460226.

71. Fittingly, it was from a nun that Kaba acquired the inspiring insight that "Hope Is a Discipline." See https://twitter.com/prisonculture/status/1009621164241641473?lang=en. This notion calls to mind Pierre Hadot's account of "spiritual practices." See Pierre Hadot, *Philosophy as a Way of Life: Spiritual Exercises from Socrates to Foucault* (Oxford: Wiley-Blackwell, 1995). Complementary to this practice-minded sensibility is an approach that some have dubbed "everyday abolition." See, for example, https://everydayabolition.com/

72. Mariame Kaba, Interfaith Banquet Keynote, Rochester, New York, April 1, 2017. See Rob Warden, "How and Why Illinois Abolished the Death Penalty," *Law and Inequality: A Journal of Theory and Practice* 30, no. 2 (2012), 245–286.

73. See https://nomoremoneybail.org/ and https://believersbailout.org/. According to a social media post by Mariame Kaba, the idea of bailing out black mothers for Mother's Day was first proposed in Atlanta, in January 2017, by abolitionist organizer Mary Hooks. Hooks is co-director of Southerners on New Ground, http://southernersonnewground.org/about/staff/.

74. https://player.fm/series/radio-islam/ep-539-reflections-dr-suad-believers-bailout-05-23-2018.

75. https://twitter.com/hodakatebi/status/1004415971514298372.

76. https://player.fm/series/radio-islam/ep-539-reflections-dr-suad-believers-bailout-05-23-2018.

77. See *Montgomery v. Louisiana*, 577 U.S. _____ (2016) and *Miller v. Alabama*, 567 U.S. 460 (2012).

78. Phone conversation, October 28, 2018.

79. On truth and reconciliation in South Africa, see Desmond Tutu, *No Future without Forgiveness* (New York: Image Books, 2000). For a critical assessment, see Richard A. Wilson, *The Politics of Truth and Reconciliation in South Africa: Legitimizing the Post-Apartheid State* (New York: Cambridge University Press, 2001). On Gacaca in practice, see Kristin Doughty, *Remediation in Rwanda: Grassroots Legal Forums* (Philadelphia: University of Pennsylvania Press, 2016).

80. In the late nineties, coauthor Joshua Dubler worked for Stevenson's Equal Justice Initiative of Alabama (EJI).

81. In 2018, EJI opened The Legacy Museum: From Enslavement to Mass Incarceration, in Montgomery. See https://eji.org/legacy-museum.

82. Bryan Stevenson, *Just Mercy: A Story of Justice and Redemption* (New York: Spiegel & Grau, 2014), 12.

83. Ibid., 309.

84. For a brief encouraging religious scholars and scholars of religion to get their institutions involved with college in prison, see Charles Atkins, Joshua Dubler, Vincent Lloyd, and Mel Webb, "'Using the Language of Christian Love and Charity': What Liberal Religion Offers Higher Education in Prison" *Religions* 10 (2019), 169; doi:10.3390/rel10030169.

85. Keramet Reiter, *23/7: Pelican Bay Prison and the Rise of Long-Term Solitary Confinement* (New Haven, CT: Yale University Press, 2016); Personal Interview with Sam Smolinsky, March 31, 2016. We reproduce here Smolinsky's account—certainly one story among others, with details that others would report differently.

86. Workshop handout, AALAC Collaborative Workshop: Engaging College Communities In and Beyond Prison Education, Bryn Mawr, Pennsylvania, June 3, 2017.

87. Personal correspondence from Charles Boyd, September 8, 2017.

88. Personal correspondence from Felix Rosado, July 9, 2017.

89. Senate Bill 492 (2017), which garnered ample support, would make all life prisoners in Pennsylvania parole eligible after serving fifteen years. See http://www.legis. state.pa.us/cfdocs/billInfo/billInfo.cfm?sYear=2017&sInd=0&body=S&type =B&bn=942. Pennsylvania is the global leader on sentencing people to die in prison. See the Abolitionist Law Center's report, *A Way Out: Abolishing Death By Incarceration in Pennsylvania* (September 18, 2018), http://abolitionistlawcenter. org/2018/09/18/a-way-out-abolishing-death-by-incarceration-in-pennsylvania/.

90. Susan Burton and Cari Lynn, *Becoming Ms. Burton: From Prison to Recovery to Leading the Fight for Incarcerated Women* (New York: New Press, 2017), 79.

91. Ibid., 103.

92. https://www.guideposts.org/inspiration/people-helping-people/ how-susan-burton-is-helping-women-rebuild-after-prison.

93. Burton and Lynn, *Becoming Ms. Burton*, 145. For more on how religious frameworks motivate formerly incarcerated people to organize for justice in their communities, see Edward Orozco Flores, *"Jesus Saved an Ex-Con": Political Activism and Redemption After Incarceration* (New York: New York University Press, 2018).

94. Burton and Lynn, *Becoming Ms. Burton*, 234.

95. See https://www.prisonerswithchildren.org/our-projects/allofus-or-none/.

96. https://news.stanford.edu/news/2015/november/prison-early-release-110215.html.

97. Personal Interview with Susan Burton, October 15, 2018.

98. Smith said this to René Girard contra the latter's unifying theory of the scapegoat. See Walter Burkert, Rene Girard, and Jonathan Z. Smith, *Violent Origins: Walter Burkert, René Girard, and Jonathan Z. Smith on Ritual Killing and Cultural Formation* (Palo Alto, CA: Stanford University Press, 1998), 179.

99. Michelle Alexander, in Burton and Lynn, *Becoming Ms. Burton*, xi. Italics added.

100. Indeed, the very first policy address of Hillary Clinton's campaign was about "ending mass incarceration." See "Remarks at Columbia University on Criminal Justice and Mass Incarceration" (February 14, 2016), https://www.hillaryclinton.com/post/ remarks-columbia-university-criminal-justice-and-mass-incarceration/.

101. As Donald Trump tweeted on June 26, 2018, in proposed violation of US and international law: "We cannot allow all of these people to invade our Country. When somebody comes in, we must immediately, with no Judges or Court Cases, bring them back from where they came. Our system is a mockery to good immigration policy and Law and Order. Most children come without parents . . .," https://twitter. com/realDonaldTrump/status/1010900865602019329.

102. See https://www.vox.com/2018/8/17/17664048/national-prison-strike-2018. The 2018 national prison strike was explicitly endorsed by the Unitarian Universalist Association, https://www.uua.org/pressroom/press-releases/show-solidarity-nationwide-prisoner-strike.

103. For resources, see Critical Resistance's abolitionist tool kit, http://criticalresistance.org/resources/the-abolitionist-toolkit/ and https://transformharm.org/#.

104. Theodore Parker, *Ten Sermons of Religion* (Boston: Crosby, Nichols, and Company, 1853), 71, 81. See also Dean Grodzins, *American Heretic: Theodore Parker and Transcendentalism* (Chapel Hill: University of North Carolina Press, 2002).

105. Parker, *Ten Sermons of Religion*, 96.

106. Ibid., 100.

107. Ibid.

Concluding Meditations

At Jewish Day School, I was subjected to catechisms and taboos, but more than that, I was entrusted with an arsenal of stories. In second grade, with guidance from the medieval commentators, we went line-by-line through Genesis. Abraham smashing his father's idols: it is a story that has haunted me ever since, a story that comes to Muslims via scripture, but which comes to Jews only via the commentators. For Terah and others in his community, these were the sacred implements, but Abraham knew them to be wrong, and he destroyed them. What did my teachers want me to get from this story? I can't say for sure: what I remember is coloring in a picture of this apocryphal moment with crayons. Perhaps it was the American boy in me, filled with the residual passions of romanticism and the sixties counterculture, who connected to the tale, but the archetype left on me an enduring trace. Years later, when I first encountered Hannah Arendt's insistence that even and especially in the upside-down world of Nazi Germany, ordinary citizens nonetheless remained morally culpable for what they did and failed to do, I could only nod my head.

The Black freedom struggle is, narratively speaking, our national epic, and that goes double for those for whom the filter of Exodus lies ready-to-hand. Around the Passover Seder table, we recited, sang, and argued about the Haggadah's edict that each generation is obligated act as if they, themselves, came out of Egypt. The civil rights movement was still in the recent past, and when, long into the night we'd sing a medley of liturgical and secular Hebrew songs, we would also belt out spirituals: "Go Down, Moses," "Amazing Grace," "Swing Low Sweet Chariot." Perhaps I was resisting the rabbis, but though the stories were unmistakably ours, I found the position of the enslaved Israelite difficult to occupy. Our exodus saga was over. "Next Year in Jerusalem!" we would sing, but as everybody understood, the United States was, for us, the Promised Land. Yet for many communities, for the descendants of those enslaved in America paradigmatically, life in this country can be an indefinite desert wandering: of poverty, of neglect, and of predation. Was it my responsibility to finish repairing the world? Of course not. But as Pirkei Avot made equally clear, neither was I free to sit idly by.

When I graduated college, I followed my civil rights forebears down South, to Alabama, where I worked for a not-for-profit that represents poor people in prison, most of them on death row. Afterward, as a graduate student, researcher, and teacher, I spent long hours at Pennsylvania's Graterford Prison. There I met a group of extraordinary men, a good number of whom had been in prison longer than I'd been alive, and together we learned, and taught, and passionately argued, and killed time. Occasionally we prayed. A principled commitment to a cause is one thing; the binds of intimacy are a different order of obligation. In time, the research component of my Graterford time became my book Down in the Chapel, and prison teaching became a vocation. When circumstances began to drag me elsewhere, I promised my incarcerated friends that going forward I would strive to earn the trust that they had placed in me.

The men at Graterford were the last great shaping force in my education. One quietly righteous scholar named Robert Altland, a convert to Catholicism sentenced to die in prison, introduced me to restorative justice and pointed me to Angela Davis's Are Prisons Obsolete? That I'd never read Angela Davis before was just one facet of my enduring ignorance. My last semester at Graterford was the time of the Arab Spring. I scrapped the syllabus and instead we collectively grappled with how revolutions happen. It's a meager theodicy that points at something and shouts "neoliberalism!", but somehow, on the cusp of the new era of social movements, I had yet to fully assimilate that for the people to someday win they must painstakingly organize. I joined up with Decarcerate PA and helped push its platform of no new prisons, decarceration, and community reinvestment.

When I accepted a job at the University of Rochester, I worked with Vincent and other colleagues in the region to begin a series of convenings—discussions, conferences, performances, and exchanges—around religion and incarceration, reflecting particularly on western New York's history of prison innovation, religious enthusiasm, and abolitionist mobilization. At some point Vincent suggested that we coauthor a book. Early in my research I discovered that William Lloyd Garrison signed all his letters with a quote from Isaiah 58: "Break Every Yoke." I pulled up the biblical text and read as follows:

> *Is not this the kind of fasting I have chosen:*
> *to loose the chains of injustice*
> *and untie the cords of the yoke,*
> *to set the oppressed free*
> *and break every yoke?*

As happens not infrequently when I come across a biblical allusion in a Christian historical context, this text didn't resonate for me as particularly Jewish. But as was earlier true of Arendt's moral exactitude, so too was it with Isaiah's prophetic exhortation to abolition: by the time I first read it, it already had its hooks in me. Some months later, in the good-natured but ill-fitting congregation where my family occasionally prays, I volunteered to chant the Yom Kippur Haftorah. Even when I was in practice, I was never good at prayer, but I love chanting the Haftorah, and when I do, I sometimes creep within earshot of the numinous. The day before Yom Kippur I pulled out my Tanakh and began to cram. I came to a phrase I couldn't understand— וְכָל מוֹטָה תְּנַתֵּקוּ—and looked up the translation. Only then did I grasp that I was face-to-face with Garrison's Isaiah: break every yoke.

Analytically, I understand that my commitment to abolishing forms of human caging is at once a timeless absolute and also an historical contingency. But is my commitment to abolishing prisons religious? I'm not always certain how to think about this; but upon finding myself in the shadow of Isaiah and Garrison, it would be secularist folly to insist it isn't so.

Recently, in search of funding for educating incarcerated people in the broader Rochester area, a formerly incarcerated collaborator and I had a meeting with an executive of a foundation that funds both Jewish initiatives and education initiatives. In making my pitch, I spoke of the resonances of the Passover liturgy for the moral and social crisis that is mass incarceration. The executive found our proposed program compelling, and seemed open to supporting us, but stated with a chuckle that she didn't see how prisons were a Jewish concern. I made the case to her then as I now make the case to you:

As a people that values freedom, and a people that has been blessed with freedom, it is our obligation to stand with those in captivity. As citizens of the United States, we are, from an ethical standpoint, no longer the enslaved Israelites; rather, we are the ordinary Egyptians. While the vanities endowed by our sacred stories may make us protest otherwise, in aggregate it is assuredly so: as white, American Jews, we are not the victims of state violence; we are its beneficiaries. So long as prisons remain, it is our obligation—us Jews— to stand in unwavering solidarity with those systemically targeted by state violence: the poor, the young, the Black and brown, the undocumented. This means standing with—and fighting for—those who are already in prison, and with those who, unless things change, are demographically destined for the same fate.

Are we obligated to break every yoke? A strict reader of Isaiah might say yes; the rabbis might grant us a bit more leeway. But are we free to sit idly by? To this much easier question, the answer is plainly no.

-J.D.

Rochester, NY

***

It was 6:45 a.m. A man who was, like me, in his late twenties, picked me up at the train station in his green Volvo station wagon. He drove me a couple of miles to an elementary school parking lot in southeast Atlanta where others were waiting. There were about twenty of us, and we had to organize ourselves into a caravan quickly for the nearly three-hour drive ahead. I stayed with the Volvo; two others joined us. We were heading into rural Georgia, to Lumpkin, home of what was then the largest immigration detention center in the United States. It was early, but no one slept. We talked about how we had come to be in this green Volvo together, on this long drive—four strangers.

The driver was a Mennonite, a relatively recent convert, drawn to the church by its commitment to social justice and peaceful living. There was a young woman just out of college, participating in a year-long Catholic volunteer program. There was an immigration attorney from an Atlanta suburb, worried that the day-to-day grind of lawyering had caused her to forget the outrage at injustice that had initially motivated her career choice. And there was me, a twenty-eight-year-old religion professor at Georgia State, the huge, diverse public university in downtown Atlanta.

Our half dozen cars reconvened on the street in front of the impressive, century-old courthouse in Lumpkin's center, flanked by mostly empty storefronts. The 2000 census recorded 1,369 inhabitants of Lumpkin, 70% of them Black, 9% of them Latinx. This was not the Lumpkin we had traveled to see. In 2006, Corrections Corporation of America, the largest operator of private prisons in the nation, opened the Stewart Detention Center. With a capacity of 1,752, and housing largely Latinx detainees, on paper the demographics of Lumpkin had changed dramatically. These new statistics were not reflected in the passers-by on Lumpkin's main street, where we assembled for a briefing on what to expect when we arrived at Stewart.

How the staff would react to us—twenty city folks intending to visit incarcerated men we had never met—was unpredictable, we were told. Some guards *might be sympathetic, though many would be apathetic or hostile. Paired off, each pair including at least one Spanish speaker, we were given the name and identification number of a man incarcerated at Stewart. Then the waiting began, the waiting that would consume most of the day. In quiet voices we talked among ourselves, learned more about what had brought us to Lumpkin, about the mix of faith commitments, political commitments, sympathy, and curiosity that motivated our group. There was a core group of Mennonites—the trip had been coordinated by the Atlanta Mennonite Fellowship—but there were also several Catholics and several seekers, and atheists, too. The charismatic leader of our group, Anton Flores, lived in an intentional Christian community near the detention center. His household consisted of US citizens and undocumented women and men sharing their lives together and hosting the families of Stewart detainees who trek from all parts of the South to visit their loved ones.*

I saw myself as an anomaly in the group. I am not from the South—quite the opposite, from Minnesota. I am not a Mennonite—quite the opposite; I attended Lutheran schools (of the conservative Missouri Synod) for some years, but I did not practice any religion then, nor was I in any way a spiritual seeker. I lived in Atlanta, but I grew up across the street from corn fields; I was not one of the many urbane Atlantans biding their time while waiting for an opportunity to move to New York or Chicago. Politically, I was formed through labor and social movement organizing, in traditions that look down on protest tourism and activist "witness."

I am also not white. My father is a Black immigrant from Latin America; my mother is a white woman from rural Wisconsin. I have relatives who have been incarcerated—they are rural whites caught in the traps of drugs and despair that others happened to avoid. Everyone in the waiting room at Stewart had their own stories, unique in some ways, similar to mine in others, but in many ways I felt alone.

Close to 1 p.m. a guard announced that "my" detainee was ready for a visit. While we had been extensively briefed on logistics, it dawned on me that we had not been told what to say. It was enough, we were told, to simply be there, to be present, to have an ordinary conversation with a man held captive, a man who likely was ripped away from his family, home, and job, held captive for profit for an indeterminate length of time before he would be deposited across the border in a country he last saw a year, or two, or two decades ago. My partner in witness—a vivacious, twenty-something white woman who worked for an Atlanta nonprofit—spoke Spanish; my guilt at imperfectly mastering my father's tongue usually prevents me from speaking it at all. We were led to a row of visiting stations, Plexiglas and a telephone receiver separating us from the incarcerated man waiting for us. I watched and listened as my partner introduced both of us over the phone, made small talk, attempted to strike the right tone between encouraging, empathetic, and realistic. She was remarkably good at this; I was not. I could not bring myself to speak—to speak in my father's language, or to speak through my partner. However difficult it was to strike the right tone in conversation, it was all the more difficult to strike the right pose while mute, across Plexiglas, looking at someone I had never seen before and would never see again.

This was supposed to be my moment of witness, and I failed. I was not sure of the meaning of "witness". I remain unsure. It seemed somehow incoherent: not wrong, not morally questionable, but also not reassuring to anyone, and certainly bearing little relationship to justice. What seemed powerful was the energy of the people in the cars, in front of the courthouse, in the waiting room. What seemed powerful was the energy I knew existed but could not see behind the locked doors: the self-organization of those caged in desperate conditions demanding dignity and justice, efforts that included a series of hunger strikes at Stewart. Witness may have been important for some, but I concluded that to advance justice we needed to bring together those with faith commitments and with political commitments to magnify the voices of the most marginalized, these dark-skinned men deemed disposable, held in camps.

Before and after my trip to Lumpkin, I have visited other prisons, jails, and detention centers. But my calling is not to witness through a plastic wall. In Atlanta, I worked with colleagues in a faith-based community organizing network to train immigration court observers tracking the injustices of a broken system and pursuing legal remedies. I undertook academic research into the resources that Black religious traditions hold for advancing justice struggles. This book intends to deploy scholarship at its best, at its most meaningful, to tell stories that motivate organizing.

It is 6:45 a.m.: we can go back to sleep or join together in struggle.

-V.L.
Philadelphia, PA

Debts and Resources

This book began in a series of conversations generously funded by the Central New York Humanities Corridor through a grant from the Andrew W. Mellon Foundation. At the research and writing stages it was generously funded by the American Council of Learned Societies, the Carnegie Corporation of New York, and the University of Wisconsin, Madison's Institute for Research in the Humanities. In facilitating this support, we are grateful to the administrations and to our departments at Syracuse University, the University of Rochester, and Villanova University. At Rochester, we are grateful for the administrative support provided by Debra Haring and Caleb Rood; at Syracuse, for support from Deborah Pratt; and at Villanova, for support from Candeth Washington, Elizabeth Orkwiszewski, and Mary Polier.

We are grateful to the many thinkers, practitioners, and organizers who helped shape our ideas about what abolition is and must be. Many of these people are named in the preceding pages; some are not. This list includes Robert Altland, Gabrie'l Atchison, Hakim Ali, Precious Bedell, Chris Barbera, Dan Berger, Hannah Bowman, Charles Boyd, David Brazil, Orisanmi Burton, Susan Burton, Nicole Deane, Kim Diehl, Nyle Fort, Anton Flores, Chris Garces, Bishop Richard Garcia, Kenneth Glasgow, Chance Grable, Bret Grote, Lily Haskell, Robert Saleem Holbrook, Mariame Kaba, James Kilgore, Brian Lee, Marie Levin, Jason Lydon, Laura Magnani, Dustin McDaniel, Laura McTighe, Mecke Nagle, Lynice Pinkard, Felix Rosado, Vincenzo Ruggiero, Rob Scott, Caleb Smith, Sam Smolinsky, Ghani Songster, and Aly Wane. Supplementary research assistance was furnished by Aaran Marans and David Markakis. Eitan Freedenberg designed our beautiful cover.

Invaluable feedback on our prose and thinking was furnished by Amaryah Armstrong, Dan Berger, Joseph Blankholm, Elizabeth Bruenig, Steve Bush, Leslie Callahan, Natalie Cisneros, Charles Coley, Michael Coyle, Mark Engler, Molly Farneth, Elena Gogovska, Brady Heiner, Kathleen Holscher, Jonathon Kahn, Joy James, James Logan, Colby Lenz, Andrea Pitts, Stan Rosenthal, Dean Spade, Kathryn Getek Soltis, Molly Tarbell, Mark L. Taylor, Isaac Weiner, James Wetzel, and Terrance Wiley. We appreciate the generous feedback on portions of this work offered by faculty, students, and audience interlocutors at a joint meeting of the Academy of Catholic Hispanic Theologians and the Black Catholic Theological Symposium, the Alliance to Advance Liberal Arts Colleges, Bard Berlin, Bates College, Brown University, the Claremont School of Theology, Greenville University, Haverford College, Hope International University, LeMoyne College, The Ohio State University, Princeton Theological Seminary, Princeton University, Santa Clara University, Saint Louis University, the Tri-Co Political Theory Workshop, University of New Mexico, University of Oslo, Vassar College, Villanova University, University of Rochester, the University of Wisconsin, and the Western Political Science Association. We are especially grateful, too, to Roberto Sirvent for the panel on our manuscript that he organized at the 2017 Pacific meeting of the American Philosophical Association.

We are immensely grateful for our friends and fellow strugglers, in Philadelphia and in Rochester, and wherever else we find ourselves at home. Above all, in this regard and in many others, we are grateful for the love and support of our partners, Lisa Cerami and Dana Lloyd, and of our children.

For readers looking to involve themselves in abolitionist organizing, we would encourage you to look into one or more of the following organizations, references to which you will also find sprinkled in the preceding pages:

A New Way of Life, http://anewwayoflife.org/
Abolition, https://abolitionjournal.org/
Abolitionist Law Center, https://abolitionistlawcenter.org/
Agape Fellowship (Oakland)
All of Us or None, https://www.prisonerswithchildren.org/our-projects/
allofus-or-none/
American Friends Service Committee, https://www.afsc.org
Believers Bail Out, https://believersbailout.org
Black and Pink, http://www.blackandpink.org/
Buffalo Anti-Racism Coalition, https://buffaloantiracismcoalition.
wordpress.com/
Casa Alterna, http://alternacommunity.com/about/
Christians for the Abolition of Prisons, https://christiansforabolition.org/
Coalition to Abolish Death By Incarceration (CADBI), https://
decarceratepa.info/CADBI
Chicago Community Bail Fund, https://chicagobond.org/
https://christiansforabolition.org/
Critical Resistance, http://criticalresistance.org/

Decarerate PA, https://decarceratepa.info/
Equal Justice Initiative of Alabama (EJI), https://eji.org/
Incarcerated Workers Organizing Committee (IWOC), https://incarceratedworkers.org/
Innercity Muslim Action Network (IMAN), https://www.imancentral.org/
International Conference on Penal Abolition (ICOPA)
Jesus the Liberator Seminary (Buffalo)
Jews for Racial and Economic Justice, https://jfrej.org/
Let's Circle Up (SCI Phoenix)
Masjid Al-Rabia (Chicago), https://masjidalrabia.org/
MPower, https://mpowerchange.org/
Never Again is Now, https://www.neveragainaction.com/
No New Jails NYC, https://www.facebook.com/nonewjailsnyc/
Oakland Peace Center, https://www.facebook.com/41510peacecenter/
The Ordinary People's Society (TOPS), https://www.theordinarypeople-society.org/
Prison Policy Initiative, https://www.prisonpolicy.org
Prisoners Are People Too, https://www.prp2.org/
Project NIA, http://www.project-nia.org/
Sapelo Square, https://sapelosquare.com/
Seminary of the Street, https://www.facebook.com/Seminary-of-the-Street-184679791588986/
The Sentencing Project, https://www.sentencingproject.org
Survived and Punished, https://survivedandpunished.org/
TransformHarm.org, https://transformharm.org/#
T'ruah, https://www.truah.org/
Ubuntu Philadelphia, https://www.facebook.com/ubuntuphilly/
Zehr Institute for Restorative Justice, http://zehr-institute.org/

Index

For the benefit of digital users, indexed terms that span two pages (e.g., 52–53) may, on occasion, appear on only one of those pages.

Islam (*cont.*)
  Muslim Brotherhood and, 158–59,
    160, 162–65, 168–69, 170, 178,
    186n28, 187n33
  Nation of Islam and, 161–62, 164, 170,
    177–78, 187n33, 216
  Project NIA and, 215
  Ramadan and, 223
  Salafism and, 177–78
  War on Terror and, 177–78
  zakat (charity) principle, 216
Islamic State, 95

Jackson, George, 155, 156–57, 164
Jacobs, Jill, 214–15
Jehovah's Witnesses, 167
Jericho Ritual, 214
Jesuits, 124–25, 135–36
Jesus
  anger of, 207
  crucifixion of, 37, 71–72, 205–6, 213–14
  liberty for the captives proclaimed
    by, 204
  Pilate's exchange with, 123–24
  restorative justice and, 221–23
Jesus the Liberator Seminary (Buffalo,
  NY), 206, 243
Jim Crow. *See* segregation
Johnson, Lyndon, 78, 79, 80–83, 100n41
John the Evangelist, 153
Jonah (Hebrew Bible), 210
Judaism
  Abraham (Hebrew Bible) and, 235
  interfaith activism and, 11–12, 213
  Isaiah and, 236–37, 238
  Jews for Racial and Economic Justice
    and, 214–15
  Passover liturgy and, 214–15, 235, 237
  Pirkei Avot and, 235
  Union for Reform Judaism and,
    112–13, 143n25
  Yom Kippur and, 237
Justice Fellowship, 114–15, 130, 133, 134
Just Leadership USA, 51
*Just Mercy: A Story of Justice and
  Redemption* (Stevenson), 218–20
Juvenile Justice and Delinquency
  Prevention Act (1974), 28
juvenile prisons, 26, 28, 129–30, 217

Kaba, Mariame, 18–19n2, 52–53,
  215–16, 218
Katebi, Hoda, 216
Kennedy, John F., 73, 76, 79–80
Kennedy, Robert F., 79–80
Kerner Report (1967), 25–26, 81–82,
  111, 112–13
Keynesian economics, 6, 84
Khabeer, Su'ad Abdul, 216
Kierkegaard, Søren, 46–47
Kilpatrick, James J.
  King's debate (1960) with, 65, 66–68, 69,
    72–74, 80–81, 108
  moral law and, 67
  private property rights and, 67–68
  rule of law advocated by, 65, 66–68, 69
  secularism of, 69, 72, 83–85
  segregation supported by, 65, 67–68, 69
  sit-ins opposed by, 66–67
Kind and Usual Punishment
  (Mitford), 25–26
King, Coretta Scott, 86–87
King Jr., Martin Luther
  on the arc of history, 227
  civil rights movement and, 44–45,
    66–68, 154
  DeWolf and, 107–8
  divine justice philosophy and, 6–7, 33,
    66, 80, 84–85, 154–55
  Kilpatrick's debate (1960) with, 65, 66–68,
    69, 72–74, 80–81, 108
  "Letter from a Birmingham Jail" and,
    153, 154–55
  Montgomery Bus Boycott (1955–6)
    and, 154
  moral law and, 65–66, 67, 97n10
  private property rights and, 67–68
  prophetic style of African American
    Christianity and, 68–69
  Reagan on the legacy of, 86–87
Knopp, Fay Honey, 125–26, 127–28
Koch Brothers, 30
The Koran, 158–59, 162, 181, 182,
  200, 216
Krasner, Larry, 51, 222–23

Law, Victoria, 33–34
Lee, Mike, 30
Let's Circle Up (LCU), 221–23, 225, 243